ON THE FRONTLINES OF THE TELEVISION WAR

TO: Serge Schmemann - San.

please sharing my old stories.

We had same trip in Africa with

Anh Andy young....

Since then I always admired your

your work...

with respect

Tony Hirashiki

4/5/2017   N.J.

TO: Serge Schmemann - San.

please Shuniji rd old stories
He had some trip in Africa with
Ann Arty young ....
Since then I always admired you

ON THE FRONTLINES OF THE TELEVISION WAR

A Legendary War Cameraman in Vietnam

YASUTSUNE "TONY" HIRASHIKI
FOREWORD BY TED KOPPEL

EDITED BY TERRY IRVING

☾ CASEMATE | publishers
Philadelphia & Oxford

Published in the United States of America and Great Britain in 2017 by
CASEMATE PUBLISHERS
1950 Lawrence Road, Havertown, PA 19083, USA
and
The Old Music Hall, 106–108 Cowley Road, Oxford OX4 1JE, UK

Hardcover Edition: ISBN 978-1-61200-472-3
Digital Edition: ISBN 978-1-61200-473-0

A CIP record for this book is available from the British Library

Printed and bound in the United States of America
Typeset in India by Lapiz Digital Services, Chennai

For a complete list of Casemate titles, please contact:

CASEMATE PUBLISHERS (US)
Telephone (610) 853-9131
Fax (610) 853-9146
Email: casemate@casematepublishers.com
www.casematepublishers.com

CASEMATE PUBLISHERS (UK)
Telephone (01865) 241249
Fax (01865) 794449
Email: casemate-uk@casematepublishers.co.uk
www.casematepublishers.co.uk

This book is a translated and revised edition of the original Japanese title: *Once I Dreamed of Being
Robert Capa* (Kodansha, two volumes, 2008)

"I like to tell people about the bravest man I ever met. He's a Japanese cameraman who didn't even come up to my shoulder but I never saw him back away or even flinch when the shooting started. He could walk through the bush all day long, carrying a load of equipment that would buckle a mule's knees and never complain. He also took all the crap the war, the country, and the climate handed out and shrugged it off with a smile."

Roger Peterson, former ABC News correspondent

"Tony Hirashiki is an essential piece of the foundation on which ABC was built. From the day he approached the bureau chief in Saigon with a note pinned to his shirt saying he could shoot pictures to the anxious afternoon of 9/11 when we lost him in the collapse of the Twin Towers (and he emerged covered in dust clutching his precious beta tapes), Tony reported the news with his camera and in doing so, he brought the truth about the important events of our day to millions of Americans."

David Westin, former President of ABC News

"The cameramen were the real heroes of the Vietnam War coverage ... and Tony Hirashiki's story proves it!"

Sam Donaldson, former ABC News White House reporter

"Tony realized his dream. He became the Robert Capa of TV news cameramen. Everyone at ABC News loved working with Tony but I was so fortunate to have him as my 'sensei.' He selflessly taught me the craft. He was always patient and gracious. Tony has such a unique sense of humor. He is as loyal a friend as you can have. A truly outstanding human being."

J. W. Lower, documentarian and photographer

"Beautifully composed pictures, even in the most chaotic of circumstances, came naturally to him. Some of that, I've learned over the years, is a matter of instinct, but more of it comes from having the soul of a poet."

Ned Potter, former ABC News correspondent

"Tony Hirashiki is among the greatest video journalists, and legendary among us. His deep intelligence, stunning eye, compassionate personality, and warm wit saved our lives at roadblocks real and conceptual in many wars, sometimes literally."

Bill Blakemore, ABC News correspondent

"In his book *Dispatches*, Mike Herr wrote '....Vietnam is what we had instead of happy childhoods.' This book is an honest, sensitive and entertaining account of that family written by one of its most respected members. This translation retains the humor and gentleness in Tony's story."

Keith Kay, award-winning CBS cameraman

"Tony Hirashiki was perfect for the times. Young, with no thought for his own safety, he just wanted to show the Vietnam war as it was. He did that, filming for ABC News and the various correspondents he worked with. It's his filmic brilliance that turned the reporting then into what was called, The Living Room War."

Drew Pearson, former ABC NEWS correspondent

CONTENTS

FOREWORD

I did not witness the event, but the arrival of Yasutsune Hirashiki at ABC's Saigon bureau in 1966 has, over the years, taken on some of the resonance of the baby Moses' discovery in the bullrushes by the Pharaoh's daughter. The legendary account does not differ all that drastically from Mr. Hirashiki's own recollection; but in the version I heard on my initial tour in South Vietnam in January of 1967, Hirashiki had an envelope addressed to the ABC Bureau Chief safety-pinned to his jacket. If that image evokes a child's first day at summer camp, it is apt. To put matters into perspective, none of Hirashiki's legion of American friends and colleagues has ever called him Mr. Hirashiki, or Yasutsune. It has always been "Tony." It is a testimony to Tony's innate modesty and courtesy that he has seemed genuinely content with this arrangement, while continuing to apply the Japanese honorific to each of our names—*Ted-san*, for example.

But back to the letter: It was from ABC News' Director of Film, a man by the name of Jack Bush. It introduced Tony to the Saigon bureau chief and, in essence, recommended giving Tony a tryout. This, as you will later learn, did not precisely reflect Tony's understanding. He thought he was coming to a job and a regular salary. At the time, Tony spoke very little English. There are some harsh critics who will argue that, despite many years living here in the United States, fluency in English still eludes my old friend. The reader must understand that loving Tony is not dependent on sharing a common language; indeed, it might even have proved to be an obstacle.

I have seen this book in three iterations: the Japanese version, which was honored with one of that nation's top literary prizes but not a page of which I could read, Tony's helpful translation of the chapter relating most directly to me, and Terry Irving's splendid effort to bridge the gap between the two. To give a flavor of Tony's English, I am providing part of an email Tony sent informing me of the good news that his original book was being honored in Japan:

> June 19, at imperial hotel Tokyo, the organizer will held award ceremony. They invited me to attend. I also getting 10 thousand award cash!
>
> So if you are coming down NY area and have time, I'll buy good Sushi Dinner (not lunch special). The book had great reviews by big news papers and magazines in Japan, but sale was slow due to economic situation, good book but too expensive and two volumes. well at least people know how we had covered the Vietnam war.
>
> I wish you are attending at ceremony..., meanwhile please share with me this honor...it's yours too. Please don't forget wash hands, gargle, no shake hand, no hug, and no kissing air or cheek and keep away from Japanese cameraman who write funny story.
>
> One article said [71 YEARS FRESH WRITER WAS BORN, PROBABLY WITHOUT SECOND BOOK]
>
> So I have to challenge!
>
> Best regard to all your family.
>
> Love and respect
>
> Tony HIRASHIKI

Tony would have been the perfect intelligence agent. He conveys the impression of a complete innocent, a man without guile. Tony makes people smile. His own smile is beatific and infectious, but it is his generosity of spirit, his deep sense of humanity that transcend language and culture. Tony Hirashiki was simply one of the best television cameramen to cover the Vietnam War. His soaring video, often acquired only at great personal risk, gave wings to even the most mundane narration. For those of us who worked with him he was also a source of gentleness and joy in a place where both were in terribly short supply.

But those were just surface impressions. I am more than a little embarrassed to discover that Tony's impressions of Vietnam, the war, and the people he worked with were infinitely more sophisticated than my own. Tony Hirashiki, it turns out, has also been a canny, if gentle, observer of a generation of American television journalists. While cataloguing and gently tweaking our failings and exaggerating our virtues, Tony has produced a memoir of Vietnam unlike anything previously written.

I have only recently re-read Michael Herr's brilliant memoir of the Vietnam War, *Dispatches*. It is, by far, the best book of its genre. It makes the horror and madness of anticipating, experiencing, and dealing with the consequences of intense combat palpable. Tony Hirashiki's book is "shot" through a softer lens, but none the less true. If I had only spoken Japanese, I would have known for fifty years what a truly eloquent man he is. I kept a diary for a couple of weeks during my several tours in Vietnam. Tony was a constant diarist and a keen observer.

This is a particularly important book for Americans to read. We have a national inclination toward solipsism—the notion that only those things we personally experience exist. That's how too many of us covered the Vietnam War; the Vietnamese becoming almost incidental to the battles being waged by our troops, the demonstrations on our college campuses, the expediencies of our diplomats and politicians. Tony was an Asian observer of the war and its victims, capable of viewing both with an objectivity and compassion that gave equal weight to the Vietnamese experience. There were, among the camera crews and photographers in Vietnam many Japanese, Koreans, Singaporeans, ethnic Chinese from Hong Kong and Taiwan and, of course, Vietnamese. There was a tendency among American television correspondents to view them largely, if not exclusively, through the prism of their technical abilities.

They, meanwhile, were casting a far more observant eye on us; on the frequent triviality of our coverage. Like the military and government spokespersons who parceled out meaningless body counts as a way of "keeping score," our reports provided little depth or analysis: "New York" was obsessed with combat footage involving American troops and we obliged. Vietnam was a dateline. We rarely engaged with its people or paid much attention to the impact that our massive presence had on their communities.

I doubt that my friend, Tony, has an acquaintance with the Scottish poet, Robert Burns, but he provides an answer to the poet's plea:

> O wad some Pow'r the giftie gie us.
> To see oursels as ithers see us!

Read on.

Ted Koppel

EDITOR'S NOTE

I want to make it clear to the reader that this is a memoir and not a history. It is what one young photojournalist saw and remembered and is not meant to be a definitive record of the people, places, and battles he witnessed. In my experience as a producer, camera operators put the facts into their lenses and often aren't paying all that much attention to the details of what's going on around them. If anyone who was in Vietnam during that period feels that we've made an error—for instance, which unit was in which particular town at what date—please let me know, we do want to get it right. But no one should assume that any error is intentional, or any oversight is meant as a slight because to do that would be to misunderstand the care and attention that Mr. Hirashiki has given to this project.

Tony's English is, as his children say, about "grade school level" so, as editor, I needed to move around some clauses, fix a verb or two, and find different words for the ones he found in his Japanese–English dictionary. However, the more I worked on this extraordinary book, the more I realized that what I was doing was very much what a jeweler does when he polishes a diamond. All I had to do was to make Tony's observations and comments clear and, occasionally, figure out what he wanted to say. I hope that the result matches the original as a warm, intelligent, and extraordinarily observant man's record of a very complicated period and the men and women who tried to present it honestly and truthfully.

Terry Irving

PREFACE

Not long ago, I had the opportunity to visit the Vietnam War Memorial in Washington D.C. and pay my respects to those who paid the ultimate sacrifice. As I looked at name after name carved on the black marble wall, I found myself searching fruitlessly for the names of those friends, colleagues, and mentors who had died doing their jobs during the nine years I spent in Vietnam.

I searched for their names although I knew I wouldn't find them.

Their names aren't chiseled into the Vietnam Memorial because that honor is reserved for soldiers, sailors, Marines, and airmen. The names of my comrades have a place in my heart instead: Terence Khoo, Sam Kai Faye, Howard Tuckner, Craig Spence, Kyoichi Sawada, Larry Burrows, Henri Huet, Kent Potter, Keizaburo Shimamoto, "Moon Face," and many others. They were my comrades and our war was on the battlefields next to the soldiers, encountering many of the same dangers, and making many of the same sacrifices.

They were journalists: television correspondents, cameramen, soundmen, photographers, and many others. They didn't carry weapons; they carried pens, typewriters, film cameras, and microphones. They used these tools of their trade, powered by intelligence, empathy, wit, and creativity, to stand side by side with the troops and witness and record the war as it actually happened and to document the courage of the young men who fought it.

In 1966, I came from Japan with a 16-millimeter film camera, a dream of becoming a legendary war photographer like Robert Capa, and no job. I was hired by ABC News and worked with the brave men and women who came to cover the war until the last helicopters lifted off from Saigon in 1975. I was hardly alone. Hundreds of journalists from dozens of countries would come to cover this war. Some were experienced journalists, well-known writers, respected historians, and legendary photographers, but most were inexperienced and unknown young men and women like me who were driven by youthful enthusiasm and a determination to report the biggest story of their generation.

None of us had been taught how to cover a war before we arrived; we had to learn the hard way. War took the place of journalism school, and battles were our classrooms. We were armored by the conviction of invincibility that is the hallmark of all young people, and we worked together, learned together, competed against each other, and built friendships that have endured for the rest of our lives. There was a wealth of stories to cover and the veteran journalists, well-known experts, and experienced troops who stood by our side became our professors. Although tuition was free and doing a tour in a war zone was, and still is, one of the fastest ways to succeed in our profession, a failure in these classes far too often meant terror, pain, and death. All of our bravery and courage was no shield against the cruel and random nature of war, and we all had to master the harsh truth that fear and sorrow would always be a constant companion.

Vietnam was the first time that all of the television networks covered all of a war, and ABC's entire news division was only a few years old. Consequently, I had the opportunity to learn in the wide-open atmosphere of a young company, and I took full advantage. I tried to collect and keep everything: reporter's scripts, the caption sheets that told the producers and editors back in New York who the people were in the stories, the "dope sheets" that accompanied every reel of film—filled with details of when and where it was shot, the names of the correspondents and crew, the events we were covering, and even how many feet of film we'd used. In addition to collecting many of the telexes, memos, and letters from the time, I have spoken and written to my co-workers many times since the war to make sure that my memories are accurate.

Thousands of personal accounts have been written about the Vietnam War but very few about those who brought it home to America. These are the memoirs of my war and a testament to my wartime comrades. We shared moments of joy, bouts of bitterness, and hours of fear. In the end, we survived Vietnam together, and together we mourned those who did not. Some might see these pages as sentimental but I'm proud of the ABC News correspondents, editorial staff, and crews that I worked with, and I want to present them to the world.

Yasutsune "Tony" Hirashiki

"The television cameraman is rather a new breed. There is no exact profile of the man. First of all, he is an artist, a craftsman, not just a picture-taker. The camera is an extension of the man himself. his knack for composition is built in. He is not only the eyes for the viewer but, often, the creator of the most dramatic part of the story."

Elmer Lower, President ABC News, London 1973[1]

PART I

GOOD LUCK *OMIKUJI*

For a cameraman covering a war, good luck meant getting good pictures, which meant risk and danger. Good luck lived side by side with bad luck. Growing up in Japan, I sometimes went to Shinto shrines to find out my fortune. Written on tiny pieces of paper called *omikuji*, there were four types of luck that you could end up with: "ordinary bad fortune," "very bad fortune," "good fortune," and "extra good fortune." If you drew one with "bad fortune "or "very bad fortune" written on it, you would fold it and hang it on a tree branch at the shrine and pray that it would change into "good fortune."

I have divided this book into two parts because, for me, there are two stories: one of very good fortune and one of very bad fortune.

In fact, they were side by side the whole time.

Previous page: Tony smiling with an Auricon camera in c. 1966. The camera weighed about 30 pounds and had to be supported by a brace that went down to a belt around the cameraman's waist. However, since the system that drove the film was inside a metal case, it was quieter than any other portable camera that recorded both sound and video. (Courtesy of Yasutsune Hirashiki)

CHAPTER I

HAPPY VALLEY

The early morning sun made the plain below us shine like a golden carpet. We had a bird's-eye view from our "Huey," the UH-1 helicopter that had picked us up an hour before sunrise.

Now, as the sun rose, we were somewhere over Central Vietnam. A Huey heading into a combat zone has to have both of the big sliding doors open, and this means that the cold morning air blows through the cabin along with all the power, and noise, of the 1,000 horsepower main engine.

The public information officer, who was our escort, shouted into my ear as he pointed at our destination, a mountainous area far to the southwest. He had to shout twice before I understood that he was saying, "That's Happy Valley."

The helicopter dropped us off on a low hill. Beautiful rice fields reached to the horizon in all directions, each filled with golden rice, ready for harvest. I could tell that it would be a bountiful crop because the weight of the rice was making all the plants gently bow in the breeze. These fields were the "golden carpet" I'd seen from the air.

By and large, Central Vietnam is a tough place for farmers. It's squeezed in between the South China Sea and the Central Highlands and, compared with the Mekong Delta where farmers can grow two crops of rice a year, in Central Vietnam it's a struggle to raise a single crop.

There are exceptions where the land is fertile and well watered. Often these areas were given names such as "Happy Valley." We were actually in the Song Ve Valley in Quang Ngai province, a region where good harvests brought devastating conflict.

Every harvest season, the North Vietnamese Army regulars and the Viet Cong guerrillas of the National Liberation Front would come down from the safety of their mountain bases for rice to feed their troops. The Army of South Vietnam, and now their American allies, would fight to stop them.

It was war as regular as the seasons.

On May 12–14, 1967, the First Battalion of the 327th Airborne, 101st Airborne Brigade was sent in. Ken Gale was the ABC correspondent on this story, a slim and handsome guy from Texas, who was only 29 years old—a year older than I was. Unlike most of the reporters, correspondents, and camera crews in the Saigon press corps, who tended to be energetic and talkative show-offs, Ken was quiet, gentle, and serious—much closer to my image of a college professor or a doctor than a television correspondent.

I later learned that Ken had planned to cover China but was blocked by the emergence of the Red Guard and the rise of Chinese xenophobia. He worked in Taiwan, went back to New York for some graduate study, and when correspondent Ron Nessen was wounded, NBC hired Ken to replace him.

Ken said that he had never done a television report before Vietnam, so his time at NBC was on-the-job training. He lasted six months before being let go and then freelanced for ABC. Ken was an excellent writer when he had time but he was not fast, and that's a problem in the deadline-driven world of TV news.

By nature, Ken always challenged himself to try new things and cover tough stories. The determination to overcome fear is an essential part of combat journalism, but Ken had a reputation among the camera crews as going too far too often.

In other words, a dangerous partner.

Once Ken asked me to join him on a report about a small 12-man long-range reconnaissance team, but a friend of mine had told me that this particular team not only searched an area but acted as a decoy to draw out enemy soldiers. I had no desire to be a decoy.

ABC News correspondent Ken Gale works on a script in the field. On May 12, 1967, Gale, Hirashiki, and soundman Nguyen Thanh Long went on a search and destroy mission with the 1st Battalion, 327 Airborne, 101st Airborne Brigade. On the second day, they were hit by a large force of North Vietnamese, a battle unofficially named "Mother's Day Hill" by the troops. (Courtesy Ken Gale)

I seldom refused assignments but that time I turned him down. Looking back at this period from the viewpoint of decades later, Ken wrote of his dangerous reputation:

> It wasn't bravery; it was idiocy. I remember that I was very afraid the first several months in Viet nam. As time went on, I gained more confidence, but mostly I think I got wholly caught up in what was then the biggest story of the times in America. The more I learned, the more I wanted to know.[1]

Our soundman, Nguyen Thanh Long, was a native of South Vietnam who loved to drink, play, and enjoy life. Most Vietnamese men are thin, but Long was really skinny despite the fact that he loved to drink *Ba Muoi Ba* beer. Ken Gale wondered if this frail-looking guy could handle the soundman's job—which involves carrying a lot of heavy gear—but Long always kept up and did his job well.

Long was planning to go to college, and I remember him as very smart, an avid reader, and a man who enjoyed arguing about any subject; including the war. He was an outspoken guy and, like many Vietnamese, just wanted the Americans to go away and let the Vietnamese people work out their own future.

Long and I became good friends even though for a long time I would unwittingly embarrass him every time we worked together. I knew that the word "long" in Vietnamese meant "dragon," so I didn't see any problem with loudly calling "Long! Long!" in the rush of changing reels or catching natural sound.

ABC News correspondent Ken Gale doing a stand-up report in South Vietnam. He was attending university and studying China Policy when a chance to cover the war in Vietnam came and he, like so many others, leapt at the chance. (Courtesy Ken Gale)

He finally begged me to call him by his family name, "Nguyen." He said the problem was my accent. When I said his name, it sounded like the Vietnamese word for female genitalia. Long knew how hard it was for a Japanese to speak his language but he just couldn't stand being so embarrassed every time we worked together.

This morning, the Airborne soldiers were gathering in the middle of the rice paddies. From here, they would be climbing west into the mountains—a long, tough march. Ken said that this was going to be a battalion-size operation and would involve hundreds of soldiers so he decided that we should stick with the command group so that we could get a better idea of what was happening when things got scattered and confused.

When the operation kicked off, the soldiers moved single file at a slow and steady pace and tried to step in the footprints of the man ahead to avoid booby traps and mines. When we reached the thick jungle on the first mountain, I looked back at "Happy Valley" with its golden fields stretched out in the sun.

It was dark and cool under the trees that made up the thick jungle canopy. The trail was narrow, less than 10 feet wide. The first soldiers in line, a job called "walking point," used minesweepers to clear the trail. Along with the machines, a trained German shepherd scout dog ran back and forth sniffing trails and bushes for any signs of the enemy. I worried that the dog would think Long and I were enemies because we were Asians but he was smart enough to realize we were on his side.

Ken came up and asked me to film the dog, and when I told him that I had already done it, he was pleased. Good communications and a shared vision are crucial to creating a good television story.

Today, you can see your video instantly, but it wasn't like that in 1967. The film had to be raced to an airplane and shipped back to the States or to one of the big Asian cities like Hong Kong, Tokyo, or Manila where it was developed and edited. The final story was transmitted over one of the few satellite links to New York.

If a correspondent expected to have certain pictures to write to and the cameraman had missed it, the result was frustration and anger.

Mistakes like this could create friction and flare up into angry words, but when the whole team was in sync, it was pure pleasure. After we'd worked a number of stories together, Ken knew when I would shoot and when I would turn off the camera to save film, so he seldom gave me specific directions.

For my part, I learned Ken's style of reporting and made sure that I got the right pictures and sequences. The truth is, a combat cameraman had to be a journalist, not just a technician. If I didn't understand what the reporter wanted to talk about or missed the unexpected moments that make a good story great, we would all fail.

The fact is that genuine combat rarely happens within the range of your camera and if you waited for what the New York producers cynically called "bang bang," you could well end up with nothing at all.

So I filmed images that could illustrate story concepts. If it was raining, I took close-up shots of boots slogging through thick, clinging mud that would show how physically exhausting it was for soldiers on the frontlines and sunsets and sunrises that were like postcards but also an excellent way to begin or end a piece. I was fascinated by everything I saw, and I tried to capture that on film.

There was no school for Vietnam. Like all the other young photographers and cameramen, I learned as I went along. My work had to address the essentials: who, where, when, what, why, and how. I couldn't write those answers, so I tried to be sure they were in my camera and to get them, I had to be on the scene, and ready to shoot at any second.

These days, many people think the press was against the war and distorted the coverage—that simply wasn't true out in the field. Nevertheless, our bosses in New York wanted to be sure our coverage was fact-based, and so they sent out what became Rule Number One: "Do Not Stage Any Scenes."

We were told in no uncertain terms that our coverage of the war was not to be scripted, dramatized, sensationalized, exaggerated, or biased in any way. Our job was to record what was happening "as it is" and then be sure we reported it "as it was."

After two hours of walking, we took a short break. When we started moving again, we heard the flat *crack* of a shot from an M16 up ahead. The captain jogged forward, and we followed.

When we arrived at the scene, a young North Vietnamese soldier was lying on the ground, and blood was softly bubbling from a wound in his chest. Except for the blood, he could have been taking an afternoon nap.

What had happened was that the sergeant walking point had rounded a hairpin turn in the trail and almost bumped into the Vietnamese soldier, who had been walking down the trail. The man wasn't in a uniform; he was wearing the black shirt and pants that were the everyday clothes of Vietnamese farmers—American soldiers called them "black pajamas"—but he was armed, and there was no question he was an enemy.

Both men reacted quickly. The Vietnamese soldier tried to throw a grenade, and the sergeant snapped off a rifle shot. The sergeant was faster. He was very lucky, his first bullet struck the other man in the heart and killed him instantly.

A soldier standing next to us pulled a card from a strap around his helmet and put it on the chest of the dead soldier. It was the Ace of Spades. Ken interviewed the man, and he showed us an entire deck made up of the same card and told us that his family back home had sent it to him. According to the soldier, both Americans and Vietnamese believed that the Ace of Spades was bad luck, and they hated the idea that it would be placed on them after they were killed.

Then we did an interview with the sergeant, whose name was Gerard Simpson, but who was usually called "Bernie." We could see that he was still in shock—his face was pale, and he was shaking. This was the first time that he had ever killed another human being. His comrades were treating him as a hero, but he was very honest when he spoke to us, "I spun around to fire at him and he started reaching for something. I fired in the general direction of his chest. I wanted to get the round out there before anything else.... If I hadn't killed him, I and my fellow soldiers would have been killed by the grenade. I had no choice."

His relief at being the one left standing was clear. He told us that "In three more days I'm going to Hawaii, and my fiancée will be flying out

Many GIs carried packs of cards—all the Ace of Spades—to place on the bodies of enemy dead. Both Americans and Vietnamese saw the card as unlucky and it was thought to increase fear among the enemy. (Film shot by Yasutsune Hirashiki; courtesy ABC News)

there, and I'll meet her there." They were going to get married and for the first time, he showed us a slightly shy but happy and smiling face. His fellow soldiers teased him by chanting "Honeymoon! Honeymoon!"

The plan was to reach the top of the mountain by evening, but we ended up camped by the side of the trail not far from the summit. Ken, Long, and I got ready to spend the night under a good-sized tree where the roots were good and thick—at least a foot high where they stretched across the ground. We had just finished our C-rations when a soldier came up with a message from the commanding officer. Apparently, he wanted Long to act as translator, but we all decided to tag along.

They had laid out the meager belongings of the young soldier on the ground; his rifle was old and worn, he had a few hand grenades, a canteen, a cooker, and a toiletry kit in a worn canvas bag. In his pockets, there had been a picture of a young Vietnamese woman and a diary, which the officer wanted Long to translate.

Long began to translate the soldier's diary. It began in 1963 when the soldier had left his small village near Hanoi. He wrote about his mother, saying that she cried when he was chosen to go south. The rest of his neighbors celebrated with a farewell party for him, but he was miserable because he had to leave his girlfriend.

In the diary, he wrote about her as his "sister," but Long explained that this was a poetic way of speaking; she was the woman he loved and he said that being separated from her was the worst part of going to war. The young soldier wrote about how he had to remember that he was a patriot and that it was his duty to go and help the people in South Vietnam suffering under the American occupation.

Long soon began to skip pages because they were filled with what he said was "a beautiful poem" about the soldier's love and how much he wanted to be with her. Long claimed that his English wasn't good enough to translate it, but I think that he was trying to protect the young man's privacy.

As the years passed, the diary began to have gaps, and the sentences were shorter—no more beautiful poetry. Long read about how life in the mountains had become more and more difficult for the young soldier as American ground troops began to take over combat duties. In the early days, he had been relatively safe because it would take the South Vietnamese troops days to get close to the secret bases in the mountains. The GIs, on the other hand, were using helicopters, which could get them into combat range very quickly. He feared the American artillery and described what it was like to hug the ground as the big shells came in.

As the Americans steadily tightened their grip on the roads and trails, he wrote about how it became more and more difficult to get medicine and supplies. By the end of the book, he wrote that he was hungry all day every day. Finally, Long translated the last page, dated only a week ago:

> The other day I cut trees and turned them into charcoal. Today, after dusk, I put a sack of charcoal on my shoulder and went down to the village to sell it. The villagers were not interested in buying my charcoal. I asked the villagers if they wanted to barter my charcoal for a little rice and salt but nobody wanted to deal

with me. It has been quite a long time since I left my home village. Everyone must have forgotten about me except my mother. I'm sad and very hungry. I want to go home. This moment, if I could get a bowl of rice and a spoonful of salt in my hand, I would never complain about food for the rest of my life.

After translating the last page, Long took a deep breath and fell silent. No one said anything for a while. When Long handed the diary back, the commander thanked him and said, almost as if he was thinking aloud, "This young man was a good soldier, too."

Long was quiet as we left the command area but once we'd settled down under our tree, he began to talk. "I hate both the VC and the NVA soldiers, but after reading this diary, I'm unable to hate this guy even though he's my enemy. He's just a Vietnamese guy like me. He believed that he had a duty to his country, and so he came down here and was killed. His life was simply wasted; any possible achievements lost forever. How stupid he was but..."

Long fell silent after the word "but."

I think that Long was genuinely shocked by this young soldier's story. It was one thing to see someone as an "enemy," a shadowy and unknown image, but the diary had made this man real.

Long had always spoken very frankly and openly with me, never hesitating to be honest about his thoughts, emotions, and opinions. He once told me about his plans to avoid being drafted into the army. He thought he could make it across the border to Laos—at the time, it was safer there. Or he could get enough money together to bribe an officer who would just mark his name down as "present." If these plans didn't work, he said he would cut the first two fingers off his right hand. He would keep the thumb and the other two fingers, but he was sure that the Army wouldn't draft a man who couldn't pull the trigger on his weapon.

For a long time, we lay quiet on our sleeping bags. I didn't fall asleep for a quite a long time. I kept thinking about the last glimpse I'd had of the young soldier laying on the ground. He'd looked like he was sleeping except for the ace of spades on his chest.

I wasn't sure if I'd be able to fall asleep at all.

Ken Gale remembers that for most of that night, heavy artillery shells aimed just yards away were whistling so close over our heads that some of the shells brushed the tree tops and showered us with leaves and twigs and the explosions were deafening. I have to take his word for this because I was sound asleep.

The commander had apparently called in a "danger close" fire command to keep enemy troops away in the darkness. "Danger close" means the shells needed to be precisely aimed because the attackers being targeted were extremely close to friendly forces.

In the early morning, we had to wait until a thick fog cleared, so we had breakfast with the soldiers. I can still remember the delicious taste of the coffee that they shared with us. The fact is that we had all gone through some stressful events the day before, and we had bonded with the men.

The fog cleared in the late morning, and we went back on the march. I called to Sergeant Simpson as he walked past and he greeted us with a big smile. The other soldiers were still teasing him with shouts of "Two more days to the honeymoon!"

After about half an hour of careful travel, the trail widened, and we started going up another mountain ridge. Suddenly—in war everything happens either suddenly or very slowly—we heard heavy machine-gun fire and grenades exploding not far ahead of us. The firing was so close that I could hear bullets whiz past my ears, making a noise that I remember as *pyunn, pyunn.*

My camera was rolling as soon as I heard the first shot.

This wasn't a single quick incident like yesterday; we were under heavy attack. The soldiers immediately moved off the open trail and into cover, and we followed, scrambling to the left and into the shelter of thick trees and bushes.

On the now-deserted trail, we saw the first casualty heading to the rear. It was the German shepherd scout dog that had led us so bravely the day before. Severely wounded and covered with blood, it was crying like a puppy as it ran down the trail.

Very soon, wounded troops appeared, supported by their comrades. I was surprised by how many were injured. The unit was ordered to fall back and form a defensive position right where we were crouching. From that position, the Airborne soldiers fought back, kneeling behind tree trunks and lying behind the big roots. The undergrowth was so dense that we couldn't see more than a few yards. One of the soldiers told us that we'd made a mistake when we jumped off the main trail. We'd moved to the left, and that's where the attack was coming from. Sadly, no place was safer at the moment, so we huddled in what cover we could find and filmed the troops from only inches away.

After a time, Long and I began to move to where other soldiers were fighting—crawling or crouching low all the way. At one point, you can hear on the film a soldier saying, "You better get down, cameraman, or you're gonna catch a bullet." So I stayed down behind the massive tree roots and would just raise my camera high enough to film. Since we couldn't move, I kept changing angles and using different lenses to get as many different images as possible.

A lot of my shots were very tight close-ups: a tense young soldier's face, frightened eyes flicking in search of a target, an unlit cigarette hanging forgotten from the side of lips pulled tight with fear and concentration.

Long was right next to me, pointing his microphone to record the sound of explosions, commands, and the cries of the wounded. Medics had set up an aid station near us because it was the safest location they could find and were tending to the wounded as a steady stream of injured soldiers kept arriving.

Ken had already put away his notepad and still camera and was doing his best to help the wounded. In a letter, he recalled how difficult it was:

> At one point a wounded soldier asked me to re-insert the needle of the serum drip bag he'd had hooked up. I crawled up to him and made several attempts to insert the needle into a vein, but I think I may have been a bit nervous, probably from idea of jabbing a needle into someone's skin as much as from all the shooting going on around us. After several failed attempts, the soldier hollered, "Goddamit. Just stick the fucking needle in the vein!" or words like that. I concentrated and got it in right.
>
> Later, after I had crawled back to my place and chattering into my tape recorder for radio story, but mostly to keep my wits about me, I felt a bump on my back. It was the same soldier, passing me his rifle and pointing out towards the perimeter. I think that's when I got scared and stopped chattering into the microphone. He meant for me to watch our flank and use the M16 when needed. It was never needed.[2]

About fifty feet to our right, I could see the command group with the captain alternating between calling commands to his troops and yelling into a radio. Long and I crawled over and filmed, but we didn't hang around. We'd been told by soldiers on earlier assignments that it was a bad idea to remain near a commanding officer and his radioman because they were always a target for snipers.

Within minutes, shells began to come over our heads and slam deep into the jungle. They made a loud whizzing sound followed by an enormous *BANG* that shook the ground like an earthquake.

With only a small number of men, many of them wounded, the captain was calling in artillery fire as close as possible to drive back the enemy. It's a dangerous tactic because it depends on everything going precisely as planned.

There was an enormous noise, and I thought I'd been struck by lightning and my eardrums had burst because, at first, I couldn't hear anything. Slowly my hearing came back, and I could hear voices screaming and moaning. I was covered by branches, leaves, and everything around me was lost in a cloud of dust. Later, we were told that a shell had come in short, hit a tree, and impacted right where the captain had been talking on his radio. He was killed instantly, and most of the soldiers around him were badly injured in a crazy confusion of blood and screams.

"Medic! Medic!"

"Oh, my leg! My leg!"

I was crazily filming everything—just operating on unthinking reflex. After a few minutes, Long tapped on my shoulder and yelled, "Tony! Stop filming! Let's stop and help!"

I looked over at Ken, and he nodded in agreement. I put my camera on the ground, and we moved to do what we could for the wounded soldiers. We helped to move the injured to where the ground was lower, and there were ditches where we could get them out of the line of fire. I remember Ken, Long, and I all struggling to move one big soldier. The number of wounded kept growing until about twenty soldiers were lying in the ditches next to the trail.

"Give me water!"

"Give me a cigarette!"

We weren't doctors or even medics, but I realized that wounded soldiers were like kids. They just wanted someone to stay beside them, talk to them, care about them. We could do that.

One soldier tried to talk to me but he'd been shot in the jaw, and his head was covered with bloody bandages so I couldn't understand anything he said. He pointed to the small backup camera that hung on a strap at my waist. I finally worked out that his father back in Chicago worked at the Bell & Howell Company where the camera was made. I showed it to him, let him touch it, and with words and gestures demonstrated how well it worked. This made him happy, and he smiled with his blood-red jaw.

I collected canteens from all over and gave them to soldiers whenever they requested a drink. A medic came by and advised me not to let them drink too much water because it would make them weak. His last words to me were, "Don't let them die."

I was shocked when I moved to one severely wounded soldier and realized that it was Sergeant Simpson. He had been standing very close to the captain, and the explosion had blown one of his legs off at the knee. I realized that the agonized cry of "Oh my leg! My leg" that I had captured on film had been his voice.

This was one of the first times when what I did in my job as a cameraman became extremely personal and horribly real. It would be far from the last.

Now, Simpson was much calmer—probably because of the morphine—he even gave me a faint smile. He asked me for water and a cigarette.

While I lit the cigarette, he asked, "Have you seen my leg?"

I shook my head.

"No more honeymoon in Hawaii." He said softly, "It's stupid."

I pretended that I couldn't speak any English, but the truth was I didn't know what I could say. I just sat beside him for a while and wiped the sweat from his face.

Eventually, he repeated, "Stupid!" and closed his eyes.

Sitting beside him, I thought about what he kept saying. What did "stupid" mean to this man? Was he talking about his lost leg? Or about his honeymoon? Was the war itself "stupid"?

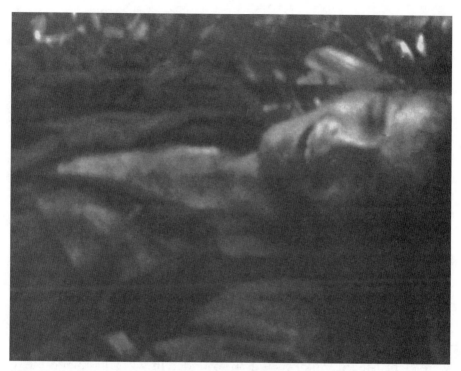

May 13, 1967. The pain of his lost leg shows on Sergeant Bernie Simpson's face. He was intending to take a leave to Hawaii and marry his fiancée only two days later. In 1968, he was the first amputee to become a New York City policeman. (Film shot by Yasutsune Hirashiki; courtesy ABC News)

I remembered that yesterday, Long had said "stupid" after he'd read the diary of the young soldier.

There was a lull in the fighting and soldiers moved quickly to prepare for a new attack. There weren't all that many left who could still fight, at least two-thirds of this small unit were either injured or dead. I wondered if they could hold off another attack?

A soldier came by and asked, "You guys know how to use machine guns?"

Long and I both said "No."

Another soldier came by and asked if we knew how to throw grenades.

"No way," was my answer. I couldn't even throw a baseball from the pitcher's mound to the catcher correctly. I was so clumsy that I was sure the grenade would never even leave my hand and I would end up killing myself.

The soldiers were disappointed by what terrible soldiers we were. We said that we would continue to take care of the wounded.

There was no second attack.

This battle was over.

Helicopters came in with reinforcements and medics to treat the wounded so I picked up my camera and began to film again. There wasn't enough clear space for the choppers to land so the initial load of GIs slid down on ropes. One of the first down was the company chaplain who moved about encouraging the wounded and saying prayers over the dead. I filmed the scene and then we said goodbye to Sergeant Simpson and the other wounded soldiers we had come to know. Along with about a dozen unwounded Airborne soldiers, we walked another thirty minutes to the top of the mountain and were airlifted out.

This small battle happened between May 13 and 14, 1967 and I found out much later that it was part of Operation *Malheur I*. Officially, there were eight Americans killed and 36 wounded in what the men came to call The Battle of Mother's Day Hill.

It might have been a small battle compared to the massive military operations happening elsewhere in Vietnam at the time, but it was an unforgettable experience for Ken, Long, and me. I wondered if the black Ace of Spades on the dead soldier's body might have had something to do with it. Were the North Vietnamese who were attacking so fiercely seeking revenge or was it some sort of bad luck?

I had no answers.

When we left, we flew over Happy Valley again but it was far away, the weather was cloudy, and we couldn't see it clearly. I felt the contrast between the beauty of the dawn of the first day and the exhaustion and sadness we felt at the end of the second. Ken Gale remembers it a bit differently:

> I had never been so thirsty in my life. It was agonizing and like manna from heaven when someone in the helicopter handed me a canteen. Back in camp, a beer had never tasted so good.[3]

Ken had time to write a great script and ABC decided to run a five-minute story on the Evening News. To put that in perspective, almost all stories on television run less than a minute and a half. Devoting that much time was a real indication of the impact that our story and my pictures had when they were shown to the decision-makers in New York (see plate section for film footage.)

However, the Military Assistance Command, Vietnam (MACV) decided to pull Ken's press card for a month and ban him from going out on missions. Again, Ken's side of the story:

> The official reason I was given was that Sergeant Simpson's family had not been notified of his injuries before the story aired. It was a cardinal rule that pictures and names of American dead or wounded would not be aired until their families had been notified. In Simpson's case, I was told that Simpson's parents were divorced and that only one parent had been notified, but not the other.
>
> Unofficially, I think what the army was most concerned with was our reporting that the captain and others had been killed and wounded by their own artillery—"Friendly Fire." But that may not have been a legitimate "official" reason for suspending my press card. In hindsight, I wonder if the letter from the major who saw us helping out might have softened reaction. I believe they could have banned me from the military coverage permanently if they'd tried harder.[4]

The shocking pictures, the many wounded, and the sound of Sergeant Simpson's cry of "Oh, my leg!" made for a report that did not help to support the war. In fact, it could hardly have been anything but negative, and that's almost certainly why the military press officials punished us. We defended ourselves by showing that we had covered the war "as is." There had been no staging, no exaggeration, and no sensationalizing. The ABC executives supported us all the way to the Pentagon and a week later I recorded in my diary:

> Ken's suspension was lifted. I heard New York made a great effort. I believe in journalism in the USA![5]

The troops sent ABC News a special letter of thanks for the help that Ken, Long, and I had given to the wounded. I felt that Ken and Long deserved praise for their actions because Ken's example and Long's words were what woke me up and got me to stop being just an "eye in a lens."

As it turned out, Long didn't run away, bribe an officer, or cut off his fingers. A couple of years later, he joined the South Vietnamese Air Force and served until the end of the war. When Saigon fell, he wasn't able to join the ABC staffers who were flown out on the last day, but he managed to get to Malaysia in the exodus of "boat people," and later immigrated to Canada.

Gerard "Bernie" Simpson went home to Staten Island and in 1968 was the first amputee to be made a member of the New York City Police.

CHAPTER 2

ROOKIE

"How do you do, sir? I'd like to introduce myself. My name is Yasutsune Hirashiki—just arrived from Japan."

My introductory greeting went very well. It should have, I'd been practicing it for days. As I delivered my speech, I held out my letter from Jack Bush, ABC News' executive in New York in charge of all film operations around the world. The letter that had persuaded me to give up my job at a local Japanese television station and buy a one-way ticket to Saigon.

I was facing Jack O'Grady, a man with a large mustache, who was the bureau chief for ABC News in Saigon. He shook my hand with a firm grip and said "Welcome to Vietnam! New York told me you were coming. They told me you were a damn good cameraman."

"I'm ready to work, sir. When shall I start?"

"Well, this week is very quiet, so why don't you check with us next week?"

What? Did he just say that I didn't have a job this week, but I might have a job next week? I was certain he was mistaken. The letter I carried was from Jack Bush and he had very clearly said that there was a job waiting for me in Vietnam. I was going to become a photojournalist like my boyhood idol: war photographer Robert Capa.

Clearly, this O'Grady fellow hadn't gotten the message.

I began another speech that I was pretty sure was clear even though I hadn't practiced it, "Mr. O'Grady, I was hired by New York as a Saigon bureau cameraman. Because of these instructions, I quit my job in Japan and came here to work."

Mr. O'Grady patiently deciphered my terrible English and said, "Show me the letter."

I gave it to him. He read it, smiled, and said, "Look at this line."

He then ran his finger along a line of incomprehensible words as he carefully read them to me. "It says that you will have a chance if you go to Saigon but the word 'hired' isn't in here. We will give you a chance. Come back and check next week. If it's busy and we need a cameraman, we'll send you on an assignment, and you'll have a chance to show us your work."

I was in shock. I had translated the letter with a dictionary and only paid attention to what I thought were the important points.

Quit.

Go to Saigon.

Have a chance.

I truly believed that "have a chance" was the same as "you'll be hired." What else could it mean? Did New York really think I would leave a good job, say goodbye to everyone I knew, and go off to a war zone with no guarantee of a steady job?

Well, apparently, that was exactly what they'd thought.

Why shouldn't they? It's exactly what I did.

With my best manners, I thanked Mr. O'Grady and said I would check in next week; acting as if it was no big deal. I walked outside and stood on the sidewalk.

I was furious at myself, "Yasutsune, your mother and your teachers are right! You are hasty, impetuous, and absentminded, and that's why you always make big mistakes in your life! Now you've really gone and done it. All you have is $700 and a 16-millimeter film camera. No return ticket. No other job. No place to stay."

I settled down and began to think practically. If I was very careful, I could live in Vietnam for three months without a job. After that, I would have to sell the camera I'd saved so long to buy, and that would give me enough to purchase a ticket home. My boss back in Japan had told me I could come back if it didn't work out. He was a nice boss, not like this mustachioed American guy!

Yasutsune "Tony" Hirashiki writes in a journal in 1966. It's a bit odd that he's so relaxed in a sampan since he later blamed the unsteady craft for damage to several expensive cameras. (Courtesy Yasutsune Hirashiki)

Even so, I couldn't just go back. I'd told everyone what a great job I was getting and people had been jealous of me as I went off to cover the biggest story there was. They'd even given me a big farewell party! People came to the airport to see me off! I couldn't just give up and go back. I'd never live it down.

I decided that I would be the best freelancer in Saigon and get as many assignments as any staff cameraman.

I had one advantage, I really was a good shooter. In the ten years, I worked at the Japanese station, I had been taught by experts. I started in

1956, right at the dawn of the era of television news, and my teachers were old newsreel cameramen and former newspaper reporters who, from the beginning, drilled me in how to shoot and, more importantly, what to shoot. I had studied American newsreels—old and new. We used American cameras and film. Now, I had the chance to get a job at an American network and, I told myself, I was good enough to meet the challenge.

All good words but my stomach was tied in knots.

I finally calmed down and rented a tiny room from a manager of a Japanese company for $50 a month.

The next day and every day after that, I dropped by the ABC bureau just to say "Hello" as if I were a salesman. I wanted people to remember my face. Perhaps they thought I was ridiculous but after five mornings of uncomfortable visits and five of the world's longest afternoons waiting for a phone call, I got my first freelance assignment.

I was sent to cover the 1st Cavalry in An Khe. I was to go there by myself, learn how things worked, figure out who to talk to, and then look for a story. When there was a story, I was to film it, write up how it should be used, and send it back to Saigon. I wouldn't be working with a reporter—it was going to just be me, my camera, and my terrible English.

OK, it was clearly a test, not only of what I could capture in my camera but of my creativity, journalism, and resilience. I was scared, but I couldn't say "No." If a rookie freelancer turned down an assignment, it was a pretty good bet that he wouldn't get another.

Early in the morning, I set out for the 1st Cavalry's base camp, catching a ride on a military airplane. To my surprise, Jack O'Grady himself woke up at 4 a.m. to drive me to the Military Air Terminal at Tan Son Nhut. I wondered if he was really such a mean guy but I didn't have time to dwell on it, I felt like a baseball player getting his first chance at the Major Leagues.

An Khe, the headquarters of the 1st Air Cavalry, was located about midway between the coastal city of Quy Nhon and the highland town of Pleiku. When I arrived at Camp Radcliff, where the An Khe airfield was located, I was met by the Public Information Officer, Captain Hitchcock.

Tony labels film cans as he unloads his camera. The standard film for TV news was 16-millimeter color-reverse so that what came out of processing first was not a negative but a positive print—ready to go. The cameraman used a "changing bag" which blocked all light to remove the exposed film from the steel magazines and tape it into aluminum cans for shipment. (Courtesy Yasutsune Hirashiki)

I've often regretted that I never learned his first name because he was incredibly helpful.

He showed me into an almost-empty press tent where there was only one other reporter and told me the 1st Cavalry hadn't been making a lot of news in the past few weeks. I asked the captain if I could go out on an operation and he said that there was a small mission going out the next day, and I could go along with the other reporter if I liked.

He introduced me to Charles Black, a veteran newspaper reporter who worked for the *Columbus Enquirer* in Columbus, Georgia. Fort Benning, the home base of the 1st Cavalry, was in Columbus and Black was a popular reporter there because his articles were filled with soldiers' names, hometowns, the details of their lives, and especially their time in combat. Back in the States, anxious families read his reports to get the latest word on their boys.

The "operation" was little more than a jungle patrol. Helicopters would drop the troops into the middle of the jungle and pick them up two days later. It was perfect for a beginner like me.

So, the most experienced war reporter went into the field side-by-side with the most inexperienced television news cameraman. The small unit of the 1st Cavalry walked for two days without sighting a single enemy soldier.

Even without combat, I picked up a lot of the tricks of the trade. First, bring something waterproof so that you—and more importantly, your camera—can stay dry when it rains. The first night, I was soaking wet and desperately trying to keep my camera dry with a tiny piece of plastic until Black kindly let me sleep underneath his hammock, which was covered by a lovely big poncho.

The next morning, when we had some spare time, Charles Black began to teach "A Beginner's Class for the Rookie War Reporter." First, I was wearing a bright white polo shirt which might as well have been a sign saying, "Shoot Here." Not only would I be a perfect target, but I was putting anyone near me in danger as well. The proper clothes were green or khaki in color, and camouflage wasn't the worst idea.

Second, my running shoes didn't have enough traction for fields, jungle, and rice paddies nor would they protect me from the natural sharp sticks and branches of a jungle trail not to mention the points of a "punji stick" booby trap. Black told me that there were very sturdy army boots for sale at the black market of any big town or city, and the black market was also a good place to find canteens, ponchos, blankets, knapsacks, and everything else I needed.

Third, I had to take care of myself when I was in the field. The soldiers weren't there to play nursemaid for a reporter, I was a guest at best and a pain at worst. I shouldn't ask for food, water, or even a cigarette. The soldiers were carrying their own supplies and so should I.

Finally, Black said that one of the key rules of combat reporting was, "War is a waiting game. It needs a lot of patience."

I felt that I was incredibly lucky to have a legendary reporter take the time to teach me the ropes. It's just simple good manners to treat soldiers as the professionals they are and not act like some whiney kid who expects to be taken care of. For one thing, the better you treat them, the better they'd treat you, and you might get a story that a rude reporter wouldn't even know about.

When we got back to An Khe, we had no story at all so I didn't call or ship anything to Saigon. I was beat so I went to take a nap on a foldout cot in the press tent. Captain Hitchcock came by and told me about a big operation that was going to kick off the next day. It was called Operation *Davy Crockett*, and it would take place in the Bong Son Valley near the ocean in Central Vietnam.

To my surprise, the captain handed me a pair of tough military boots, a camouflage uniform, and a poncho. Amazingly, they fit me because they were made for Vietnamese soldiers and so were cut slimmer and smaller. I was a little confused because I hadn't asked for anything but I think that Charles Black told the captain that this crazy, green Japanese cameraman needed a hand.

The next morning, I hitched a ride in Captain Hitchcock's jeep, and we drove to Bong Son with a convoy filled with tents, cots, desks, phones, and typewriters; all of it destined for a press center at the staging area.

When we arrived, the captain immediately began to set up the press center, and since I didn't have anything else to do, I helped erect the tents and unfold the beds, and we finished before dark. As a reward, I got the best bed, which was the one nearest to the entrance. If anything happened, you were the first out and could either start filming or start running depending on what was going on.

As it happened, there wasn't a competition for beds since I was now the only journalist. Charles Black had flown out with the 1st Cavalry to the frontlines so I was alone in the large tent. The captain had arranged for me to go with another unit first thing in the morning, so I went to bed early because even rookies knew that "first thing" meant well before dawn.

The next day, I set off with the soldiers of the Second Battalion who were to cover the north flank of the tactical zone in Bong Son Valley.

They were some of the first "Airmobile" units and used helicopters to transport troops to the battlefield, bring in weapons and artillery, carry out the wounded, and attack the enemy from the sky.

The first day, however, we walked. We crossed rice paddies along the narrow footpaths and climbed up and down hills. The fields were beautiful, with tiny white and yellow flowers that looked like stars in the sky. I filmed low-angle shots of the soldiers' boots against the flowers.

That night, we camped on a high hill, and I set up my little camp behind a large rock for shelter. It was a cool and comfortable night with a clear sky so all the stars shone as if we were in a planetarium and not the middle of a war. I went to sleep looking at the stars.

Somewhere around midnight, I was awakened by the *crack* of small-arms fire. The enemy was firing from the bottom of the hill, and I could see the red streaks of tracer bullets. I stayed behind my rock as several shots passed so close that I could hear their sound—like furious mechanical bees. The Americans set off parachute flares, making it bright as day all around us, and then they began to pour rifle fire towards the bottom of the hill.

I wasn't a soldier, I was a cameraman and even though I tried filming when the flares ignited, I knew it was too dark to capture any detail. Eventually, I lay down behind my rock and watched the sky where the stars had been joined by stray tracers and flares.

I began to question why I was here. I thought about my friends and family back in Japan and felt some regret about leaving. I watched the fireworks of war and fell asleep. In the morning, one of the soldiers told me that the fighting had gone on all night, but I'd slept through most of it.

The second day was a different story. Heavy fighting had begun early in the morning as soldiers surrounded a village which intelligence had indicated was a Viet Cong base. I filmed soldiers as they approached the village and were hit with heavy weapons fire. The Americans immediately called in air support, jets began their bomb runs, and soon there was heavy black smoke, then flames, and the village burned.

A frightened water buffalo came running very fast out of the village and headed right for us. I followed it with my camera and filmed as the buffalo was shot just before it reached the soldiers. Moments later, refugees came running from the village—old men, women, and children.

An old grandmother pointed back at the burning village and angrily yelled at the Americans. I would have liked to know what she was saying, but it was easy to guess. The unit I was with moved into the village but all the enemy soldiers had left. In fact, they might well have left before the air strikes. No one could tell me.

I had plenty of action footage for the first day's report on Operation *Davy Crockett* so I hitched a ride on a helicopter and flew back to the base camp in the early afternoon. The press center was now filled with newsmen from Saigon. There weren't enough beds, but mine was still reserved even though there were prestigious journalists looking to claim it. Captain Hitchcock was a good guy.

A bed is nice, but the most important thing at a press center is a telephone. The military telephone circuit was called the Tiger line. If you were lucky, you could get through to the ABC bureau and, if you were incredibly lucky, in minutes instead of hours. That day, I reached Jack O'Grady in less than ten minutes.

Suddenly, I wasn't sure if I was lucky at all.

"Where have you been? Why didn't you contact us?" He was shouting and angry.

I could only guess that this was because I hadn't contacted him for four days. I hadn't tried to get through because I didn't think I should bother him when I didn't have anything to ship and the rest of the time I was in the field.

I tried to explain, "I'm here at Bong Son, sir! I followed a new operation, *Davy Crockett*. I filmed some action. Shall I send it, sir?"

O'Grady didn't believe what I was saying (although it's quite possible that is that he simply couldn't understand what I was saying) and Captain Hitchcock took the phone to explain that not only had I been unable to call because I was too busy shooting but that I had been the only cameraman out there who got film of the first day of a big military operation.

When I got back on the phone, Mr. O'Grady's mood seemed to be much improved. Apparently, the Saigon press corps had only been told about Operation *Davy Crockett* at last night's press briefing and correspondent Roger Peterson had left to cover the story with a camera crew this morning. Jack told me to give my film to Roger and then head back to Saigon.

While I was waiting for Roger and his team, I borrowed a typewriter and typed up a list of all the pictures I'd shot during the day's action. I believe I spelled most things correctly but "Davy Crockett" wasn't in my Japanese-English dictionary. When Roger arrived with Ron Headford, the Australian cameraman he usually worked with, he was very happy with my list and said it would really help in his first report.

It wasn't an "exclusive" because Charles Black had been there but I did have the only camera footage. I hoped to see Mr. Black again but I was told that when he was out with the troops, he never came back to the base camp and over the years our paths never crossed again. I was really lucky to learn from him on my first assignment.

When I got back to Saigon, I was told that O'Grady and the New York executives were quite happy with how I'd done on my first time out and I had another assignment already.

I was a real war cameraman!

After a day's rest, I was sent back to continue covering Operation *Davy Crockett* and this time, I was working with Jack O'Grady himself. As soon as we went out with an Airborne unit, I realized that this was his first time in the field. He was having a hard time keeping up with the soldiers, so I paid attention to be sure that he didn't fall behind.

In the afternoon of the second day, we were all sitting on the ground taking a break, and he told me to stop calling him "Mr. O'Grady." Just plain "Jack" would be just fine. This was a bit of problem for me because this is a violation of Japanese manners. I offered to compromise and call him *Jack-san* out of respect. He said he was OK with that, and that's what I did for the rest of our time in Vietnam.

O'Grady then said that I should only speak English at all times and all places—even in conversations with Japanese friends. I knew he was trying to make me learn the language, and I tried my best. Later on while working that same story, I met a Japanese photographer named Bunyo Ishikawa. I think that he thought I'd been touched by the sun because he would speak to me in Japanese and I would answer in my

Tony walks with an Auricon film camera c. 1971. In addition to a brace leading to a belt around his waist, a platform above the shoulder holds the weight of the camera, and the battery pack is attached to the brace. A Vietnam-era cameraman would often carry this weight, plus extra film, magazines, batteries, and a bare minimum of food and camping equipment, for days on end. (Courtesy Yasutsune Hirashiki)

terrible English. I couldn't tell him that O'Grady was close by, checking up on me.

Later, when O'Grady had walked away, I quickly explained in Japanese why I could only speak to him in English. He was relieved that I wasn't crazy and later we became great friends.

Later, O'Grady and I had a chance to ride in an observer plane—a tiny, very old propeller airplane no bigger than a Cessna. The pilot, who was a Forward Air Controller, would fly very low and slow over the jungle, searching for enemy positions, and mark the location for attack jets. The pilot was brave but not stupid, he'd find the enemy, and then move away, and let the big planes come in.

I was using the small Bell & Howell camera so I could change shutter speed and use slow motion (the Auricon only had one speed), which smoothed out the airplane's shakiness, and I ended up with a great platform to film an aerial battle with Phantom jets bombing targets with both explosive and napalm bombs. It was vivid and dramatic, but also frightening as the small plane dove in and out to plant smoke bombs and evade ground fire.

New York was impressed with our unusual footage and sent a complimentary telex to O'Grady. The way telexes worked was: if you did a good job, got fresh material, and, most importantly, beat the other networks, New York would send a nice telex that was known as a "Herogram" or an "Attaboy." Of course, if your film was shaky or out of focus and especially if the other networks had something we didn't get, the telex was quite nasty. These were known as "Rockets" and came out of New York a lot more often than Herograms.

I was very happy that in less than two weeks on the job, I already had two Herograms and not a single Rocket.

O'Grady went back to Saigon, but I stayed until the operation was over. When I got back to the press center at An Khe, I called Saigon through the Tiger line. This time, I got Bob Lukeman, who was the assistant bureau chief and assignment manager.

"What are you doing there? The operation is over. Come back to Saigon as soon as possible!" I thought I was in trouble again, but then he added, "By the way, you did a very nice job!" I was a little confused by this combination of praise and criticism, but I got used to it. It's just part of the way desk people always talk.

When I got back to Saigon and reported to the bureau, Jack gave me a firm handshake and showed me the telex he'd gotten from New York. It wasn't very long, but it was nice to read:

O'GRADY'S OPERATION REPORT WAS EXCELLENT.[1]

The next day, I received my own Herogram. It was a bit longer and began:

MR. HIRASHIKI'S PICTURES WERE EXCELLENT;
HAD GOOD COMPOSITION, GOOD CLOSE UPS,
AND CAPTURED EXCITING SCENES.[2]

I was happy at the compliments, but then I became depressed because it went on to say I needed to improve my technical proficiency because some of the pictures were over-exposed.

Wow, those guys in New York were tough!

Both O'Grady and Lukeman laughed and said that NY always found something to complain about.

Now I was consistently getting freelance jobs and I'd only been in Saigon for three weeks. I'd passed the first test.

In those days, there was continuous tension between the Catholic-led government of General Nguyen Cao Ky and Nguyen Van Thieu and the majority of Vietnamese, who were Buddhists. Da Nang, on the central coast, was the second-largest city in South Vietnam and was the stronghold of the opposition. At first, the situation was peaceful with non-violent demonstrations and boycotts, but when Vietnamese soldiers joined with the Buddhist activists and set up defenses in the Old City, the government sent in elite military units to root them out.

The Tinh Hoi Pagoda, one of the largest Buddhist temples in Da Nang, was a center of opposition, filled with armed soldiers and refugees.

I was sent to Da Nang for an entirely different assignment, testing out a new color film to see if it was sturdy enough for news coverage. The TV networks were changing their regular programs to color, and they wanted the news to be in color as well. I shot pictures of the Buddhist demonstrations because the clothes of the monks and nuns were bright, warm oranges, yellows, and browns that would really put the film to the test.

I wrapped up the test shoots, sent the film back, and began to work with Roger Peterson. He already had Ron Headford shooting sound so I was to be the "cutaway" camera, shooting silent footage that could be worked into his stories. I wasn't given a lot of instructions, just told to go out and find good pictures.

The streets of Da Nang were anarchic but, as a reporter explained to me, the local soldiers hadn't been fighting very hard against troops who were often from the same units. This changed when the elite troops arrived from the capital and the skirmishes between government and rebel forces became more serious.

The next day, more military reinforcements from Saigon arrived, and the Tinh Hoi Pagoda was completely surrounded with armored troop carriers and tanks. I hadn't shot anything the day before so I was determined to do well. Roger and his crew were covering the government forces near the front gate, so I searched for a high point where I could get a clear picture of the pagoda, which was buried in an old neighborhood of small streets and alleys.

A street kid about ten years old began to follow me, and after a while I asked him if he could lead me near the pagoda. Because of the language issues, I turned to acting. I took my camera and posed with it as if I were filming to show that I was a journalist and not a spy. One of my few Vietnamese phrases was "*Cho toi di*" which is what you said to a taxi driver when you were ready to go. I had no idea what "pagoda" was in Vietnamese, so I put my hands together in prayer, clapped, and chanted "*Nammaida, Nammaida.*" That's a Japanese Buddhist chant, but I'd heard it in Vietnam and knew it was pretty close.

That was all it took. The kid waved for me to follow him and took off down tiny lanes, through the courtyards of people's homes, and across small alleys. In less than five minutes, we were at a side door to the pagoda. The courtyard of the pagoda was jammed with people working, running, praying, and preparing to fight the government troops.

Tony Hirashiki in 1967. "...this wonderful man could walk through a deserted village and five minutes later, have a dozen kids following him around as if he were the Pied Piper!" (1995 letter from Roger Peterson) (Courtesy Yasutsune Hirashiki)

Rebel soldiers were digging bunkers and trenches, filling sandbags, and piling them up right next to civilians. Young monks were answering questions and giving instructions while nuns and other women cooked food and delivered tea to the workers. Even kids were helping.

It was an incredible scene so I didn't ask for permission and simply began to film. No one tried to stop me, in fact, everyone was friendly, and some were eager to show what they were doing. After I had filmed in the courtyard, I went to the front gate and took pictures of the rebel troops standing ready to fight off attackers.

At one point, I was behind sandbags in a machine-gun nest, and I could see all the other newsmen gathered with the government troops only 200 yards away. I even recognized Roger because he was taller than anyone else.

At one point, rebel soldiers began to move out in several lines along the wall of the pagoda and behind the trees along the road. I heard the loud and sharp *da, da, da, da* of machine-gun fire and soldiers near me fell down wounded.

The government hadn't fired warning shots; they'd shot to kill!

The attack didn't last long, but more than a dozen soldiers and civilians were killed or wounded. I got scenes of the advancing soldiers, of rebels evacuating the wounded, and medical care in the temple courtyard.

Yesterday, I hadn't shot a single worthwhile frame of film but this morning, my camera was rolling almost continuously. The scenes were shocking, ugly, cruel, sad, and unreal. There were so many victims in the courtyard, and the shooting had only lasted a minute. If the government launched an attack with the tanks and heavy guns lined up outside, I couldn't imagine the bloodshed.

I thought that this was just a political protest by the Buddhists and, even though some soldiers had taken their side, I never expected that it would come to killing each other. In Japan, I had covered many demonstrations and the police only used tear gas, but here they had fired live rounds immediately and, as far as I could tell, the wounded soldiers and civilians in the courtyard and on the floor inside the pagoda couldn't be evacuated to a hospital.

In fact, everyone inside appeared to be trapped, including me. I had filmed everything that was happening in the pagoda, and I needed to get my film to Roger. For the first time, I was worried about my own safety. I sat on the stone steps of the pagoda to think. Inside the pagoda, women were chanting and praying louder than ever in front of the main altar. It was a beautiful sound and very reminiscent of my home in Japan.

I don't remember how long I sat on the steps, but it was at least an hour before a young monk walked up and began to speak to me in clear and easily understood English.

He said, "I need your help. We wish to have a press conference in here this afternoon. We are all thought of as rebels. We want to have a chance to explain our point of view and the situation we're in. As you know, no journalists have been here so no one has heard our ideas. Could you bring your reporter and other international reporters—as many as possible?"

It was a demanding request. Should I bring journalists into such a dangerous place?

I told the monk that I'd come in by the side door with the help of a street kid and wasn't sure how to get out, much less bring other journalists back in. He promised me that he would show me a way out and arrange a way back in. I asked how they could guarantee the safety of the journalists. The young monk told me that he would order the rebel soldiers to hold their fire, and the newsmen needed to wave white handkerchiefs or something else white and shout "*Bao chi*," the Vietnamese word for journalist.

I told him that I'd try my best, but I couldn't make any promises. He gave me an escort and they led me out of the pagoda and back through the maze of alleys, lanes, and back roads. My escort vanished as soon as we reached the main road.

When I arrived at the press center, I found that Roger had been worried about me, but when I told him that I had footage from inside the Tinh Hoi Pagoda, Roger simply couldn't believe it. He thought I must have been confused, and filmed some other smaller pagoda.

I finally convinced him, and now it was Roger's turn. He had to decide whether he and his colleagues should go to the besieged pagoda on the word of a brand-new freelance cameraman.

Roger grilled me for more details about the situation inside the pagoda and then talked it over with the other reporters. Finally, about ten decided to follow me into the pagoda. The wire service reporters from Associated Press and United Press International, some still photographers, and Roger and the ABC sound crew.

Before we left, I made sure that everyone had a white handkerchief, a towel, or a white shirt and I taught them how to say "*Bao chi*." We crossed the dividing line in the gathering darkness and followed the route I had memorized. As we twisted and turned through the maze of streets, the newsmen were tense but followed me without question.

When we approached the pagoda, we waved our white handkerchiefs and polo shirts, and loudly repeated "*Bao chi. Bao chi*." The rebel soldiers were cautious, peering at us suspiciously from behind their sandbag barricades, then they waved us forward. The young monk's word was good, no one even raised their weapons, and we all walked safely into the pagoda.

The young monk welcomed us and for the next hour or so, he answered the newsmen's questions. Roger had his own sound crew, so I filmed cutaways: shots from the side, close shots of pencils writing on pads, or tight shots of Roger listening.

I felt good because the Buddhists got to give their side of the story openly and completely and face the questions of real journalists. I also decided that Roger Peterson looked like a great guy to work with.

When we made it back to the Da Nang press center, several reporters shook my hand in appreciation and said that getting the other side's story made their reporting better. Roger shook my hand with his powerful grip even though I tried to tell him that I should be thanking him for trusting me in such a dangerous situation.

Two nights later, it poured rain from midnight on. I couldn't sleep, partly because of the thunder of the rain on the tin roof of the press center and partly because I kept thinking of the Buddhists, wet and cold at their positions behind walls of sandbags or in inches of water at the bottom of bunkers and trenches. The government had announced that they would launch a full-out attack if those in the pagoda didn't surrender by dawn.

In the morning, we were told that all the Buddhist civilians and rebel soldiers had vanished from the Tinh Hoi Pagoda.

All of them just gone!

I imagined that everyone, including the young monk, had used the cover of the rain to disappear into the maze of lanes and alleys.

I knew that not favoring one side over another was essential if I was to be a real journalist, but in the time I'd spent with them, I had become sympathetic toward the Buddhists and the rebel soldiers. Perhaps I was impressed by people who would fight for their cause even when they knew that defeat was only a matter of time.

ONLY ABC NEWS HAD PICTURES OF BOTH SIDES AND OTHER NETS DID NOT.[3]

Exactly one month since I had left Osaka, and already my third Herogram!

After Da Nang, ABC hired me almost every day through May and June and into the beginning of July. I was happy for the work, but my finances were running low. Finally, with only $40 in my pocket, I asked Jack O'Grady when ABC was planning to pay me. Jack was so surprised that he scolded me, asking why I hadn't simply asked for my pay. Then he ordered me to sit down and write up how many days, what assignments, and then add up the total. As soon as I handed that in, he wrote me out a check for almost two thousand dollars.

A couple of days later, Jack called me into his office and told me that I was being sent to Hong Kong the following week.

My time at ABC was at an end!

I assumed that the news from Vietnam had quietened down, and I knew that Jack was leaving for the States and a new bureau chief, Elliot Bernstein, was already on his way to replace him. They simply didn't need me any longer.

I decided to be a man about it.

"*Jack-san*, you have been very great about helping me and you gave me a lot of chances. And I enjoyed working with you and ABC News. Thank you for your help. And I wish that someday I will work with you and ABC again!"

Then I made a deep bow, showing my respect in the traditional Japanese manner. It was an honest and sincere speech, and it was completely in English! I was proud of my *Sayonara* speech.

I couldn't understand why Jack looked so confused. Then he burst out laughing and said, "You're crazy! You're not fired! You're going to Hong Kong for a vacation, or 'R&R' as we call it. In fact, you've been officially hired as a full-time staff cameraman for ABC News. From now on, you'll work three months without vacation, and at the end of that, you get 10 days of R&R in either Hong Kong or Bangkok with your round-trip ticket, hotel, and meals all paid by the company."

Then he gave me a vigorous handshake and repeated just in case I hadn't understood, "Congratulations! You've been hired!"

I was happy, stunned, and embarrassed all at the same time. I'm not sure I've ever had so many different strong emotions at the same time. Later, I found out that ABC had made the decision to put me on staff quite a while before but, as with my pay, they'd just forgotten to tell me.

Jack O'Grady sent a letter to my boss in Japan, thanking him for giving ABC the chance to hire an excellent cameraman like Mr. Hirashiki. This O'Grady guy, who I'd thought at first was mean and mustachioed, had turned out to be a classy boss.

When I returned from Hong Kong, I was told to learn how to operate the "Auricon," which was the big sound camera that the number one cameramen carried. Ron Headford, the Australian I'd met when he was working with Roger Peterson, was known as the "artist of the Auricon" and he taught me all the techniques and tricks. When I'd mastered the big camera, I found out that Roger Peterson had specifically asked for me to work on his team.

There were moments when I hadn't believed it, but the letter that Jack Bush had written me in Osaka had come true: "If you go to Vietnam, you will be given a chance."

CHAPTER 3

TEACHER

It was a scorching day. In general, my memory insists that the sun in Vietnam moved much slower than it does in other places. This was a perfect example, even though it was late in the afternoon, I felt as if I was going to get sunstroke right through my hat.

It didn't matter. I was not going to fall behind.

It was October 13, 1966 and, after weeks of working by myself or as a second camera, I had been assigned to a correspondent!

Roger Peterson was only a year older, but he was about twice my size; 6 foot 4 inches tall, two hundred and fifty pounds, and all the strength of a Minnesota farm boy. Roger said that, from the age of eight, he would be out from dawn to dusk; planting, weeding, or picking crops. As soon as he was old enough to work legally, he took jobs doing everything from hauling wheelbarrows of cement, to cutting and laying sod, to loading grocery trucks at a warehouse.

Roger wasn't just big and strong; he was one of the best reporters at ABC and one of the nicest guys in the extremely competitive Saigon press corps.

I was not going to let him down.

We were out on a maneuver with the Marines. Roger was in front, I was following him, and Frank Eddy was third. If you could have heard me, you'd have thought I was insane. I was muttering "Roger, Roger, Roger" over and over. Most Japanese have trouble with the letter "R" and my pronunciation was worse than most. Whenever I tried to say "Roger," the word that came out from my mouth instead was "Logger" or "Lodger."

"When will you be able to say my name correctly?" Roger often asked me, so instead of singing marching songs, I walked to a rhythmic chant of "Roger, Roger, Roger."

Frank Eddy was working as my soundman. From Sydney, Australia, he was an experienced sound engineer, always pleasant, easy to work with, and willing to work hard when we had to. The problem was that Frank was my first teammate in Vietnam and so, by default, my first English teacher. I was determined to learn English as quickly as I could so I soon began to speak exactly the same way Frank did.

In a very short time, I had a relatively large English vocabulary—most of it American and Australian obscenities. In fact, you could say I was fluent in Cursing. It wasn't a problem in the field; most soldiers talked the same way, the problem was when I tried out my English in Saigon.

"Tony, I'd love to have you join me for dinner, but please keep your mouth shut!"

"Please, don't talk like that in front of my wife, OK?"

To Frank Eddy's credit, when the camera began to roll and sound was being recorded, he never used foul language in case it might get on the air.

As I would have said back then: "He might not have been the best [expletive deleted] English teacher, but blast it, he was always bloody damn good—a professional who never cocked up in the field!"

★★★

On the first day we worked as a team, Roger asked, "Do you have a nickname?"

"A what?"

"Yasutsune Hirashiki is too long. Don't they have shortened names in Japan? Like we call someone Bill when his name is William, or Dick for Richard, Bob for Robert."

"No, I've never had a nickname."

So, Roger simply decided that I was to be "Tony" in the field. I asked Roger why I needed to have a short name and he told me he didn't want to be working his way through "Yasutsune Hirashiki" in the middle of a firefight. Just like that, "Tony" became my "battlefield name."

"Don't run, Tony!"

"Don't move—stay there, Tony!"

"Keep your head down, Tony!"

In the times of greatest danger, Roger's use of my short name was a source of information, directions, and essential warnings. Since I could depend on him watching over me, I could concentrate on filming the war without worrying about my own safety.

It did create a minor problem for Roger. On his most dramatic on-scene radio tapes, the natural sound of battle and his descriptive narration of the scene would be suddenly interrupted by shouts of "Watch out, Tony!" or "Tony! Keep your head down!" The editors in New York complained of the trouble they had cutting them out.

To be honest, I don't like my nickname but it's been picked up by just about every other American I've ever worked with and being "Tony" has saved my life many times in many wars.

In order to become Roger's primary cameraman, I had to operate the Auricon. I hated that camera from the first day I picked it up and I shot with that or something very like it for the next ten years. The networks weren't satisfied with silent black and white film that looked like World War II so there was really no choice. It weighed around thirty pounds—so heavy that it had a shoulder mount with a brace that went down to my waist and helped distribute the weight. It was so heavy because it was soundproofed so that the ratcheting of the shutter wouldn't attract enemy attention.

It was only after I began to use the Auricon that I realized the importance of sound. Whizzing bullets, explosions from bombs and incoming shells, the shouts of soldiers, the rhythmic tramp of feet, the sad voices of refugees, the thunder of helicopters and tanks, and, of course, the ability to do interviews quickly—all of this added an urgency and immediacy to the footage. In addition, the correspondent wasn't limited to a "voice-over" narration recorded long after the action, he could stand up right in the middle of the action and describe what was going on. These were, naturally, called on-camera "stand-ups" or "stand-uppers" and would end with the correspondent's name, network, and the location.

Roger often did exciting stand-ups during the middle of a battle with soldiers firing behind him and bullets *zipping* past. He'd have to crouch down to stay safe but I could usually film while standing up because of my height.

★★★

One early morning, I followed Roger to a battlefield where a major battle had been fought all through the night before.

It was a scene from hell.

We went to the hilltop where American soldiers had fought off a massive attack by North Vietnamese regulars. It had come down to hand-to-hand combat and, despite the fact that they'd won, the GIs were exhausted, some shouting and others weeping. Bodies of dead North Vietnamese were everywhere; killed while charging forward, while lying down, and while simply standing still.

I had never seen so many dead before and I felt as though the ground was spinning around me. I almost vomited. I know I filmed the scene but I can't remember doing it. Roger never said anything to me but I later was told that he'd asked the other correspondents, "Why is Tony never afraid of combat but unable to handle bloody scenes?"

In truth, I felt that if I concentrated on a bloody scene through the viewfinder with the other eye closed, I could shoot the most gruesome images. Focusing on doing my job well—capturing the images, watching the focus and the exposure, worrying about how much film I had left, all of this kept me distanced from the horror that surrounded me.

Roger used to be a city reporter so he had some experience with blood and gore but like the rest of us, Roger was learning "on the job." Roger worked the war as if he was back on the streets of Chicago; he covered the fundamentals; he went to the scene, witnessed events, talked to everyone from generals to privates, and then went and got confirmation of the facts. In the end, he dispatched accurate and unbiased reports.

The American and South Vietnamese military authorities seldom censored what we reported before it aired. There were certain rules to obey; a few sensitive areas were off-limits and there were rules about revealing the precise location of a patrol or a gun battery. As a courtesy, we did not broadcast faces or tell the identities of wounded or dead soldiers until we were confident that their families had been notified.

Roger and I made a memorable first impression on most people—particularly soldiers—because of the enormous difference in our size. I was always reminded of John Steinbeck's *Of Mice and Men*, which revolves around the friendship between the short, smart George and the dim, very large Lennie. Of course, in our case, the characters were just the opposite: Roger was not only more intelligent and more experienced but he also moved a lot faster.

I maintained that I was slower because of what I had to carry. The big Auricon was on my right shoulder, a battery pack slung on my left shoulder, another on my waist, and a heavy knapsack on my back. The knapsack held extra cans of film and pre-loaded film magazines made of heavy steel so that I wouldn't have to reload during a firefight. I also carried my little Bell & Howell silent camera as a backup. That was a lot of weight.

Along with his personal gear, Roger only had to carry a notebook and a light Philips tape recorder the size of a hardcover book for his radio reports. I have to admit that occasionally as I was walking along, I would think about the unfairness of the small man carrying so much and the big man carrying so little.

More evidence of the inequity of the universe was that for every step Roger took, I had to take two. In the beginning, he would stop and wait for me to catch up and ask, quite sincerely, "Would you like me to carry the camera?" They were kind words compared to the complaints I'd get from some of the other correspondents but I'd still answer by saying, "The camera is the soul of a cameraman same as a sword for a samurai. How can I give my soul to you?"

When we were in the field, Roger always walked first, and Frank and I carefully stepped right in his footsteps. There are no safe places in a war zone—a country road, a small trail, a footpath between rice fields; any of these could be mined or booby-trapped. Sometimes, I worried that Roger was too heavy and would trigger a mine that other, lighter men might have walked on without danger. I never thought about the fact that every other of my steps could hit something that Roger would have just stepped over.

If you worried too much about such things, you'd never go into the field at all.

On a battlefield, the situation usually changed quickly and unexpectedly. I learned from Roger how to stay calm, judge a situation, react quickly, and stay safe while still getting the story. Roger was very brave but never reckless. I always thought that I would make it back to Saigon as long as I was with Roger. Shield, good-luck charm, and *sensei*; I was sure that I had the best partner imaginable.

Roger's knapsack was the biggest I'd ever seen and it was so heavy that I couldn't even lift it. He used it to carry it easily, and it contained just about everything imaginable. When he set up camp for the night, it was like watching a magician pulling an endless stream of odd objects from a tiny hat. First would be a neatly folded rubber mattress which he would blow up in less than five minutes—something that would have left me gasping for breath on the ground. Next, Roger would take the shovel strapped to the side of the knapsack and dig foot-wide ditches along the sides of the mattress to keep away the torrential rains that would fall almost every night. Using a large knife, he cut down tree branches for tent poles and with these, he supported his big poncho over the mattress. If we were in deep jungle, he wouldn't use the mattress but just hang a hammock and a mosquito net between two sturdy trees.

A few of the other items in his knapsack: towel, soap, toiletry kit, shaving kit, portable radio with spare batteries, flashlight, antimalaria pills, salt tablets, pills to sterilize water, powder for athlete's foot, insect spray, aspirin, antidiarrheal medicine, can opener, coffee pot, portable fuel, socks and underwear for three days, several notebooks, writing kit, paperback books, picture of his fiancée, corn cob pipe, pipe tobacco, and at the bottom there would be a bottle of Jack Daniel's wrapped in extra clothes.

I couldn't carry a big knapsack because my first priority was the camera and anything else was very carefully chosen. I had to take cans of unexposed film and extra magazines and a number of tools and spare parts. A rubber-coated, hooded poncho was essential; it was a raincoat, the roof of a tent, and ensured a dry bed to sleep on. Folded in half with poles on each side, it was an emergency stretcher strong enough to carry a wounded man or to serve as a final shroud for the dead. A poncho and a light nylon blanket made up the total of my creature comforts.

When I was packing, it always came down to a choice between film and food. A 400-foot roll of 16mm film weighs twice as much as a can of food so I would always end up carrying more film and leaving the extra canned food behind.

I hung a canteen of clean water on my belt but Roger carried two canteens and I knew that one was filled with water and the other with Jack Daniel's. At the end of a long day, when he had finished writing the script for that day's story, Roger would relax, open the correct canteen, and, with a gentle smile, sip from it while smoking his pipe.

Roger loved to spend time with the troops and preferred stories of muddy foot soldiers on a battlefield to generals in their Saigon headquarters or fortified bases. Roger taught me that soldiers could be photogenic and they didn't have to be brave action heroes. They were just as interesting when writing or reading letters from home, shaving, cutting their hair, or simply kicking back and enjoying themselves with their comrades. It was unbelievable to see how these tough, hardened soldiers would change into playful and boyish young men the instant the bullets stopped flying.

Up at the front, we were right out there with the soldiers, facing the same hardships and danger, and so they were friendly and open. They taught me a lot about how to survive in the field, even making room for me in their trenches when shells began to rain in.

I was still very much a "greenie" and made many mistakes. In a quiet moment one day, I was with a group of men, and we shared cigarettes. I used my Zippo lighter and lit two cigarettes but the third man jerked his away and said, "Don't do that to me!" They told me that the first man who lit up caught the eye of the enemy, the second gave the enemy time to set his aim, and so the third man would be shot. I didn't make that mistake again.

One day Roger, Frank, and I were following a Marine unit on a mission to clear out active guerrilla forces reported to be near the base at Con Thien. We'd left base at around nine o'clock in the morning and had walked for nearly four hours without coming across a soul—not the Viet Cong and not even local villagers. The lack of villagers made the Marines uneasy, they knew that this region was dangerous and the absence of civilians meant either that they were afraid or had been ordered away.

In front of me, Roger's canteens made a rhythmical banging sound; behind me, Frank was cursing steadily about the hot sun. We finally turned on to a small village road after walking a long footpath between two rice paddies. I looked ahead and saw bushes and trees and dared to hope for a bit of shade for the next break.

I could hear the sound of cicadas singing and thought, this is just like a forest in Japan.

Crack! Crack! Gunfire rattled in front of us. As soon as he heard the shots, Roger ran toward the sound with a microphone in his hand, recording as he ran. Frank and I followed but he was too fast for us to catch up.

Then we heard him shouting. "Tony, don't move! Don't come here! Stay there and keep your heads down!"

We stopped, found some cover, and I began to roll film as bullets snapped over our heads.

By the road, a young black Marine was screaming in pain while his comrades poured bullets into the woods. A Navy medic crawled to the soldier and gave him morphine. Suddenly, everything was quiet, and I could hear the cicadas again.

Then Roger came around the bend leaning on a Marine. His right hand was completely covered in blood!

Roger was wounded!

I screamed and rushed toward him, dropping my camera on the ground, and completely forgetting about taking pictures or the news or anything but the fact that Roger was hurt. I simply couldn't believe it. He was the big one, the strong one, the guy who always ran straight towards where the guns were firing; his tape recorder switched on and recording everything that happened while he calmly described the scene.

This time, the audio recording included the sound of the bullet as it smacked through his right hand and arm.

Even though he'd been wounded, his first thoughts had been for his camera team, telling us to stay back and keep our heads down. In contrast to my panic and worry, Roger was calm even though he grimaced from the pain.

Now, I was furious at myself. My camera was on the ground, I was acting like a green and inexperienced rookie, and had forgotten everything Roger had tried to teach me. I had gotten scenes of the fighting, but no pictures of Roger wounded. I got my camera and tried to do my job.

October 13, 1966. While following a unit involved in searching for guerrilla bases near Con Thien, correspondent Roger Peterson was wounded. A bullet passed through his right hand and lower arm. (Photo John Schnider; courtesy Roger Peterson)

"Roger, are you interesting in doing a stand-upper?"

Roger was a little surprised by my question, but I thought that he might forget his pain if he was concentrating on something else. Roger thought for a few moments and then nodded. He even managed a smile.

I put my camera back on my shoulder and started rolling. Roger held the microphone in his left hand and began to do an "ad lib" report, just making it up as he went along. He went on for a while but then stopped and said, "I can't think anymore, and my brain just can't focus. I've got to stop." The morphine and loss of blood overcame him, and he leaned back into the tall grass and fell asleep until the medevac chopper took him away.

October 13, 1966. Roger Peterson, wounded and waiting for a medevac chopper, attempts to record a "lay-downer." However, as he remembers, the morphine hit hard and he never finished. (Photo John Schnider; courtesy Roger Peterson)

Decades later Roger recalled the events for me in a letter:

As far as my memories of my getting shot—it was on October 13, 1966, just south of Con Thien as I recall. I can't remember the Marine battalion or company we were with. We had just linked up with them, and I don't think I'd even gotten the name of anyone. I remember thinking it was going to be a nothing operation because we didn't see anything for a couple of hours, then we got ambushed on the left flank.

I went up to see what was happening. One Marine had been shot through the right forearm as he started across a clearing and they were patching him up when I got there. I remember the wounded Marine was black and his buddy, who was very concerned about him, was white, and I thought maybe we could do something with that angle when the shooting died down.

I thought I saw something moving in a treeline. I pointed and asked a sergeant if he had any men over there. He said no, and then the firing started again. I got hit at an angle from above—guy must have been in a tree and thought I was an officer or somebody directing fire—anything's possible.

I remember some Marine yelling for a corpsman, saying "We got a photographer hit over here!" I wanted to tell him I wasn't a photographer, but it didn't seem too important at the time. The corpsman came, patched me up, and then the firing started again, and we both dove down. I got my face in the mud and blood from my wounds so I didn't look too good when we went running back to the middle of the company and saw you and Frank.

Then I ad-libbed a piece and got medevac'd out. I've never seen that film—some ABC idiot managed to lose it.

Hope this refreshes your memory. It seems like such a long time ago—and then sometimes, it seems like it just happened last week. I wish we could have a chance to work together again someday on a good picture story, but that's probably not possible. But we had a hell of a time for a while, didn't we?[1]

Roger went straight from the field hospital to the States and was operated on there. Frank and I continued following the Marines and made it back to the base just before sunset. Frank even stopped cursing.

October 13, 1966. In a shot by Tony Hirashiki, a medic holds Roger's microphone as he struggles to order his thoughts. (Film shot by Yasutsune Hirashiki; courtesy ABC News)

CHAPTER 4

HAWKS OR DOVES

Back in the States, those who supported the war were known as "hawks" while those opposed were "doves." As I learned more about war and those who covered it, I found out that those terms were far too simple but in those early days, it was easier to get the right shots if I knew I was working with a "hawk" or a "dove." In my youthful simplicity, I often reduced it to "hawks" being reporters who wanted to get right up to the frontlines as and "doves" as reporters who wanted to cover stories away from the battles.

Don North was a handsome Canadian who reminded me of Alan Ladd, the movie actor who starred in *Shane*. Richard Pyle, reporter and Saigon bureau chief for the Associated Press, knew Don in the early days:

> ...as a freelancer, [North] could work for anyone and soon found himself working for everyone. Colleagues in the Saigon press corps joked about "North, the one-man band," going afield with a clumsy, 20-pound tape recorder, a 16-mm film camera, two 35-mm still cameras, and last, but not least, a pen and a notebook. Not all were so versatile, but North embodied the adventurous spirit and professional ambition that drew hundreds of journalists and would-be journalists to Vietnam in the 1960s.[1]

In a letter, Don described his first days in Vietnam:

> I had taken some army training as a youth in Canada but was not interested in being a soldier. As a journalist, I could experience the comradeship and excitement of war without having to shoot anybody. I went to Vietnam believing that the US was trying to save this little democracy from the threat of International Communism. It soon was apparent to me that this was essentially a civil war and

the little democracy was a corrupt dictatorship that did not deserve our assistance. Motives for going to Vietnam!

As a young journalist I believed war was a prime story to be covered and as a freelancer, you could always sell "bang bang" pictures to somebody. The closer you got to where the bullets were flying, the fewer reporters you had to compete with for the story. So it was possible to make a living as a freelance war correspondent in Vietnam. Later with some Vietnam experience, I was asked to join ABC News if I would sign up for at least a year of Vietnam duty.

To be a network correspondent was a dream I had followed for many years and finally because of the war it was possible. The networks needed young correspondents who would go to Vietnam. By 1967 most staff correspondents of the networks had gone to Vietnam for six months to a year, and they were not willing to go back. So the nets had to bring in new correspondents who would go to Vietnam for at least a year, and they hoped perhaps two or three if the war lasted that long. I doubt if I would have been hired by a network until much later in my career if it had not been for Vietnam.[2]

In their off hours, members of the Saigon press corps would engage in heated discussions about many things—one of the favorites was the wisdom of carrying handguns for their own protection. Were you safer carrying one or just more likely to be seen as a combatant? Are you supporting one side by standing ready to defend a position along with American soldiers? One of the few things that protected a journalist in a combat situation or if they were picked up at a checkpoint or ambush was their civilian status. For that reason, many argued that journalists should not carry any weapons because we were civilians reporting on the military and not members of the military. Others felt that journalists should be able to defend themselves so that they didn't put an additional burden on the troops they were with—just like you shouldn't ask a soldier for a drink or a cigarette, you shouldn't depend on them to take care of you either.

Most camera crews made the decision very simply; they had to carry enough weight and more film or extra food beat a pistol any time. I wouldn't have known what to do with a gun and would have been more likely to shoot myself than an enemy. That made the choice quite simple.

Don North did carry a pistol for a time and remembers that the executives in New York knew he was armed but never told him to stop or complained in any way.

On February 27, 1967, correspondent Don North records a stand-up as Airborne troops move out as a part of Operation Junction City. Takayuki Senzaki is mixing the audio which is then fed by cable and recorded on Tony Hirashiki's film. Since Roger Peterson had assigned Yasutsune a "battlefield name" of "Tony," for quicker communications, Takayuki Senzaki had become "Yuki." Nicknames are not a part of Japanese culture. (Courtesy Don North)

In 1967, Don North, Takayuki Senzaki, and I were in a helicopter with soldiers from the 1st Infantry Division. They were going into War Zone "C" near the Cambodian border for Operation *Junction City.* With more than twenty-five thousand troops, this was billed as the largest search and destroy operation since American forces took up a combat role in Vietnam. The target area was believed to be an enemy stronghold where they based their headquarters, supply depots, and even hospitals.

My soundman, who I had given the battlefield name "Yuki," had recently arrived from Tokyo where he'd been a still photographer. He'd been lucky enough to follow the Japanese ping-pong team to China and his photographs were carried in *LIFE* magazine. He showed up at the ABC News Tokyo bureau with "*LIFE* Magazine" printed on his business cards and through sheer self-promotion managed to get a job as a soundman in the Saigon bureau.

On this trip, Don did a stand-up where he very coolly described the situation with soldiers exiting a helicopter behind him amid smoke from earlier bombardments. A still photographer took a nicely framed picture; on the left Don standing up with his microphone, in the middle Yuki was operating the sound gear, and on the right, I was manning the camera. Don recollected in an email:

> This was the time that the Pentagon called ABC News and said: "We don't mind if your correspondent North chooses to carry a firearm. Just tell him not to strap it on when he does a stand-upper to camera."

In another email, Don expanded on his going armed.

> Operation Junction City. I carried a gun, a .45 that I'd bought for $10 from another correspondent who was leaving. I'd gotten separated from the US troops I was with in heavy jungle one time and it scared me to think what would happen to me if I met a VC. I was dressed almost like any GI. I thought it might save my life if it came to a matter of who shoots first. But I found it heavy and cumbersome and it was unlikely I would be wandering around by myself without troops, so I decided to trade it for a smaller .35 caliber Police Special which would fit in my jacket pocket. I packed that around for a while, then a GI offered to trade me for an even smaller .22 caliber pistol that was very small and fit in a shirt pocket. An officer later told me the .22 was not powerful enough to do much damage and if I fired it point blank at a VC it would probably just piss him off. So I stopped carrying it around and finally sold it for $10 which is what I paid for the .45 in the first place. Most GIs, I found were pleased to see a correspondent carrying a "piece," it sort of showed them you were ready to fight if need be.[3]

In 1968, Don North covered the Tet Offensive in Saigon, and his report was the first report broadcast on American TV because of an error by his cameraman; a very lucky mistake as it turned out. Cameraman Peter Leydon had scrambled to the US Embassy where enemy troops were within feet of taking the building. Unfortunately, he'd left so quickly that he and North had crossed signals and each thought the other was bringing the extra film. In the end, they only had 400 feet of film.

That's about 11 minutes of pictures.

They made those 400 feet last through the biggest event in the entire Vietnam War, carefully choosing each scene. Don explained how this ended up giving him a scoop on the other networks in an article originally

On the first day of the Tet Offensive—January 30, 1968—Vietnamese sappers blew a hole in the wall around the US Embassy in Saigon. Correspondent Don North recorded his reports lying down to avoid gunfire as American troops fought to clear the Embassy grounds. (Courtesy Don North)

published in *Vietnam Magazine*. It's also a good example of how field reporters often disagreed editorially with the bosses in New York.

> The film from all three networks took off from Saigon on a special military flight about noon. When it arrived in Tokyo for processing, it caused a mad, competitive scramble to get a cut film story on satellite for the 7 p.m. (E.S.T.) news programs in the States. Because we had only 400 feet to process and cut, ABC News made the satellite in time, and the story led the ABC-TV evening news. NBC and CBS missed the deadline and had to run catch-up specials on the embassy attack later in the evening. On the last 30 feet of film, I recorded my closing remarks in the embassy garden:

> "SINCE THE LUNAR NEW YEAR, THE VIET CONG AND NORTH VIETNAMESE HAVE PROVED THEY ARE CAPABLE OF BOLD AND IMPRESSIVE MILITARY MOVES THAT AMERICANS HERE NEVER DREAMED COULD BE ACHIEVED. WHETHER THEY CAN SUSTAIN THIS ONSLAUGHT FOR LONG REMAINS TO BE SEEN. BUT WHATEVER TURN THE WAR NOW TAKES, THE CAPTURE OF THE US EMBASSY HERE FOR ALMOST SEVEN HOURS IS A PSYCHOLOGICAL VICTORY THAT WILL RALLY AND INSPIRE THE VIET CONG. DON NORTH, ABC NEWS, SAIGON."

> A rush to judgment before all pieces of the puzzle were in place? Perhaps. But there was no time to appoint a committee to study the story. I was on an hourly deadline, and ABC expected the story as well as some perspective even in those early hours of the offensive—a first rough draft of history. My on-the-scene analysis never made it on ABC News. Worried about editorializing by a correspondent on a sensitive story, someone at ABC headquarters in New York killed the on-camera closer.[4]

In 1967, Don won the Overseas Press Club Award for his reports from Vietnam. I'd always thought of Don as a hawk, looking back, I'm not so sure.

★★★

Bill Brannigan was the first correspondent I worked with who, I felt, really disliked covering combat. In 1967, Bill arrived for a two-year tour to cover for a correspondent whose wife was having a baby. Bill had worked on the Assignment Desk in New York, except for a three-month stint in Vietnam in 1966.

When the camera teams talked, we would always try and work out whether new reporters were "hawks" or "doves." I wonder if the reporters realized how intently we would watch them or that we would compare notes. The other cameramen said that Bill seemed to avoid going up to the frontlines or covering major battles, and the consensus was that he disliked the "bang-bang" aspect of war.

In fact, Bill did do many feature stories that weren't directly connected to a battlefield. Although it was certainly true that covering these stories was less dangerous, it certainly wasn't any easier on the camera crews because we had to work to get the right pictures for the story the reporter was writing instead of the reporter writing the story to the pictures we had.

For example, for a story on American soldiers involved in the booming Vietnamese black market, we spent days tracking how supplies meant for military post exchanges (PXs) were diverted and sold, and waited, sometimes for hours, to get pictures of GIs in the act of selling goods to black marketers.

The truth was that, while going to the front and covering war scenes was dangerous, it was simpler and more exciting. From an academic standpoint, I suppose feature stories were better, but there was a good likelihood that they would be left on a shelf in New York and forgotten. A combat story, on the other hand, had to be run right away, or it would be outdated. Even if a feature was scheduled to run, very often something new would come in, and it was shoved out of the way.

At times, Bill had to cover combat, and when he did, I realized that he was completely involved in that story as well, and the results weren't like other reporters.

They were better.

We went into the small town of Quon Loi, where soldiers from the 1st Infantry Division, fresh from the States, were gathering for a major push. The young men, most just out of basic training, were nervous and milled about as they found their units, got their orders, and lined up for their helicopters.

Bill walked around first, talking to officers and senior noncoms until he finally found the right unit. They were all fresh recruits with creases still in their uniforms. As I watched them, I realized that a year ago I had probably looked just like them.

Bill picked out one soldier, PFC Ronnie Compton, from a tiny Kentucky coal town named Pinsonfork, and told me to stay with him, film him as he ate, as he talked to buddies, as he checked his equipment, and as he did all the other things that soldiers do in the "wait" part of "hurry up and wait." Every once in a while, Bill would ask him a question—not an interview but just quick things like "What are you thinking about?" or "Are you scared?"

The young soldier had just turned twenty, but he wasn't nervous around a television camera, he answered Bill's questions simply and sincerely. "Honestly, I am scared. It's my first combat. I want to make sure I don't make any mistakes." (See footage in plate section.)

Bill had gotten permission for us to go in the same helicopter and follow Compton right onto the field of battle. I had some doubts, going into combat with an entirely green unit seemed dangerous, but Bill wasn't scared so I wasn't going to complain.

The target area had already been pounded by air strikes and artillery fire, and we would be going in right after the bombardment ended. Wave after wave of helicopters loaded with tense but determined soldiers headed for the frontline. The unit we were with boarded their helicopters and checked their weapons for the last time.

I sat next to the door so I could jump out first and during the flight, I kept on filming the faces of these grim and determined young men— including PFC Compton.

There was gunfire at the drop zone, and the pilot yelled for everyone to get out fast. He wasn't even going to touch down but just hover, and we would all have to jump. I'd done this before and so was ready as we tumbled out into a chaos of smoke and noise.

A "hot LZ" is both deadly serious and amusing at the same time. Some soldiers dropped into a roll and just kept on rolling, others fell backward. Then, of course, their comrades jumped right on top of them.

Our Kentucky boy did indeed fall on his butt, but he stood up quickly, carefully checked his gear, regrouped, and moved out briskly with his rifle in position. We stayed right behind him and caught up just as he

ABC News correspondent Bill Brannigan interviews an American officer in 1967. Tony began working with Brannigan in 1967 and found him to be the first correspondent who wasn't interested in shooting combat footage every day. Even though he was more interested in stories than simple "bang bang," Brannigan was wounded at Khe Sanh on March 6, 1968 along with his cameraman, Jim Deckard. (Courtesy Bill Brannigan)

reached the tall trees of a rubber plantation. I could hear the sound of bullets whizzing by as his unit began to return fire.

Right as the firefight began, we got close, and Bill spoke quickly, "How's everything going with you? Were you scared when you were jumping from the helicopter? How do you feel now?"

Compton stopped firing for a moment and when he answered, it was as if the young boy had somehow disappeared, and been replaced by a soldier. "I was tense when the helicopter landed. At that moment I was scared, but I'm not scared anymore."

Even as he spoke, his eyes stayed carefully focused on the enemy line, and as soon as he was done, he moved forward and was moving deep into the trees. He walked confidently, all his training coming back to him, as step by step, tree by tree, he disappeared into the forest.

Bill did a stand-up at the entrance to the rubber plantation then we headed back to the staging area. When there was a break, I asked Bill why he chose that one soldier out of so many others?

He explained that he had been impressed by the young man's innocence and pure heart, an American boy next door who believed that fighting in this war was a part of his patriotic duty. Bill felt that through the story of this one boy, we could tell the stories of thousands of American soldiers.

At the US Military's press office in Saigon, we would all gather on Thursday or Friday evenings and watch the news programs that had been broadcast during the previous week. Videotape was still a new and very expensive technology so they were recorded through a kinescope machine which simply shot a live television screen with a black and white film camera. The resulting film was flown to Saigon and, although the quality wasn't very good, it was our only chance to see how our work had looked as well as the reports of our competitors.

The first report was Howard Tuckner for NBC News. As expected, it was filled with dramatic combat scenes and close-up shots of battle. Tuckner did the end of the report under heavy fire in the half-standing, half-crouching position that people already referred to as "Tuckner's Crouch." As a cameraman, I noticed that the camera didn't shake and the scenes had excellent composition. It was really great work under severe conditions, but I already knew that his cameraman, Vo Huynh, was one of the best. When the report ended, the entire audience applauded.

The second report, from CBS correspondent George Page, was also on Operation *Junction City* and was filled with scenes of combat. During Page's stand-up, a bullet had come quite close, and he'd flinched and paused for a second but then continued. When the screening of George's report ended, there was even louder applause.

Bill Brannigan's report came last. It opened with our footage of a twenty-year-old soldier anxiously waiting for his orders at the staging area. The recruit from Kentucky was introduced with a lot of pictures and very few questions and answers. The close-ups of his good-natured face showed his tension. My shooting had brought out the bravery and common sense of this young man without losing sight of the fact that he was still just a boy.

When he talked to the camera with his southern accent, it was so strong that many in the audience chuckled. Then came the scene of green soldiers jumping and falling in complete chaos at the landing zone—the press burst into full-throated laughter. Most had gone through the same experience on their first landing on a hot LZ, so the laughter was born of understanding and empathy. Then our young "Sergeant York" made his appearance as he faced his first real battle. His last words on camera were "I was scared, but I'm OK now." Then he marched into the woods and disappeared.

When the report was over, there was silence in the screening room. I thought no one had liked our story because it didn't have enough combat footage. After all, they'd loved the first two stories with all their "bang-bang" shots, and stand-ups shot under fire.

Then the room erupted with applause and shouts of praise. Everyone stood up in a "standing ovation" for the report. I could hear people shout "It's beautiful!" and "Fantastic report!" and "Wonderful story!" When the lights were turned back on, Bill was surrounded by members of the press corps shaking his hand and patting his shoulders. This is how Bill remembered the story in a letter:

> I remember the "New Soldier" report very well. I was motivated by the fact that many Americans at home, at least those who did not have relatives in the military, might not be aware that GI turnover was a fact of life, since most of the GIs did a year's combat tour and then were sent home. So, in effect, there were "newcomers" arriving all the time. We, of course, were very lucky to encounter PFC. Ronnie D. Compton, of Pinsonfork, Kentucky. He was an unassuming, sincere young man who wasn't at all intimidated by a TV camera and microphone.[5]

In the same letter, Bill wrote about his feelings on covering the war:

> As an individual, as a journalist, as a US citizen and as a former officer in the US Navy, I was interested in seeing first-hand what was happening in Vietnam, while also recognizing the physical danger involved. From my Navy days, the

only travel I had completed outside the US was in Asia—Japan, Okinawa, Hong Kong, Thailand, and the Philippines, I did feel some affinity for the region in general.

I recall writing down my impressions about the war while flying across the Pacific on my way to Saigon. I believed that the US had gotten involved in Vietnam with good intentions—protecting the South from communist infiltrators and also shielding other nations in S.E. Asia from pressure by Hanoi and Beijing. I was not sure that the direct involvement of Americans in the war was the best way to carry out these intentions and was interested to see if the South Vietnamese were doing their utmost, politically as well as militarily, to repel the Viet Cong and North Vietnamese. And this goal to see if and when the US role could begin to diminish as the South Vietnamese took over more and more of the effort, remained one of the main areas of my attempts to cover the war—in all its aspects, pacification, combat, politics, etc.

This is one of the reasons that I was not so eager to cover battle itself all the time because I felt the "boom-boom" gave the audience only a fragment of the picture. After all, in most cases, combat was taking place in only one percent or less of the country on any given day—what was happening to shape political attitudes or to affect the course of the struggle in the ninety-nine percent of the country that was quiet? Obviously, combat was the point of contact for most Americans at home, whether they had family in Vietnam or not. And, major combat, of course, had a political impact in the US. And on a bureau level, I recognized that it was only fair that the risky assignments, such as combat was, should be shared among the correspondents and crews on as equal a basis as possible. But, I am not an admirer of warfare and get no personal satisfaction from having my adrenalin run and breath grow short. I never have and still don't like guns. I also felt responsibility for the camera teams that accompanied me—after all, my decisions on whether to turn right or left go forward or stay put affected them as well as me.[6]

So, I learned that Bill might have hated war, but he was not simply a "dove." In fact, he was an excellent war correspondent because he was always trying to find a deeper meaning instead of only the events of one particular day.

★★★

The military command in Saigon used to hold press briefings every day at 5 p.m., and these became the intense and often angry exchanges between the media and the American spokesmen known as the

"Five O'clock Follies." As reporters got out in the field and saw things for themselves, many stopped trusting the military to give them the facts. My own disillusionment with the Vietnam War began when I covered the aftermath of The Battle of Hill 875 in November 1967.

Hill 875 was outside a small market town named Dak To in the mountains of Central Vietnam. Special Forces had been operating in the area for years, befriending and training the local Montagnard tribes to fight the Communists. In turn, the enemy had built bunkers, roads, and command positions on the peaks. In 1967, the US Military Command sent in American troops along with several South Vietnamese battalions to take those positions.

More Americans would die taking Hill 875 than any other piece of land in the entire war.

The enemy had retreated, and the fighting had ceased, but ABC had gotten the word that the Americans had taken the summit late so I was sent in to Dak To with correspondent Ed Needham and soundman Dick Harris a day after the battle. Dick came from Minnesota, and he had taken on the task of retrieving my English from the gutter where Frank Eddy had left it. He said that my constant cursing just wasn't what you expected from a network cameraman. Ed Needham was a veteran print reporter who had worked for several magazines but had only recently joined ABC. He was older and appeared to be a calm and experienced reporter.

The next morning, we were waiting for a helicopter to take us to the top of Hill 875 when the soldiers began to be brought down. Since the wounded would pass in front of the press, a press officer had put up a rope along the edge of the path and asked us not to badger them with questions. The network crews, reporters, and photographers all agreed to go along, and we stood in a line along the rope.

When the first wave of helicopters landed about a hundred yards away, there was silence as dozens of black plastic body bags were unloaded along with bodies that had been quickly swathed in green ponchos. As the choppers continued to shuttle between the hilltop and the base, the badly wounded were carried past, and then the walking wounded. They were walking past only fifty feet away, and no one in the press said a word.

The soldiers' faces were filthy and unshaven, their uniforms stiff with a mixture of mud and blood and, in their eyes, you could see anger and frustration. The wounded were covered with blood-soaked bandages that had turned such a dark red that it was almost brown. Their feet were dragging and they walked past in complete silence. It was anything but a victory march by these brave, elite American soldiers.

When the second group was walking past, a reporter finally called out, "What happened?" and another asked, "Tell us what happened on Hill 875."

At first, the soldiers just kept walking without the slightest reaction. We were surprised when a few turned around and faced the cameras and microphones and began to talk. It was an eruption of anger, frustration, and sorrow. In the beginning, the soldiers spoke one by one but soon they began to talk over each other, shouting, and even weeping as terrible memories poured out. We all stayed behind the rope but the soldiers came closer, and their stories became more intimate.

They were giving us testimony of the shocking, brutal, bitter, and cruel nature of the fighting on that hill. They were so angry that curse words came pouring out; they were speaking from the heart and those were probably the only words that could begin to express their feelings. It was the reality of war being told in a more sincere manner than I had seen in all the time I'd been in Vietnam.

Yes, they had taken the hill, but it was not a victory. The tunnels and trenches that the North Vietnamese had built all across the mountaintop had made it an almost unbreakable fortress. We were told that when they got close to the top, the enemy set off smoke grenades that confused the Marine and Air Force bombers and led to a "friendly fire" catastrophe where high explosives had slammed into an area where medics were frantically working to save the wounded.

This was our first report, and we shipped it to Saigon as soon as possible. We knew that the next important scenes would be from the top of Hill 875. The other networks had two crews but ABC, as usual, had only sent one so we decided to split up. Dick took the sound camera and went with Ed to finish the story at the bottom of the hill while I took my faithful Bell & Howell silent camera. I followed the reinforcements and walked up the hill where so many had given everything.

When we finally reached the top, I could see the deep bunkers and sandbagged trenches that the enemy had built. While I was filming, an Airborne soldier who was standing next to me said emotionally, "When we took those bunkers, the US Air Force jet dropped bombs. And it wasn't just explosives—it was napalm! Look how the bodies of American and Vietnamese soldiers are all together. They died in the same bunkers when the bombs hit."

Just after 4 p.m., helicopters landed with a general and other command-level officers and, to my relief, Ed Needham and Dick Harris. There was going to be a memorial service for the soldiers who given their lives for this scrap of land. They attached bayonets to the rifles of the dead soldiers and then rammed the rifles point first into the ground and placed the men's helmets on top. In front of each rifle, a pair of newly shined boots was carefully positioned. It struck me that the long line of rifles, helmets, and boots looked as if the soldiers themselves were lined up at attention.

There were no flowers, no candles, no photos, and no eulogies. It was a simple ceremony, but a very emotional one all the same. A chaplain gave a short prayer, and a soldier played a beautiful, sad tune on his trumpet. The sad tune of the trumpet echoed across the mountain and down to the valley below. The Airborne soldiers stood motionless, but I could see tears flowing down their cheeks.

I had trouble focusing because I was crying as well.

I didn't know why I was crying; it wasn't my war. These weren't my people.

Perhaps the tune was simply too sad.

Perhaps. But even I don't believe that.

CHAPTER 5

THE BUREAU

The ABC News Saigon bureau was on the sixth floor of the Caravelle Hotel at the corner of Tu Do Street. Just up from the Caravelle was what was once the city's opera house, and across the street was the very classy Continental Hotel. Back in the 1960s, the Caravelle was new and had better electricity and plumbing so a lot of the press stayed there rather than in the older, colonial-era Continental. On the other hand, the terrace bar at the Continental was world-famous so a lot of journalists stayed there just for the conversation.

In Caravelle Suite 606, which faced the street corner, the bureau chief, the assistant bureau chief, and manager Tran Dinh Hong (usually known as Lam) sat near the windows. The desk of the secretary, Miss Do Thi Thuy Hien, was next to the pounding telex machine near the entrance.

Room 605 was the crew room where we would wait for assignments and play a considerable amount of cards.

Most crews would have at least one Vietnamese member who usually ran the sound gear and could give a rough translation of what people were saying. These guys came from all parts of Vietnam and usually, we got along very well. There was usually a game in progress. The Vietnamese guys soon found out that I loved to gamble so they let me join in. In the beginning, I was usually the chump until I learned the game and then I would slowly turn the tables and get my money back. No one in the bureau really cared about our games—they just wanted to be able to find us instantly when something happened.

The local manager of the ABC News bureau in Saigon, Tran Dinh Hong, or "Lam" as he was usually known, was an excellent reporter as well as manager. Correspondents soon learned to check with him before embarking on any story about Vietnamese politics or military infighting. (Courtesy Yasutsune Hirashiki)

ABC's Vietnamese staffers were a very talented and experienced group and almost fearless. Don North once showed me a copy of a report on the brutal Con Thien battle. His crew, cameraman Nguyen Van Qui and soundman Nguyen Xuan De, shot a heartbreakingly sad scene where a Marine squad was trying to save another Marine, who had just been critically wounded by a North Vietnamese rocket.

The film showed the men attempting CPR and mouth-to-mouth respiration. When one would run out of breath, another took over—even while new rocket attacks came crashing in all around them. In the end, they couldn't save him and the camera caught their sadness and bitter

Crews would work 24-hour days in the field so no one worried about their near-constant poker games while on standby. From the upper left is a government press officer, soundman Hoang Dinh De, Tony Hirashiki, and Paul Lam. (Courtesy Yasutsune Hirashiki)

disappointment, they had no tears, but their heads were down, and they were silent.

After it had reached New York, Correspondent Executive Nick Archer sent them all this telex:

> **I WOULD LIKE TO SIMPLY STATE THAT I HAVE COVERED THE NEWS AS REPORTER AND I HAVE SCREENED A GREAT AMOUNT OF FILM IN THE PAST TWENTY-ONE YEARS BUT NEVER HAVE I BEEN MOVED AS I WAS YESTERDAY WHEN I SCREENED YOUR STORY OF A MARINE DYING IN CON THIEN. YOU ALL DISPLAYED GREAT COURAGE AND GREAT PRIDE IN YOUR WORK. GOD BE WITH YOU.**
>
> **SINCERELY**
>
> **NICK ARCHER**[1]

In the early days of my time in Saigon, most of the Vietnamese crew members were either stringers or freelancers and most of them quickly learned to shoot with the Bolex or Bell & Howell silent 16-mm cameras so that we would have a second angle on any event. In fact, one of the soundmen, Tran Van Than, known as "TV Than," had been a cameraman and we became quite good friends. He was a quiet guy, always smiling but not talking much. It was a great surprise to find out how brave he was.

One day, Tran Van Than was covering one of the big generals (I think it was Nguyen Cao Ky) as he visited South Vietnamese troops. North Vietnamese mortar shells began to hit directly on the VIP visiting area, and everyone threw themselves into bunkers except tiny Tran Van Than, who pushed Ky down and protected him with his body.

The other soundmen were Tran Van Kha, who would play a critical role in our coverage of the Easter Offensive in 1972 and my friend Nguyen Thanh Long whose name I so terribly mispronounced. Truong Kha Tien was the most educated sound technician—he had even gone to University in California to study audio. He often helped us as a producer as well as recording sound.

In my early days in Vietnam, my soundman was Dang Van Minh, who was severely injured in a helicopter crash while he was doing reserve military service. Once he recovered, he came back to work for us. ABC evacuated Dang Van Minh in 1975 along with many other staffers and he worked as a cameraman in the Los Angeles bureau. There, his talent blossomed and he became one of the best shooters at ABC News.

The other Vietnamese staffers were two female typists; Nghiem Thi Loi worked during the day and then Thuan T. Dinh-Banh, who worked as a telex typist at the Presidential Palace during the day, and would work the night shift at ABC News. Trinh Van Kim was responsible for getting the film shipped quickly to places like Hong Kong or Manila, a reticent man named Thieu ran messages, and the three drivers: Nguyen Dang Thiep, Dan Van Ho, and the very first driver ABC ever hired and the most dependable: Chu Dang, which means "Uncle" Dang in Vietnamese.

In 1970, Hoang Dinh De and Jean-Claude Malet joined the bureau. Malet became my regular soundman and an excellent friend. He had been a cameraman but preferred to work sound. This meant that he could see like a cameraman and, while I had my eye screwed into the lens, he would be my producer and tell me what was going on outside

Before getting his own camera, Dang Van Minh (left) was Tony's soundman as was Truong Kha Tien (center), and Jean-Claude Malet (right). Jean-Claude was the soundman Tony worked with the most in the later years of the war and they became fast friends. (Courtesy Dang Van Minh)

the tiny fragment that fits into the viewfinder. The result was that, even though I seldom opened both eyes to shoot, I still got excellent coverage because Malet was my eyes and ears and, in many ways, my bodyguard because he would warn me of danger on a battlefield.

Along with the Vietnamese crews, we usually had some foreign shooters working with us. Cameramen Jim DeSylva and sound tech Dick Harris from the United States, Terry Khoo from Singapore, cameramen Ron Headford and Peter Leyden and my infamous English teacher soundman Frank Eddy from Australia, and soundman Hartmunt Kunz came from Germany. Whenever something exciting happened, we'd get "big-footed" by the crews from the other Asian bureaus: Ted Koppel from Hong Kong with Y. B. Tang and Patrick Lett or Lou Cioffi out of Tokyo with Robert Jennings and Harry Weldon.

In the mixed military gear that crews generally wore in the field are (left to right) AP photographer Nick Ut, who would take the iconic photo of a young girl hit by napalm; Dang Van Minh; an unknown photographer; and T. D. Suu, a soundman who would often work with Tony in Cambodia. (Courtesy Dang Van Minh)

Bureau chiefs came and went, but the fact was that a good deal of the real work at ABC News Saigon was directed by two very smart and accomplished Vietnamese. Paul Lam was the local manager and hired local staffers to fill our needs on a freelance or stringer basis. Lam was an excellent reporter himself and covered all the South Vietnamese government and military briefings. A new reporter soon learned to go to him if they wanted to speak to a politician or an expert, he would help gather news materials for the correspondents, and do the final translations of Vietnamese interviews so the reporters could write about them accurately.

While Lam handled people and politics, the senior secretary, Miss Hien, was briskly handling mountains of paperwork. She would arrange press IDs with the Military Assistance Command Vietnam, work with the Immigration Office to extend visas, and ran the mailbox-sized telex

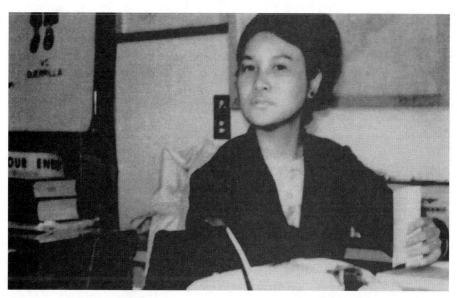

Senior secretary Do Thi Thuy Hien took care of the paperwork, visas, and cared for the telex machine. Crews and correspondents would hang around the telex to see if their latest work had received an Attaboy or a Rocket from New York. (Courtesy Mrs. Hien Boase)

machine that would pound away like a jackhammer all day with scripts, shipping bills, customs reports, and Rockets and Herograms from New York. She had a joyful character and frankly, for all her efficiency and precision with the paperwork, she could be a real "ditz" which only made her more charming to be around.

Here is an example. At one point, the boss of bosses, ABC corporate president Leonard H. Goldenson, was going to stop by and visit the bureau. Everyone ran around cleaning and getting rid of clutter and then was quite tense when the time came for our VIP to arrive. Miss Hien very graciously welcomed him with her best smile and said, "Welcome to Saigon, Mr. President Goldfinger."

We were in shock. She had mixed up his name with the villain in the James Bond movie!

Looking back, I'm sure he thought it was just a humorous event and a good story but all the local staff were quite worried that she would be fired and relieved when she wasn't.

I had my first real Vietnamese dinner when Miss Hien invited me out to a restaurant in the countryside. I guess most of the food was good but what I remember was when she introduced me to a Vietnamese delicacy: *hot vit lon*. It was a duck egg where the farmer had waited until the little duckling began to grow in the shell and then it was boiled and you ate it right out of the shell.

When the top of the shell was broken open, I could see the neck and half of the body of the duckling inside. Apparently, I was not cut out to be a gourmet because I only managed to eat one egg to be polite.

Over this dinner, our conversation turned to the people who came to work as journalists in Vietnam. Miss Hien had decided that there were three types of people in the press corps. The first group was young and usually unknown reporters who were determined to make a name for themselves. It wasn't hard. All they had to do was go right to the most active frontlines, work day after day, and cover battle after battle. If they did that (and survived) they'd have a good chance of beating out the older and wiser veterans. Then, their stories would begin to show up on the front page with their byline underneath. With that change, editors and executive producers who wouldn't previously have allowed them into their offices would begin to pay attention to their reports, film, and stills. You had to be pretty determined to cover a war, but you have a shot at seeing your name on the front page of the *New York Times*, the *Washington Post*, or the *Chicago Tribune,* or a photo gracing the front of the now almost-extinct news magazines like *LIFE, TIME,* or *Newsweek*.

The downside were the dozens of journalists who were killed, went missing and were never found, or returned home with injuries.

The second group, according to Miss Hien, were experienced free-lancers who were dreaming of that stroke of luck that would get them a staff job. Like me, a lot of young and cocky cameramen would show up and go to where the fighting was so fierce it was hard for the assignment managers to find a staff reporter or photographer to take the assignment. The freelancers would sell their stories and photos to anyone who would pay and then they would head back into danger in the hope of another paycheck. You'd find them in places the were tough to get into, tough to get out of, and they spent most of the time in the mud dodging North Vietnamese artillery, rockets, and mortar shells.

When the day came that a freelancer's picture was on the cover of *TIME* or *Newsweek*, or better yet, the large-format magazines like *LIFE* or *LOOK*; he'd probably only collect $400 but photo editors and assignment managers would know his name. He'd be a real war photographer and could hope that this new reputation would mean a staff job with a steady income and perhaps, a future.

Miss Hien said that the third category were those who had become so deeply involved with the war and the people, the land, and the scars we were putting on it, that they simply couldn't escape. It was as if they were addicted to the Vietnam War and couldn't get by without their fix. She named several famous journalists, historians, photographers, and writers who would leave and then keep coming back or simply find a home and move in. It wasn't just the war; it was also the people. Writers like Graham Greene who wrote *The Quiet American*, or Bernard Fall who wrote *The Street Without Joy* about the French war and predicted that, like the French, the Americans would fail as well. There were photographers like Robert Capa, the Hungarian who is probably still the world's most famous photojournalist and who had stepped on a land mine right here in Vietnam.

Miss Hien poked a spoon into her third duck egg and asked me, in a joking manner, which category I was in. I had only just arrived in Vietnam and thought I was all categories and none. I wanted fame, a reputation, and money but I hadn't even begun to accomplish anything of significance. Deep inside, my secret ambition for years had been to become as good as Robert Capa. I thought it was an impossible dream but in Vietnam, at least I had the chance.

I never answered her.

Along with Lam and Hien and the rest of the Vietnamese supporting staff, there was always an American bureau chief and an American manager. Most bureau chiefs were assigned for one to two years although New York also sent Nick George and Syd Byrnes for shorter periods when they simply had to find someone to fill in. My first bureau chief

Dick Rosenbaum, the youngest Saigon bureau chief ABC ever assigned, with Tony Hirashiki on Tony's 30th birthday. (Courtesy © Rosenbaum Family Trust.)

was, as I've mentioned, Jack O'Grady, Elliot Bernstein followed him. and in 1967, Dick Rosenbaum was promoted to be the youngest bureau chief ever.

Dick was tall and a little heavy with a carefully trimmed mustache. His wife, a very bright and brave woman named Thea, came to Saigon with him. Dick went out with the troops from time to time which was expected; no one would have predicted that the bureau chief's wife would train as a parachutist with the US Airborne but that's exactly what she did.

In those early days, many bureau chiefs went up to the frontlines with the crews to gain experience so they could better direct the correspondents and crews. At one point, even ABC News President Elmer Lower was scheduled to go into the besieged Marine base at Khe Sanh but the shelling was so heavy that their flight was canceled. Recently, Dick Rosenbaum wrote about how it came about:

> Elmer Lower arrived on the first commercial flight allowed into Saigon during the Tet Offensive which lasted from January–February 1968. On his arrival at the

bureau he said "I'm sure you are happy to see me, but don't let me get in the way. Is there any way I could help out?"

I said in jest, "Would you mind being Jim DeSylva's soundman? I've got crews all over the country and need some help here in Saigon." He said he would really like to be Jim's soundman. So, what the heck; I put him to work. For the next several days he worked nearly every Saigon story as a soundman.

In early January, Khe Sanh, a forward hilltop base for the Marines near the North Vietnam border, had been under mortar and artillery attack for weeks. So Mr. Lower asked if I could get him into Khe Sanh. My first thought was "Great, I can see the headline: ABC NEWS PRESIDENT ELMER LOWER KILLED WHEN STUPID VIETNAM BUREAU CHIEF DICK ROSENBAUM ALLOWS BOSS TO FLY INTO KHE SANH."

But we flew to Da Nang anyway and then waited until there was a pause in the constant shelling. We boarded the C-123 and the crew chief gave us each two combat vests. I put one on then asked the crew chief, "What should we do with the second vest?" He chuckled and suggested we put one under our feet and sit on the other to protect us from incoming bullets from below.

The flight in was bumpy, but uneventful. As we were about to land, incoming rounds starting hitting the runway and the pilots immediately aborted the landing and roared back into the sky. The plane, now low on fuel, had to return to Da Nang. As they were refueling the aircraft, I asked Elmer if he was ready to try again.

"Nope," he said, "I'll try anything once."

We flew back to Saigon.[2]

The bureau chief and the assignment manager often acted as the buffer between the producers and executives in New York and reporters and crews in Saigon. We all knew that New York was always looking for exciting footage since intense visuals were the best way to capture the war and the ratings.

Eight thousand miles away in Vietnam, the correspondents and crews were exceptionally brave but the ones who survived weren't crazy and there were times when an assignment was simply too dangerous. This was the bureau chiefs' daily dilemma, whether to push crews into situations where they could be hurt, hire a freelancer or stringer who'd be more willing to take the risk, or refuse to even allow crews to go to places where it was simply too perilous. If we missed the footage and it appeared on CBS or NBC, the Rockets would come in on the telex but if a staffer was wounded, the bureau chief took the responsibility

Dick Rosenbaum (right), the youngest man ever to be hired as Saigon bureau chief for ABC, waits with ABC News President Elmer Lower (left) and cameraman Terry Khoo, for their flight into the besieged Marine base at Khe Sanh. (© Rosenbaum Family Trust 2016)

and lived with the guilt. As for great pictures, after all the planning, it was often just a roll of the dice, as Dick Rosenbaum described in 1967:

> If our crew goes out the right side of a chopper, it may get no action. If the competition goes out the left side and finds action, how does your crew get over to that side under fire? Sometimes you can best describe getting good combat footage as luck.[3]

CHAPTER 6

CON THIEN

In late September 1967, I was sent to cover the siege of Con Thien, a Marine base about two miles south of the Demilitarized Zone. The North Vietnamese had been pounding it for months: artillery mixed with ground attacks. Thousands of the enemy had died over the summer, and now they had settled into a long-range artillery versus air power duel. In just over a single week, between September 19 and 27, over 3,000 rounds of mortar, artillery, and rockets landed on Con Thien.

Weeks before, the CBS team of John Laurence, Keith Kay, and soundman Pham Tam Dan had broken the story of the brutal siege, coming in on a truck convoy. Now, the military decided to fly other network crews in but said that it was too dangerous to let all the reporters to go in at the same time so we had to take turns. One crew would go into Con Thien, shoot for two hours, and then pull out as a new crew came in.

The two hours that I was in Con Thien, the North Vietnamese gunners must have been taking a break because no shells came in the entire time. All I shot were Marines firing mortars into the jungle where they thought the enemy might be and a sequence of troops coming out of their bunkers for a break. It was good footage, but it wasn't "bang bang."

When we left, a CBS team was coming in, and they got slammed. The artillery barrage was intense, and they had great footage of explosions, men scrambling for cover, and all the "bang bang" you could ask for.

The next day, I got my first Rocket from New York.

WHY DID CBS HAVE EXCITING INCOMING SCENES AT CON THIEN, BUT ABC HAD ONLY OUTGOING SCENES?

Dick Rosenbaum stood next to me as I read the telex and saw the disappointment on my face. His telex to New York was clear:

WE CAN'T FORCE OUR CAMERAMAN TO WAIT AND COVER INCOMING SCENES AT BESIEGED OUTPOST CON THIEN

Sam Jaffe relaxes in 1967 during coverage in Saigon. During the Tet Offensive in January 1968, Sam Jaffe, the former ABC bureau chief in Moscow and currently in charge of Hong Kong was called in to assist in coverage. After three weeks, he told Time Magazine *"the longer you stay here, the more inevitable it is that you're going to be hurt, maimed or killed." (Courtesy Don North)*

I appreciated Dick's support but I was even more determined to take chances to get better footage.

On January 31, 1968, the North Vietnamese and Viet Cong broke what was an informal but traditional truce held during the Tet holiday, attacking cities across South Vietnam. I was with Bill Brannigan and Nguyen T. Long in Hue, and we were at the Da Nang press center, relaxing and watching the annual fireworks celebration. As we found out later, it wasn't holiday fireworks but a major rocket and mortar attack.

When the sun came up, we moved to the South Vietnamese Army headquarters and shot all the film we could. Then we hitched a ride with Vietnamese Marines into the Citadel—as the old walled part of the city was called. We were told that almost the entire city had been taken except for one small corner where South Vietnamese troops and American advisors were still holding out against two battalions of the enemy. It was so bad that the People's Liberation Front flag flew over the Imperial Palace. Between the South Vietnamese troops and the US Marines, Hue was retaken from the Communists, but it took a month and casualties were high.

Bill, Long, and I followed an ambulance to the closest battle, but it was far too dangerous to stay there. The battleground was covered with piles of the bodies of soldiers from both sides. In the end, we were stuck inside the Old City for two days before we managed to get out on an American helicopter. Saigon was worried that we had been hurt or killed but Brannigan had told us not to take any significant risks, like following South Vietnamese troops too closely as they advanced. Once again, we stayed safe but we didn't bring out very exciting footage—it seemed as if we could stay sheltered or get great shots but not both.

Meanwhile, the fighting in Saigon had tied up all the crews, so the Y. B. Tang crew and Sam Jaffe, a veteran and well-respected correspondent were sent in from Hong Kong. Y. B. Tang was one of the first cameramen to be hired by ABC, he came from Cuba, and might have had more experience than any other news cameraman.

As soon as they began to cover the battle for Hue, Sam, and his crew were caught in a dangerous situation and almost killed so Sam demanded that the Saigon bureau replace them because the story was simply too hazardous. The Saigon desk tried to calm him down and asked if he would continue to cover the story but not take any unnecessary risks.

American troops struggle to save a wounded comrade during intense fighting to retake the city of Hue after it was captured by the Viet Cong during the 1968 Tet Offensive. (Courtesy Don North)

Sam refused, and Don North and the Jim DeSylva crew were sent up from Saigon. They managed to get excellent film of American soldiers fighting in heavy incoming mortar fire, but New York wasn't satisfied, saying that they simply weren't competitive with NBC and CBS during this crucial battle. CBS had great footage of Hue including film shot by a South Vietnamese cameraman who had been captured by the North Vietnamese but allowed to continue filming.

Sam Jaffe and the Saigon bureau had their argument on the telex wire which meant it could be read in every ABC News office around the world—publicity that made the New York executives very unhappy. A *TIME* magazine article titled "The Men Without Helmets," quoted Sam about the situation:

> ABC's Hong Kong Bureau Chief Sam Jaffe also decided after three recent weeks in Vietnam that "I won't cover Khe Sanh, and I refuse to go back to Hue." Summed up Jaffe, 38, who saw action as a merchant seaman in World War II and with the Marines in Korea: "The longer you stay here, the more inevitable it is that you're going to be hurt, maimed or killed."[1]

Sam Jaffe shoots a stand-up in Saigon during rocket attacks in 1967. His crew is the Y. B. Tang crew usually based in Hong Kong. (Courtesy Don North)

I have to assume that Sam's honest comment damaged his career because he was soon assigned to covering the United Nations in New York, widely considered a backwater job. Sam had been at the height of his career, based in Moscow during the Khrushchev years, the first correspondent to interview Prince Norodom Sihanouk, and recipient of the prestigious Overseas Press Club Award but he soon left broadcasting altogether.

What did that mean for the rest of us? Could we refuse a dangerous assignment? Well, I believed I could but up to this point, I had almost never said "No," so I really couldn't be certain.

It was always a confusing situation: New York was very concerned about our safety when we were in danger but, at the same time, they expected us to deliver the goods—in many ways a bit like soldiers on the frontlines.

CHAPTER 7

MEET THE BOSSES

In the fall of 1969, I was told that I was going to have to undergo "orientation" in New York. I was worried about this; was this "orientation" related to my being "Oriental?" Did non-Japanese employees need to go through "orientation?"

Once they had stopped laughing, it didn't take long for my bosses to assure me that it just meant flying to New York and meeting with the senior producers and executives of ABC News. These days, ABC News occupies almost the entire block of West 66th Street between Columbus Avenue and Central Park West but, back in the 1960s, it was packed into a single building known affectionately as "7 West 66th."

I had a very good time watching how the daily operation worked and taking pictures of my bosses at the round table—essentially the brains of the ABC Evening News. At this point, there were no morning or evening programs, so this was the only ABC News program we had, and it had only been increased from 15 to 30 minutes two years before.

Phil Starck, who was assigned to the Saigon bureau in the 1970s, told me that during that period, the executives were changing and improving ABC News in an attempt to catch up to the older and stronger network news divisions:

> ABC News was finally beginning to act like a first-rate news organization. Elmer Lower had just hired Av Westin along with Dick Richter and Dave Bucksbaum from CBS to run the ABC Evening News. Av demanded excellence. He was not one to suffer half-assed efforts and second-rate reporting.[1]

ABC News was a young organization and President Elmer Lower's hiring of Executive Producer Av Westin away from CBS was seen as a big step towards making their broadcasts more professional. Phil Starck wrote in 2008 "Av demanded excellence. He was not one to suffer half-assed efforts and second-rate reporting." (Courtesy Yasutsune Hirashiki)

Along with Westin, Dave Bucksbaum and Dick Richter came from CBS News to add even more strength to the ABC Evening News line-up. (Courtesy Yasutsune Hirashiki)

Executives and show producers confer on the day's news during Tony's visit to New York in the fall of 1969. Meeting all the bosses was nice but going to Shea Stadium and seeing the Mets win the World Series was heaven. (Courtesy Yasutsune Hirashiki)

Apparently, it was working since the show was improving, the ratings were up, and ABC News was generally more competitive. As Executive Producer, Av Westin was proving that he was a strong leader. Taking Vietnam as an example, Av had to be certain that the reports were factually correct, editorially well-balanced, and avoid tensions with the Nixon Administration by not letting the broadcast appear to be too negative or anti-war.

This was why many of the young war correspondents felt that New York didn't understand them and didn't realize what was really going on in Vietnam. Some of them even complained that New York would do more to censor their stories than anyone in Saigon.

Alongside the new hires, there were experienced executives who had built ABC. Vice President Bill Sheehan, Show Producer Walter Porges, Vice President in charge of Correspondents Nick Archer, and my direct boss, the Director of Newsfilm, Jack Bush. These were the people who watched what we sent in, encouraged us when we were down, criticized

Show Producer Walter Porges and VP Bill Sheehan share a moment of humor. (Courtesy Yasutsune Hirashiki)

and advised us when we weren't working up to par, and sent the infamous Herograms and Rockets that we waited to read every night.

They all knew my name and had heard plenty of stories about the crazy little Japanese cameraman. I was treated with friendship and warmth—in fact, when they found out that I was a baseball nut, Nick Archer took me out to Shea Stadium and Bill Sheehan gave me tickets to the World Series so I could see the Mets win. As a result, I'm still a Mets fan today.

★★★

Everyone said that Jack Bush, the Director of Newsfilm, was a tough man to work for. Everyone but me. In 1966, Jack was the man who had written me the letter that said, "If you go to Saigon, you'll have a chance to work."

It may have been tough to get the job, but once I had it, Jack could not have been a better boss. He protected and defended me and was a source of endless support. In early 1968, the network faced massive budget cuts because a planned merger with ITT had failed. I was told that the news division alone would have to cut out 15 million dollars in costs. The day that the "massacre" happened, thirty people lost their jobs, including several from the Saigon bureau. I was saved by being cut from the Saigon payroll but transferred to the Tokyo bureau and assigned to work with Roger Peterson.

The clearest proof that Jack had my back was that I kept my job for 40 years despite the number of times I broke expensive cameras. The Auricon sound camera was just too big for me to carry and, while it was made of steel, the C-mount where the lens was attached was made of soft aluminum. Unfortunately, this fragile part was essential and, if broken, the camera was useless.

And I broke them all the time.

Several times when I jumped from a helicopter into a hot LZ the drop was as high as 10 feet. The joke at the bureau was that, when there was an accident in the field, the bureau chief would ask about the camera first and the cameraman second. A cameraman could be replaced, but a broken camera was a real problem because the delicate parts had to be shipped in all the way from New York.

At one point, I was covering the war in Cambodia and spent days running across fields and crossing streams. In one terrible week, where I had a mixture of bad luck and personal carelessness, I broke three cameras. Even for me, this was a new record, so a telex came in from Jack Bush, asking how I could have broken three cameras so quickly and pointing out that they simply didn't have the budget to keep replacing equipment at this rate.

I wrote a long letter to Jack, my stomach hurting the entire time.

18 November 1970

Dear Bush-san,

How are you in these days? Many thanks for your helping and advice. Today I'm trying to explain what's happened my lenses.

Nov/10–11/1970 I was in the field, following ARVN operation Takeo Province in Cambodia riding tanks. We had to stay overnight. In the midnight, the rain

The man who brought a young Japanese cameraman into ABC News and stood behind him with a faith in his ingenuity, moral values, and artistic ability; Director of Newsfilm, Jack Bush. (Courtesy Yasutsune Hirashiki)

starting. I kept my camera gear inside the tank for prevent from wet. But there were no space for us (we stayed outside tank) only for gears. Suddenly heavy rain came. The soldiers rush back into their tank—yes it was happened—one of them kicked my camera broke lens. Of course not their faults. I regret why I should stay with gear even wet. The attachment part between camera and lens was broken.

Nov/12/1970 We went North, another battle field was there. On route 7, the big bridge were blown up by VC so we have to cross small lake by tiny sampan. We took it. Suddenly Sampan lost balance, sinking. less than one minute later, our sampan was under water. I tried hold camera. and before sampan sunk, I throw camera to bank. Soundman Malet also helped it but another gear, amplifier, power pack, mike all went under the water. It's lucky that camera still beside bank without wet but lens part was broken again ... so we could picked all other things up from under water, after dry, clean but amplifier had to send Saigon.

Nov/13/1970 We went same way. I hate this small sampan—so tiny. so unsteady—however we passed safely in the morning, after finish work we have to return same lake, same sampan. Yes, finally our sampan reached bank. I was trying to landing so carefully because we still remember how dangerous this moment, I'm too nervous and then I slipped down again same place yesterday. Lens was gone—attachment part between camera and lens—How I was sad. Please understand my feeling that moment.

I believed 13th Fridays since it. My nervous made mistakes too. First attachment and second attachment, I broke little difference part, so I combined them and used until new lens came today. As such my experience the most of my cases when I jumped from helicopter, when jumped from LST, when slipped down in muddy rice fields etc I never broken it at town believe me. So If I can get extra attachment same amount for one lens, I don't make you trouble so much. I heard Angenieux (lens company) can give us extra attachment for same lens. Forgive my several mistakes. I'll be more careful...I promise you.

By the way we have to go cross same lake again and again by nasty sampan, I'm still nervous it, but I have to go. I'll have duty here until 26th of November.

Best regards to you and madame

Jack wrote me back with a very kind letter instead of issuing a pink slip.

Dec/07/1970

Dear Tony,

Thank you very much for your explanation of your equipment difficulties in Cambodia. I did not intend to imply that you were not careful with your equipment. I know how careful and dedicated you are to keeping your equipment in running condition. However, when I heard that a sampan had been sunk, I became concerned for you and your crew. I'm relieved that you and Claude Malet did not sustain any injuries. The equipment can always be repaired or replaced....

Sincerely,

Jack Bush

Director of Film/ABC-TV News[2]

Steve Bell was the correspondent with me on that trip and he says the memory of me writing that letter has stayed with him:

We had to take sampans because our cars could not get across bombed-out bridges. I remember hearing a splash when your sampan overturned. When I looked across I could see only your arms and the camera above water before you got the camera ashore. But the amplifier was under water. The next day when I walked into our office at the Royal, I found you sitting at my typewriter surrounded by wads of paper from failed attempts at writing to Jack Bush. The line in your letter that I've never forgotten was, "Tony hates the dirty sampans.[3]

Jack Bush and Nick Archer, the Vice President in charge of Correspondents, had been friends for a long time and they made an excellent team. When they joined ABC News, it was just starting to produce a news program, so it was Nick, an editor from Movietone News and Jack who set out to create a news division from scratch. Nick worked at finding young, unknown reporters with the talent and charisma to grow to be stars. In later years, those young unknowns would take ABC News to the number one position.

During the Vietnam War, one of the toughest jobs Nick had was to find good reporters who were willing to go to Vietnam. Some of the reporters who were willing weren't all that good and a fair number of the good reporters simply didn't want to spend time in a war zone.

Every new correspondent would have a meeting with Nick before he or she embarked for Saigon. His advice: "Don't take risks. Nothing is worth your life, but keep sending good reports." Standing next to Nick, Jack Bush would often add, "Listen to your camera crews. You'll be fine!"

There was a twenty-fifth reunion of Saigon bureau staff in 2000, organized by the wonderful bureau secretary/managers, Miss Loi and Miss Thuan. At that event, we asked Nick, "What were the best and worst moments of the Vietnam War for you?" He thought a minute and then answered:

> The best moments I recall were when correspondents came to see us and offered to go voluntarily to cover Vietnam. Then I wouldn't have to force someone to go. It was a tremendous relief. The worst part what when our people were in a dangerous situation and I couldn't sleep at night, worrying about them and anxiously waiting for the morning phone call to Saigon to find out if anyone was injured. If anyone was hurt or, sadly, killed, it was all my responsibility and it was a heavy thing to bear.

Steve Bell told me his favorite Nick Archer story:

> There were many days in 1973 when we had no assignments. We would send Asia story ideas to NY every morning, but there were too many things happening elsewhere. In the afternoons, a number of us from all three networks who had been in Vietnam together would occasionally gather in one of the bureaus for a friendly poker game.
>
> A young administrator recently assigned to our bureau from the US was scandalized and sent a private letter to Nick Archer exposing us for our

Nick Archer, ABC News' Vice President in charge of Correspondents, smiles as he and Tony Hirashiki watch the Mets win the 1968 World Series. Vice President Bill Sheehan provided the tickets and as a result, 50 years later, Tony is still a Mets fan. (Courtesy Yasutsune Hirashiki)

transgression. My first knowledge of the episode came when Nick sent his reply as an open telex. It said:

RE YOUR LETTER. WHEN YOU HAVE BEEN WHERE THEY'VE BEEN, AND DONE WHAT THEY'VE DONE, YOU, TOO, MAY PLAY POKER.

REGARDS, ARCHER

I still consider it one of the best compliments we ever got.[4]

★★★

When I was hired in the spring of 1966, the President of ABC News was Elmer Lower. It wasn't until much later that I found out that he was famous in the world of photography having spent World War II working with photojournalist Robert Capa. Elmer was Capa's editor, handling and sorting the pictures he took during the Battle of the Bulge and jumping with the 101st Airborne across the Rhine. It was interesting to know that Capa described him as "Elmer Lower, the wily head of *Life*'s Paris office." However, Capa was well known as a loose cannon, and Lower was probably one of few editors who could handle him.

After World War II was over, Elmer worked for CBS and NBC News and then became President of ABC News in 1963. Lower discovered talented young correspondents, including Frank Reynolds, Peter Jennings, Ted Koppel, Sam Donaldson, and Steve Bell. His discovery of the young Peter Jennings as he was covering a political event for Canadian TV was a well-known story.

His concerns weren't limited to reporters and anchors, he felt the cameraman was integral to the final product. I think Elmer's friendship with Capa was one of the reasons why he loved and valued film cameramen. In 1973, he spoke about the role of the TV cameraman in a presentation to the Royal College of Art in London:

"I think that too little credit has been given to the men who actually are in the field who make these pictures," Mr. Lower said. "The correspondents generally get the accolades, but all three networks have displayed the work of the finest

Elmer Lower had been in the field before he became the President of ABC News. Proof was that he not only worked as soundman for cameraman Jim DeSylva in Saigon but attempted to go into besieged Khe Sanh with a crew. (Courtesy of John Lower & University of Missouri Journalism School)

cameramen in the world. Sometimes it seems the cameraman's dedication becomes a simple challenge 'How close can I get to the action?' The question always is 'What can I get my camera to see that no one else can see?' 'What will the human eye miss that I can get my camera to record?'"

"The television news cameraman," Mr. Lower said "is rather a new breed. There is no exact profile of the man. First of all, he is an artist, a craftsman, not just a picture-taker. The camera is an extension of the man himself. His knack for composition is built in. He is not only the eyes for the viewer but, often the creator of the most dramatic part of the story. Like his bravery, his patience is congenital. Hours of waiting for something to break, hours of waiting to get from one place to another don't seem to faze him. He offers no excuses for the weather—if there's a picture, he'll get it. The location is immaterial. A battlefield? He'll go. Gunfire? Well, that makes it a little tougher for him to take his time on production values, but he's the first man in."

"The television news cameraman is really most comfortable in a place where the action is. He has a seventh sense about impending movement. He'll tell you he 'lucked into' a sequence, but I often feel he knew it was coming."[5]

I actually met John Lower before I got to know his father. John was a talented photographer making a living as a freelancer in California. When Jean-Claude Malet and I were assigned to travel to Thailand, Japan, India, and Bali and shoot for a series of documentaries on the "Religions of the Orient," for Edward P. Morgan, John Lower was assigned to be my assistant cameraman. As soon as we began filming, I realized that John had the ability to truly "see" through the lens and the sort of creativity needed for documentaries, so I decided he should be on his own to film whatever he thought was appropriate. When the programs were released, John was credited as a "cameraman," and I was a "Director of Photography."

In 40 years, that was the only time I was credited as a "Director of Photography."

New York was very impressed with John's work, so they created a new position at the Tokyo bureau for him. It wasn't a staff position, he was only a stringer, and I was puzzled why he couldn't be staff considering his father ran the company. I asked John about that, and he said that father and son weren't allowed to work for the same company to avoid being accused of nepotism. I was amazed as in Japan, nepotism was a common and expected business practice and the son of a company president would be educated and groomed to run the company from the time he was a kid.

I suggested to John, "Why can't your father become a stringer president and you can take a staff job?"

Of course, I said it as a joke to cheer him up.

When Irv Chapman was assigned to be the ABC News Tokyo bureau chief, there was a small welcome party and, since I happened to be visiting Japan at the time, I was invited. John's parents flew in from New York and were on the receiving line along with Irv Chapman and his wife, Arlene. I was at the end of the line of guests, and when I reached the end, my boss said to me in a serious manner, "Welcome. May I introduce myself? I'm 'Stringer President, Elmer Lower'."

He shook my hand and started laughing.

My heart almost stopped, and I broke into a cold sweat. John must have told his father what I'd said as a joke. It was in poor taste and I regretted it. In Japan, this sort of rudeness to a superior would have been grounds for instant dismissal. However, I did not receive a pink slip and in fact, according to Vice President Bill Sheehan, everyone on the executive floor enjoyed teasing Elmer with his new nickname of "Stringer President" or "Freelance President."

In September 1974, Elmer Lower handed over his position as ABC News President to Bill Sheehan but remained as a corporate Vice President. In effect, he really did become a "freelance president" and John Lower finally got a staff job. Later, Elmer Lower wrote to me about it:

> I have always enjoyed your little "joke" about being a "freelance president." Instead, I became "president emeritus." Ask Pete Hively (then the bureau chief in Saigon) to explain to you what that means. I still am working with the news department on political conventions and elections, which are a specialty of mine. I love to work on them.
>
> I have always been very fond of Cameramen, ever since I became acquainted with photography in 1937. I will continue to speak out in their behalf... Keep up the good work, Tony, you are a fine cameraman and ABC is proud of you. I think you have fine touch when you take films of people. That is what television is really all about ... PEOPLE.
>
> All the best wishes. Sincerely yours
> Elmer Lower[6]

★★★

In October 1970, a young manager named Phil Starck showed up to take over the Saigon bureau. A former major in the Marines, Phil looked like a young version of Clint Eastwood. He stood six feet two inches tall, looked neat and cool, and had not lost the tough discipline of the Corps. He was very soft-spoken, likable and dependable. I guess he must have liked Vietnam since he served two tours as a Marine and came back as a civilian. His experience in Vietnam as both a soldier and a journalist gave him a unique perspective:

> When I joined the Saigon bureau in October 1970, I was 33 years old. I had come back to Saigon because I wanted to. I had met and worked with a few of the camera crews, correspondents, bureau chiefs, and producers while I was with the Office of Information to know there were some really great people in the

Saigon bureau. I was also determined that we strive to be number one and get "the story right."

It was important to me that all members of the bureau be treated with respect and fairly. There were still instances where crews, local staff, and correspondents might be treated differently either by bureau management or NYC management. This wasn't right. We all should have been working for the common goal of providing the best and most accurate news coverage possible. I believe we succeeded in having everyone, office staff, drivers, shippers, crews and reporters worked their butt off to make it happen. We did have a few people, both American and Vietnamese, who didn't pull their weight, but they generally were dealt with by sending them back to the States or off the payroll in Saigon.[7]

The atmosphere of the bureau changed drastically after Phil took over. We became more serious and worked more as a team. We'd had some problems right before Phil arrived: in general, a lack of discipline and very low morale.

It's possible that we were influenced by the negative mood of the soldiers and Marines up at the front. When the troops began to withdraw, those who remained seemed to have lost their fighting spirit and their faith in their officers and the whole concept of winning the war. That was one of the reasons New York sent Phil to Saigon and it worked. Everyone, even the Vietnamese staffers, could feel Phil's leadership and sense of mission and we all began to work in the manner that a first-class news division should.

During Phil's three-year stay, the Saigon bureau made significant progress, and we became very competitive against the other two networks. If we did a good job, we were immediately recognized and complimented. If we did a bad job, we heard about it quickly and privately.

Although Phil was not a bureau chief—his official title was Manager, Business Affairs for Southeast Asia—we considered him the backbone of the Saigon bureau. Phil was the type of leader who you could trust, depend on, and even love. Phil also shared his observations about that period:

Overall the ABC News team was even-handed. From my observation point, late-1960s to mid-1970s, the ABC film crews—cameramen and soundmen—were outstanding in covering news and were excellent in helping bureau management and the correspondents develop stories that were not always evident in the ordinary course of the day's events.

I regret not developing more Vietnamese sources independent of our local bureau staff. There was always a nagging suspicion that we (the bureau as a whole)

Two men who worked together to get the Saigon bureau through times of crisis. Phil Starck (left) arrived in 1970 and weathered the Easter Offensive and the departure of American troops, and Kevin Delany (right) was directly responsible for the successful evacuation of 101 ABC local employees and family members during the 1975 fall of Saigon. (Courtesy In Jip Choi)

was not always getting the correct scoop, and that we may have been force-fed information. I can't prove it, but I wish we had better sources in the [South Vietnamese] government and also in the US government operations....

I can honestly say we had some of the best cameramen in Asia; Choi, Khoo, and Hirashiki were the best. Later Minh graduated to a full-time cameraman and did a great job. All news people who covered the Vietnam war in the field were at risk of becoming a casualty. And there were many news people wounded and killed. In retrospect, the Vietnam War was covered as well, or better, than any war in which Americans were involved. Current events in Iraq and Afghanistan prove this out.[8]

In December 1971, Kevin Delany became the Saigon bureau chief. Kevin was a forty-four-year-old veteran journalist and an expert on Asia—experience gained first as a correspondent for CBS and then as a director for the Peace Corps in Thailand. He was a tall, quiet man with a very gentle manner. Under the leadership of Kevin and Phil Starck, the ABC News Saigon bureau became one of the stronger network teams, and we were no longer a laughingstock when compared to the other networks but instead right on their heels.

★★★

I suppose that it would be more accurate to refer to Peter Jennings as a colleague rather than one of my bosses but, when I joined the Saigon bureau, he was the anchor of the Evening News and a strong voice in what made it to air. Since he was always knowledgeable and decisive, I'm going to add him to this chapter as one of the people I worked for. I certainly cared about his opinion and wanted to impress him.

Peter was born in 1938, the same year as I was born, and when he took over the anchorman job in 1965, he was only 25 years old. For two and a half years, Peter was ABC's leader as we went up against Walter Cronkite and the team of Chet Huntley and David Brinkley. Peter was the first anchorman to cover the Vietnam War in person.

On his first trip to Vietnam, both his cameraman Larry Johnson and soundman Wally Oaks were injured by the accidental explosion of a hand grenade. US 1st Division troops were clearing a minefield near Bien Hoa airbase and soldiers were preparing to detonate unexploded munitions. Peter and crew were filming the scene, the crew got too

Peter Jennings was the brash young anchor who'd been hired to anchor the brash new ABC News. Tony worked with him for years after the war but missed his 1965–66 visit—the first network anchor to report on the war in person. (Courtesy ABC News)

close, and were struck by shrapnel. An AP photographer ran a picture showing Peter taking care of his own wounded crew.

I remember a big black and white photo that used to hang in the wall of a corridor at ABC in New York. It showed Peter and the Saigon staffers posing on the roof garden of the Caravelle Hotel. He was one of the anchors who would wear Lou Cioffi's famous "TV correspondent suits" rather than a coat and tie. Peter wasn't a "pretty-boy" anchor, he was a good TV correspondent. All of the camera crews knew that he could do an ad-lib report live and get everything right the first time. He was natural and comfortable in front of a camera, never stiff or worried. Most of my years of work with Peter were after Vietnam: Lebanon, Northern Ireland, and many assignments in the United States.

Peter was a heavy smoker but was always trying to stop or at least cut back. He would do this by not buying any cigarettes, but then he usually ended up bumming smokes from other reporters or the crews. He finally did stop smoking but, during the emotional coverage of the 9/11 attack on the World Trade Center, he began to smoke again. When he developed lung cancer, it took his life very quickly. I wrote him a "get well" note and said I regretted giving him cigarettes for so many years, but he passed away before it arrived.

I regret that I wasn't able to get Peter's thoughts and memories about Vietnam for this book. We were both working in New York, so I always thought there would be plenty of time.

Sadly, there wasn't.

CHAPTER 8

INDEPENDENT GUY

The first time I heard the name "Ted Koppel" was when my friend Terry Khoo told me, "Watch out for this guy named Ted Koppel. He's the new correspondent." I hadn't actually met him yet, but I was told that he seemed young, quite charming, and very friendly. On the other hand, I had learned to trust Terry Khoo's judgment. He had been covering Vietnam since the early 1960s and was both my mentor and my best friend.

Every time a new correspondent arrived in Saigon, the camera crews all tried to find out what kind of person he or she was. We wanted to know if they were a good reporter, could they get a script done quickly, and would they take our suggestions for shots? Easy to work with or a screamer? Were they willing to eat sushi?

We figured the new reporter was asking the bureau managers and other reporters the same things about us. These are important questions when you're going to have to live with someone for days or weeks in the high-pressure world of a war zone.

So what was the problem with this Koppel guy?

"He might be one of the best correspondents we have." Terry said, and then added, "He is very smart and quite an independent guy!"

This didn't help a lot.

What was an "independent guy"?

And why would that be a problem?

Terry proceeded to give me a rundown on Ted. He was two years younger than I was although he looked much younger, almost like a kid who had just graduated from college. But it turned out that Ted had

ABC senior foreign correspondent Ted Koppel c. 1967. Tony Hirashiki initially competed with him and ended with a friendship that has lasted over 40 years. (Courtesy In Jip Choi)

already had a lot of experience. He'd started working in radio in 1963 and already covered several big stories in the States—among them, the civil rights protests in the South.

In 1963, a few months before President Kennedy's assassination, Elmer Lower took over as the first President of ABC News. His priority was to build a strong foundation by hiring the right people; ABC president Leonard Goldenson described those early days in his biography, *Beating the Odds*:

> Elmer Lower had a very tough challenge. His first priority was to hire experienced people, and that meant getting them from our competitors. We could never afford enough of the top people, so Elmer also had to find promising newcomers who could be developed, over time, into first raters.
>
> One fellow, who had joined ABC only a few months before Elmer came aboard, was Ted Koppel. At that time, he was about twenty-four years old, working on "Flair Report," newsy, radio features for the entertainment department. When Elmer began to pull things together, he asked ... to transfer that whole production unit into his department. That's how Ted got into News, a very lucky break for ABC.[1]

In 1967, Ted came to cover Vietnam. Ken Gale, who had only started working at ABC News a few months earlier, remembers their first meeting. Ken was at the bureau struggling to type his script for that night's news report, a task that never came easy to him, when a boyish-looking man came into the room:

> I was sitting at a typewriter in the Saigon office with terrible hangover from too much of too many things night before (I won't go into detail) when this young cheerful guy in chino pants with a buckle in the back (That was sort of the yuppie fashion of the time) and a natty button-down aloha shirt walked in the door. I thought he was probably some young corporal or buck sergeant from an army public relations office. I think I may have been a little gruff.
>
> To back up a little bit, we all knew a new correspondent named Ted Koppel would be joining us soon. I don't think anybody knew much about him. But shortly before he arrived I had read a very clever, well-written article by him in *The New Republic* magazine. It was called WHAM, Winning Hearts and Minds in Vietnam. I was very envious that I had not written something like that, and I was probably a little intimidated until he showed up in the bureau. Then I think I was incredulous. Who would believe it?
>
> A short time later I heard him recording a piece he'd written for radio and knew he was definitely the real thing.
>
> Doubt went away, envy continued.[2]

I fear Ted may have had a terrible first impression of me. The first day he joined the Saigon bureau, he witnessed what had to have been an exceptional "conversation" between me and the bureau secretary, Miss Hien. I had just returned from an assignment in the field, and I bowed deeply to Miss Hien in my best traditional Japanese manner and asked, "Miss Hien, any motherfucking mail arriving for me?"

Yes, this was the period when my only English teacher was the foul-mouthed Frank Eddy. Today, I would be mortified at what I sounded like and would have fully expected Ted to take an instant dislike to me. It was true that he was stunned but, after many decades of working together, I now know that he has one of the best senses of humor I've ever known, and I had just made him a gift of a story that he would repeat at every opportunity.

In the middle of April 1967, Ted and I, along with soundman Dick Harris, were given our first assignment together: two weeks working out of the US Marine base at Da Nang. I'd only been in Vietnam about a year, and none of us were over thirty years old. My first impression of Ted, despite the warning from Terry Khoo, was that there wasn't anything to worry about; he was smart, a fast writer, and easy to work with.

We spent two days walking with the Marines across rice fields and through wrecked villages. In one village we found written in English on the wall of a destroyed house "Don't burn or destroy the people's houses, paddies, and property." We also had pictures of jets flying over, dead bodies, and several captured Viet Cong. Ted decided that it wasn't enough for a report because it would have to compete with the death of former German Chancellor Adenauer.

On the morning of the third day, Dick and I were sitting down to breakfast in the mess hall when Ted came in and told us that we had a new story. We rushed out without eating and then proceeded to march along after another Marine unit. I had decided, based on my "long" experience with the US military, that the Marines were the toughest soldiers to keep up with. They always started out walking and would then continue to walk until they found the enemy or the South China Sea. I've never understood why the Marine Corps was associated with the Navy and not with the Army since they walked more than the "foot soldiers" in any infantry unit I ever covered. As a newsman, once you were assigned to the Marines, you had to be prepared to keep up because you knew you wouldn't be allowed to catch a ride in a jeep or a lift in a helicopter unless you were wounded.

For the next two days, we climbed from rock to rock, hill to hill, and mountain to mountain. At times it seemed as if we were always climbing uphill, never down, and so would soon reach the clouds. Even when we did reach the summit of something, we couldn't take it easy going down because the Marines would always avoid all trails, saying that the enemy might have set booby traps or land mines on them. Often we'd go right across large rocks, and large rocks were hard to climb, especially near the bottom of the valley and along the cliffs, where they were slippery.

Don't get me wrong, it wasn't easy for the Marines either, they had to do all this climbing and clambering with heavy machine guns and mortars. Sometimes they had to use ropes to lift their gear from the bottom of the valley to the top of a hill. On the other hand, the harder it was, the more the Marines appeared to enjoy it. We hadn't had any "contact" with the enemy, so I kept filming scenes of them working their way up and down the roughest terrain they could find. I kept thinking that my film was more suited to a sports show than a news program.

We were all exhausted, but Ted never gave up. He would just keep going, never losing his smile, or his gentle manner. We were all young men and so it became a bit of an unspoken contest to see who was tougher. At one cliff, it looked like I wasn't going to make it with my sound camera and a nice Marine offered to carry it for me. I said, "No, thank you" and made it to the top somehow. I was stubborn and, I suppose, showing off a bit for my correspondent.

Along with the physical effort, we had to fight another enemy, hunger. I usually carried several cans of food with me on late assignments but we'd rushed out, and I'd forgotten to pack any rations. We could have tried to get something from the Marines who had supplies for several days but, as I've explained, in a war zone, one of the unwritten laws was that a journalist never asked a soldier for food.

On the first day, I was able to manage by drinking water from my canteen, but the pangs in my stomach actually woke me up in the middle

In 1968, Ted Koppel works with his audio recorder and a sheaf of notes while out on a frontline mission with American troops in Vietnam. (Courtesy of Terry Khoo Family)

of the night. I had never experienced such hunger in my life and so far, it had only been twenty-four hours. The fact was that all that climbing and marching had just used up all my energy. Ted didn't say a word, but I was sure he and Dick had to be starving as well.

We still wouldn't ask the soldiers for food.

The next morning, I pretended to be asleep while the Marines next to me were having their breakfast. The smell of freshly made coffee actually hurt my nose, but I wasn't going to break down. Whenever I'd followed Army units, they always had helicopters bring in solid breakfasts like eggs, bacon, sausages, and pancakes. They called it "hot chow." Sharing "hot chow" wasn't like asking for rations that a soldier had to carry on his back. I dreamed of a breakfast chopper run but, just like their determined marching, the Marines only used their helicopters for moving in ammunition and evacuating wounded soldiers.

At 10 a.m. Dick Harris finally collapsed from heat and exhaustion and was evacuated with the wounded soldiers. As Dick was being loaded into the helicopter, Ted asked me if I was OK. I lied and said I was fine.

I really wanted to say, "No, I'm not all right. I'm starving to death, and I want to go back and eat," but I was not about to show any weakness in front of this fresh, youthful reporter. Somewhere in the back of my mind, I thought of Terry Khoo saying, "Watch out for the new guy."

Was this what he was warning me of?

I wasn't sure, but I was certain that I wasn't going to give up before he did.

After Dick was evacuated, Ted picked up and carried the sound gear that Dick had left behind. Sound gear, with its amplifiers, cables, and microphones, is one heavy load.

At that point, I almost admitted that Ted had me beat.

Later that day, when the Marines had climbed to the top of yet another mountain, they took a break for lunch. I sat next to the soldiers, closed my eyes, and pretended to take a nap. I concentrated on not letting on that I was so hungry I might start to eat my boots. Ted had apparently gone to sleep as well, but I'm sure it was the same act.

Even with my eyes closed, I could tell what kind of C-rations the soldiers were eating. My act would have worked, but my stomach refused to cooperate and began making very loud and very strange musical sounds. I tossed and turned, but nothing I did would make it stop.

An enormous black Marine sitting next to me very politely offered me an unfinished can of food. Even as my mouth was saying, "No thank you," my hand went out of control and grabbed the can. It was franks and beans. I don't even like franks and beans—they give me heartburn.

I'll never forget how delicious that first spoonful tasted.

Out of the corner of my eye, I saw that Ted was watching.

I handed the can over to him along with the spoon as if I wasn't really hungry at all. He took it and gingerly dug out a spoonful and carefully put it into his mouth. Then he returned the can and spoon to me.

I took another spoonful, ate it slowly and carefully, and then passed the can back to him. It was almost like taking part in a formal Japanese tea ceremony. After a few of these exchanges, the food was gone.

It took a tremendous act of will not to eat the can and the spoon.

When the food was all gone, so was my feeling of competition with Ted. I knew we would make a great team. There's an old Japanese saying, "If we share the same pot of rice, we are close friends."

I told Ted that I wanted to go back, and Ted instantly agreed to return to the base. We were on a helicopter an hour later. I still regret that I didn't ask the name of the black marine who gave us his unfinished can of franks and beans. On the other hand, it seemed like an Act of God, and he might have been an angel.

A sweaty, uniformed angel with a rifle.

When we arrived back at the Marine base, a public relations officer took us to the cafeteria in the officers' club. There was an enormous amount of food laid out like a holiday feast. The funny thing was that I wasn't hungry anymore so I just took a few pieces of fruit and got some fresh coffee.

It was a hard but memorable trip, and now I knew how tough this new guy truly was.

A month after our rock climbing trip, Ted, Nguyen T. Long, and I went back to Da Nang for a large-scale operation. The area several kilometers north and south of the line which separated South and North Vietnam had been designated as a Demilitarized Zone. Recently, American intelligence said that North Vietnamese and Viet Cong forces had infiltrated into the Zone and were using it as a safe refuge to stage attacks on the South.

For that reason, the Marines were planning an all-out campaign to clear all enemy troops from the Demilitarized Zone. Most of the land they would be fighting in was small farms so before the operation began, the population was warned to evacuate to safer places further south. Thousands of Vietnamese peasants fled by land and sea.

Among all these refugees, Ted had found a particularly interesting story. There was a village of farmers who were now being forced to flee their homes for the second time. In 1954, they moved from North Vietnam, but they always hoped to be able to return to their homeland. They found an area inside the Demilitarized Zone that was as close as they could come to their old home, settled, and grew rice and other crops.

Now, they were being told to move again, and Ted decided that following their sad journey to yet another home would make a good story. For the next two days, we stayed with these impoverished people and filmed them, beginning as they had to leave their farms with the rice ready to harvest in the fields and then had to stand in long lines to get rice in the overcrowded refugee centers. We stayed with them and filmed as they waited on the shore for a boat, watched them board a Navy Landing Craft Utility with what few belongings they could carry, stand and watch as their home slipped away over the horizon, and come ashore in a new and strange place in the South. Long talked to many of them and translated their stories and anecdotes so that they became real people and not just "refugees."

Ted was completely soaked when he did his stand-up on the beach at Dong Ha because he had traveled with the refugees and gotten wet right alongside them. His approach was very sympathetic and Long and I were very impressed with his angle on the story. We were also a bit worried because this was only 1967 and almost all the news reports sent back to the States were about soldiers in action and filled with shots of "bang bang."

I remember that the Saigon bureau chief, Elliot Bernstein, appeared to be unhappy about this story and the stand-up specifically and said that Ted was a little too emotional and displayed too much sympathy towards the refugees. Recently, Ted wrote me about this story:

> Dear Tony,
> How nice to hear from you: and how especially nice that you have such good memories of our time together. I do too. For a very short period (only a few weeks) during 1967, I kept a diary in Vietnam. By coincidence, the assignment you wrote about is one that I referred to in my diary. I am copying it for you exactly as I wrote it back then:
>
> *Saturday, May 20, 1967—Dong Ha*
> *Predictions of leisure easily made, but much more difficult to fulfill. Jim Pringle of Reuters told me about an LCU (Landing Craft Utility) shuttle run between Dong Ha and Demilitarized Zone—Purpose to pick up some of the 12,000 Demilitarized Zone residents who will be a dead-on target when that section of the Demilitarized Zone below the Ben Hai river becomes a free–bombing zone.*
> *It took most of the day to get up to Green Beach, which is the Marine designation for the stretch of coast-line where they began their amphibious assault into the Demilitarized Zone. Now it is the clearing point for the evacuation, not only of civilian refugees, but the Marine shore party which has been mercilessly clobbered by artillery and mortars since they first landed two days ago.*
> *When we reached the beach aboard a Navy LCU, there was hardly any activity. The sun was broiling hot. A small group of Demilitarized Zone villagers was crouched in a confused heap on the sand at the water's edge. They had practically nothing with them but the clothes on their back—and even that is a misleading cliché, because their clothes were just about falling off. They were so ripped.*
> *They were loaded aboard the LCU almost immediately. At first they huddled together under the wheel-house. Then, an hour or so later, as we were making our way down the coast, they started lining the rail—not, as one might have expected, to take a last lingering look at their home, but at an American carrier, anchored off-shore about a mile away.*
> *I get the impression that these people are almost beyond emotion now. Their reservoir of grief appears expended. We reached Dong Ha at dusk, and the refugees were put on a truck and taken to a school house. We'll rejoin them again in the morning and follow them to their new "home."*[3]
>
> *Sunday, May 21, 1967—Cam Lo*
> *At 0800 we went back to the school house. There were about 100 refugees remaining at the school. Later in the day, they would be taken to a central gathering point at Cam Lo. Since we had transportation with us, I decided to move on to Cam Lo right away.*

The camp looked like something the "Okies" (Tony, those were people who lost their farms during a Depression in the 1920s or '30s and piled all their belongings onto cars or trucks—many of them were from Oklahoma, which was especially hard hit. Therefore, the term "Okies.") had lived in during the '30s. Rows upon rows of tents.

Some of the 2–3,000 people already there had managed to bring few sticks of furniture— others had brought some chickens, ducks, and pigs. There were even a few water buffalo.

All in all, it was a pretty barren sight, though. Drinking water has to be brought in by truck, and the rice, which these farmers were just about to harvest around their homes, is now doled out to the accompaniment of loudspeaker announcements telling whose turn it is to pick up his rice ration.

It is more desirable than being bombed, but I doubt that either the American or South Vietnamese government will harvest much gratitude here.[4]

So much for the diary, Tony,

Oh, one of your earlier questions—did I ever get any criticism from New York about the refugee story?

NO.

From 1969 to 1971, Ted spent a lot of time in Vietnam when he wasn't covering stories across Asia and the rest of the Far East as an ABC News foreign correspondent and, eventually, as the Hong Kong bureau chief. He came in and out of Vietnam so many times, covering the war and its people, that he became an expert on the region.

I never knew how my best friend, Terry Khoo, who was a talented journalist himself, could instantly predict that the boyish-looking guy would hold such great qualities and a promising future.

However, even after all these years, I still have no idea what Terry meant when he warned me that "Ted is an independent guy!"

CHAPTER 9

HE LOVED MOZART

Vietnam was the news story of the decade, and I imagine, like me, every journalist who arrived had had a moment when they realized they had to drop everything and go cover the big story. Many followed the impulse and arrived in Saigon—each one as different as the stories they wrote but no one was quite as unconventional as my next correspondent—Craig J. Spence.

Spence was from a well-off Boston family and began his career as a reporter for WCBS in New York City. He had a reputation as a hard-working journalist but the crews said he was mean and tough to please. Liz Trotta of NBC News, one of the first female TV correspondents to cover the Vietnam War, was a longtime friend as she wrote in her book *Fighting for Air:*

> Craig J. Spence of ABC News, a great character of the Manhattan scene, headed toward me resplendent in a perfectly tailored bush jacket and matching khaki trousers. He was the only man I ever knew who wore a Cartier dress watch in combat. As he gestured me to a halt, he lit his corncob pipe—an accessory he had borrowed from his hero, General Douglas MacArthur. Spence was the dandy at war, a reincarnation of the "traveling gentleman"—adventurers of wealth and family—who visited battle fields for a thrill during the nineteenth century. He was at the same time winning and despicable, a concentrator of emotions who drove people either to loving or hating him. Although he had no journalistic credentials to speak of, with his talent for promotion, for boring from within, he had gone far on naked nerve. He could get you to do things you would do for no other person, make you bend your imagination to his own, usually for his own advancement. He was the Great Persuader.[1]

There was always a rumor going around in the press corps that there simply had to be CIA agents working undercover within the 300 members of the press and a frequent topic of conversation was trying to pick them out from the legitimate journalists. According to a Vietnamese friend, Spence had to be CIA because "he is just too smart to be a TV correspondent."

There was no doubt that Spence was a bright guy, the problem was that he seemed determined to prove that he knew more than everyone else and to keep on proving it long after he'd made those around him feel like fools. He claimed that it was merely the fact that he felt he had to call out stupidity and ignorance wherever he found it. There were a

Liz Trotta, an NBC reporter and friend, wrote of ABC News correspondent Craig Spence, "Spence was the dandy at war, a reincarnation of the 'traveling gentleman'—adventurers of wealth and family—who visited battle fields for a thrill during the nineteenth century." He is seen here with cameraman Terry Khoo. (Courtesy of Terry Khoo Family)

lot of others who thought it was just his way of showing off. Now, all of this was what others told me, oddly enough my first impression of him was that he seemed like a rather nice and friendly guy.

The first time I was assigned to work with Spence was a ten-day trip to the city of Da Nang. Right from the beginning, it was a disaster. On the first night, we had dinner because sharing a meal was one of the best ways to get to know someone. I needed to have an idea of what to shoot with the limited time and small amount of film available and the correspondent needed to know what he should be sure to ask me for and what he could just assume I would do on my own.

The Da Nang press center was operated by US Marines and, during the dry season, you could sit outside and enjoy dinner in the cool evening air in a courtyard next to the volleyball court. The menu featured T-bone steaks flown directly from the States and, usually, it was one of my favorite meals.

That night, Spence was so relentlessly unpleasant that my steak tasted like sand, and I couldn't finish my dinner. As soon as we sat down, he made certain that I knew that he knew everything about art, music, literature, and every other field of knowledge. Sure, it was boastful but, in the beginning, it was fun because I was thinking of how much I could learn from a man like this.

How wrong I was.

It wasn't a conversation; it was an inquisition!

It was as if I was back in school and trapped with one of the teachers I'd really disliked in a nightmare oral exam. Spence pressed in like a prosecutor cross-examining an opposing witness.

His first question was easy but unexpected. "What is your hobby?"

What was my hobby? My mind raced. Did I have any hobbies?

For the past decade, I had been too busy learning my craft and working in the field to have time for a hobby. I liked fishing, hiking, mountain climbing, watching movies, playing cards, chess, and any form of gambling but I didn't think they were the right kind of hobbies.

I should have mentioned those activities, but I wanted to impress him. "Sure, my hobbies are reading books and listening to music."

Oh, I wish I could have taken those words back!

He jumped right in. "What kind of books?"

"Lots of Japanese literature and English novels translated into Japanese. Recently I've been reading hardboiled detective stories."

"Detective stories? Which writers?"

"Well, I like Ross Macdonald because of his main character, private detective Lew Archer," I said.

Spence wasn't impressed. "How about classics? Have you ever read Shakespeare?"

Shakespeare? I wondered. Where did Shakespeare fit into this conversation?

Now, in Japanese schools, we studied Shakespeare, but we read only a few acts from each play in English. Did that count? Well, I decided to fight back, even if it meant pushing the truth a bit. "Sure. I've read some of his plays."

When I saw his sarcastic smile, I knew I'd fallen into a trap. "Have you ever read Othello?"

There was no way to back out now. "Yes."

"Do you remember the name of the heroine?"

"Her name is De...De...Desdemona, I guess."

"Who was the bad guy who gave bad advice to Othello?"

"His name was Iago, wasn't it?"

Here, I was saved by a lucky accident. Only a few weeks ago, I'd watched Othello on TV in a Hong Kong hotel room. Apparently, Spence wasn't buying it because he started to grill me on details. "What did Desdemona lose?"

I racked my memory, "Was it the neckerchief? The handkerchief? Something that Othello had given to her?"

In the end, I just shrugged and didn't say anything.

The prosecutor turned to the jury and declared the witness a proven liar, "I doubt you read it. That was very important to the story!"

I didn't even know I was in a fight, and I'd already lost the first round!

I had mixed emotions: sad because I'd been caught in my own lies and furious because the questions were ridiculous. What did Shakespeare have to do with news, the war, or anything else?

I kept all these emotions inside. What I didn't realize was that my time in the witness box had only just begun.

Spence proceeded to cross-examine my other hobby. "What kind of music do you like to listen to?"

"I listen to all sorts of music; Japanese popular music, American jazz, folk songs, and classical music as well."

"Who is your favorite classical composer?"

I rattled off the name of every composer I could think of, "Bach, Beethoven, Chopin, Tchaikovsky, Mozart … I like all of them."

He pounced, "Mozart? Which of his pieces do you like?"

To tell the truth, I only knew two pieces of Mozart, "I like *Eine Kleine Nachtmusik* and one of the symphonies."

"Symphony number what?" he demanded.

Number? I had no idea what number! Once again I searched my memory. Beethoven is simple, his symphonies were numbered 1 to 9. Why did Mr. Mozart have to give two-digit numbers to his symphonies? Was it Number 31? Number 40? Number 41?

As I tried to recall the number, I kept humming the melody of the opening part—trying to prove I really did know it but was just unable to remember the exact number.

In the end, once again I failed to answer.

He was quite upset, even angry. "How dare you say you like Mozart! You can't remember the titles and numbers of his symphonies! Mozart is my favorite. I know all the names and numbers of each piece."

I felt terrible. OK, I'd told him that I really liked reading books and listening to music, but I didn't expect to be examined on the details of the stories or have to recite a list of musical pieces! While I fumed, Spence went on to tell me in great detail how much he loved the classics, how Boston had a great symphony orchestra, and how often he would go to concerts.

Oddly, even though I didn't like the way he dealt with people, I began to like him. I had the impression that, while he had an incredible education, he had no street smarts, and was terrible at getting along with ordinary people. After that meal, when Vietnamese friends would insist that he had to be CIA, I'd say that was nonsense. How could he be a spy if he couldn't have a conversation with an ordinary person?

A few days after that disastrous dinner in Da Nang, I wanted to work out a ceasefire, so I wrote him a short memo. It was easier to put my thoughts down on paper and more accurate because I could look up the words I didn't know.

> We are on the same team. I'm not your competitor. Like in baseball, you are the pitcher, and I'm the catcher. Can we just try and understand each other and just drop all this competition about who is better?

After reading my reconciliation letter, he shook hands with me, and we established a working relationship and a good friendship that continued for many years.

I had no doubt that Craig Spence was an excellent correspondent; he had a fresh eye and a new way of doing television news. At least, it was new to me. He was especially aware of the importance of picture and sound and used them effectively in a "show and tell" style. This was exciting for his crew because he paid attention to what we were recording and our work would end up as the centerpiece of the story.

An example: there was a small abandoned cemetery near Tan Son Nhut airport in Saigon. It was quite old and had lines of white tombstones, the graves of French soldiers who'd been killed during the first Indochina war. One day, Spence took me to this tiny, ruined graveyard to do an on-camera segment. He stood with an old book, facing the camera, and read a few lines about the tactics that North Vietnamese defense minister Vo Nguyen Giap had used to defeat the French army at their fortress of Dien Bien Phu.

This is how I remember the end:

> "History is repeating itself. Our American military might make the same mistakes as the French military did in the first Indochina war."

I panned along the names of the French soldiers, the chipped and neglected little graveyard, and the pictures—a ruined line of white tombstones that was the only legacy of these forgotten men—worked beautifully with the script. (See footage in plate section.)

On another day, he took me to a small village in the Delta where there was another time-worn tomb. North Vietnamese leader Ho Chi Minh had died only days before, and Spence talked about the background of Ho and then revealed that decades ago, Ho himself had lived in this village, and the grave belonged to his ancestors.

Liz Trotta recalls another one of his dramatic stand-ups:

> He began one piece about how a VC would elude American patrols by submerging himself in swamp water and breathing through a tube. Rising from the depths on a close-up, he began, "This is how the VC hide. And this is the kind of war it is—you can't see the enemy."[2]

That was precisely the sort of "show and tell" that Spence liked to do where the element of surprise made it difficult for viewers to miss his point. Even though Craig Spence thought the war was the right thing for America—we called him a "hawk"—the military press officials were usually upset at him because his reports had such vivid criticisms.

Craig discovered a young Vietnamese folk singer and composer named Trinh Cong Son and used one of his songs as the background music for a report. Son came from Hue, and his songs would describe farmers, mothers, widows, lovers, children, and the ruined villages and devastated farms that used to be their homes. Son attempted to avoid controversy by calling his music "tired of the war" songs rather than anti-war songs. Spence used one of his songs to build a photo essay showing the people and the countryside of Vietnam and how it had been damaged and later devastated by the continuing conflict. He used very little narration and instead showed his cameraman's pictures and just let the song tell the story.

This time, the cameraman was Korean In Jip Choi, who was an artist with the camera and his stunning photography of village scenes and close tight shots of Vietnamese faces brought out the human tragedy so often hidden in the body counts and troop movements in our day-to-day coverage.

One day, Spence and I were on the way back from an assignment in the countryside. The story had gone well so we were in a good mood and passed the time singing or humming tunes in the car. At one point, we began to hum a famous opera aria.

Suddenly, I wondered if Craig knew the name of the opera. I didn't know the name of the aria, but I knew the name of the opera: it was Puccini's *Tosca* and I knew it because a senior correspondent, Ray Maloney, used to hum it while we were playing cards. Specifically, he tended to hum it when he was winning so it stuck in my memory.

I asked, "Do you know the name of the opera?"

He said, "Sure," but then stopped, searching his memory.

Finally, he said, "I know the opera, but I simply can't come up with it. Do you know it?"

I answered, a bit smugly, "Yes."

We made a bet that Craig had to come up with the name of the opera by the time we arrived back at the bureau. Poor Craig struggled and pondered, but the name eluded him.

When we pulled up to the Caravelle Hotel, the time was up, and I said, "It's from *Tosca*."

Craig congratulated me with a handshake. "You're right. It's the aria from *Tosca*. You do know your classical music."

In 1969, the military press authorities got their wish and Craig was banned from reporting in Vietnam. ABC based him in Tokyo as a free-lance radio reporter covering Asia and the Far East. Once, I visited him at the Tokyo Foreign Press Club where he was in charge of the library. He seemed to be relaxed and happy, surrounded by books and good conversation.

Ten years later, I ran into him in Bangkok as he was on his way to Tehran to meet with the Shah of Iran.

As he was leaving, he said with a smile, "Hey Tony, I still keep the memo you gave to me at Da Nang. It's precious."

Years later, when he was a lobbyist and became entangled in a Washington sex scandal, many of his friends abandoned him. Liz Trotta was one of the few who hung in, told him to tell the truth, but that was advice he couldn't take:

> On November 10, 1989, Craig J. Spence, dressed in a tuxedo and listening to Mozart, lay down to die on a bed in the Boston Ritz. He had barricaded the door and taken enough booze and pills to carry out the long-promised suicide. A birth

certificate, a will, which included a bequest to Mother Teresa, and antidepressant pills were stuffed together into a false ceiling. On a Walkman, a cassette titled "Eine Kleine Nachtmusik." In a postscript to the note, he apologized to the management for the inconvenience.[3]

Craig Spence was only 49. I know that others have different views but to me, he was a great journalist and a true creative artist.

During the Mother's Day Hill engagement on May 13 and 14, 1967, the number of American casualties rose to the point that the ABC News crew stopped rolling film and began to help the wounded. Here, Ken Gale gives water to a wounded GI. *(Film shot by Yasutsune Hirashiki; courtesy ABC News)*

May 13, 1967. The Airborne unit's outer perimeter was becoming dangerously thin and the wounded were moved back to the rear where there were tree roots and ground cover. (Film shot by Yasutsune Hirashiki; courtesy ABC News)

Opposite, from top: May 13, 1967.
A wounded GI enjoys a cigarette. Since none of the ABC News crew were trained medics, they helped by passing out water and cigarettes.

Ken Gale ties a tourniquet on a soldier's arm in preparation for inserting the needle for an IV bag. Gale wrote later that he was probably as nervous about inserting the needle as he was about the continuous small weapons fire all around them.

A medic applies pressure to the neck of a wounded soldier. The audio over this section of film was "You had better get down, cameraman," as Tony's interest in getting a shot became greater than his instinct for self-preservation.
(Film shot by Yasutsune Hirashiki; courtesy ABC News)

January 25, 1967: a suspected enemy soldier is marched blindfolded to the rear for interrogation during an operation where a village is sealed and then completely searched. *(Film shot by Yasutsune Hirashiki; courtesy ABC News)*

A GI keeps watch from the shotgun seat as his unit moves forward in the early days of Operation Junction City which began on February 27, 1967. *(Film shot by Yasutsune Hirashiki courtesy ABC News)*

On February 24, 1967, ABC News correspondent Don North reports on the second day of Operation Junction City. The use of a stand-up showing a reporter right on the battlefield was felt to show that their reporting was current and not gained from sitting back in Saigon. *(Film shot by Yasutsune Hirashiki; courtesy ABC News)*

A GI moving forward into the Central Highlands as a part of Operation Junction City takes time out to "monkey around." *(Film shot by Yasutsune Hirashiki; courtesy ABC News)*

On March 23, 1967, ABC correspondent Bill Brannigan interviews PFC Ronnie Compton for a report called "New Soldier." Compton, from Pinsonfork, Kentucky, had only arrived in Vietnam days before and Brannigan worked to get an in-depth picture of his thoughts and fears as he faced his first combat. *(Film shot by Yasutsune Hirashiki; courtesy ABC News)*

On November 28, 1967, American troops work to get a wounded comrade to a medevac helicopter after the struggle for Hill 875, a part of the battle of Dak To. More Americans died to take this hill than any other piece of land in Vietnam. *(Film shot by Yasutsune Hirashiki; courtesy ABC News)*

Only days after GIs took the enemy stronghold of Hill 875 on Thanksgiving Day 1967, ABC News correspondent Ed Needham reports from the peak. Even though the assault on the hill was one of the bloodiest battles of the war, it was abandoned immediately. *(Film shot by Yasutsune Hirashiki; courtesy ABC News)*

Troops from the 173rd Airborne struggle to get a wounded soldier on a medevac helicopter. Hill 875 was taken on November 25, 1967 with massive casualties—many of them allegedly caused by "friendly fire" from American pilots. Tony Hirashiki recorded soldiers yelling and weeping as they told of the "shocking, brutal, bitter, and cruel nature of the fighting on that hill." *(Film shot by Yasutsune Hirashiki; courtesy ABC News)*

ABC News correspondent Craig Spence was given to finding original video to illustrate his pieces. In August 1969, he used an abandoned French graveyard to demonstrate how the North Vietnamese would bleed the American forces until they were forced to leave. *(Film shot by Yasutsune Hirashiki; courtesy ABC News)*

Intelligent and harshly critical, ABC News correspondent Craig Spence began by berating Tony Hirashiki for not knowing enough about literature and music but, over time, Tony gained respect for his creative visuals and insights. *(Film shot by Yasutsune Hirashiki; courtesy ABC News)*

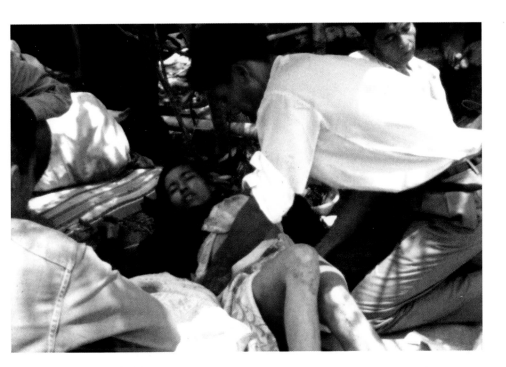

Victims of a massacre by Cambodian government troops are treated on April 9, 1970. Those attacked were ethnic Vietnamese who had lived in Cambodia for decades but were blamed by the Lon Nol government for its mistakes in the anti-Communist war. Government troops had opened fire on unarmed civilians because of false fears that the ethnic Vietnamese villagers were aiding the North Vietnamese. *(Film shot by Terry Khoo; courtesy ABC News)*

The body of a man lies in a field after Cambodia troops opened fire on ethnic Vietnamese villagers on April 9, 1970. ABC News correspondent Steve Bell managed to get the story past Cambodian censors with the help of Hong Kong bureau chief Ted Koppel. *(Film shot by Terry Khoo; courtesy ABC News)*

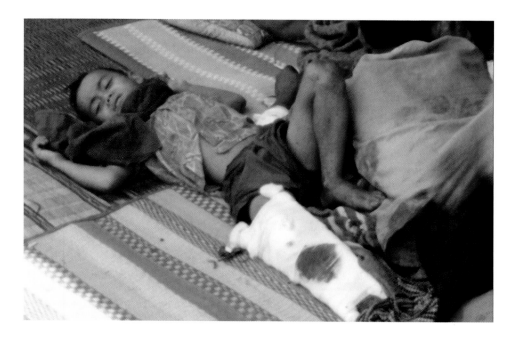

April 9, 1970. A young Cambodian boy of Vietnamese descent bleeds from a wound to the leg after his village was attacked by Cambodian government troops. *(Film shot by Terry Khoo; courtesy ABC News)*

In May 1972, Kontum City had been hammered by the North Vietnamese and their seemingly endless supply of tanks and rockets. Broken helmets littered the main street. *(Film shot by Yasutsune Hirashiki; courtesy ABC News)*

ABC News correspondent Dick Shoemaker describes the battle, with American airpower providing decisive assistance to the South Vietnamese defenders. *(Film shot by Yasutsune Hirashiki; courtesy ABC News)*

Even if it looked hopeless, South Vietnamese soldiers were holding out, fighting at point-blank range and using grenades to dig their opponents out of cover. *(Film shot by Yasutsune Hirashiki; courtesy ABC News)*

Hirashiki and Malet found an American military advisor, Major Wade Lovings, still at his post in Kontum City. They were amazed to see Lovings repeatedly race into a hail of gunfire, pick up one or two of his wounded South Vietnamese soldiers by their belts and carry them to safety. *(Film shot by Yasutsune Hirashiki; courtesy ABC News)*

As Tony Hirashiki and J. C. Malet continue their coverage of the besieged city of Kontum, an evacuation begins. At first it was organized and peaceful...

...but before long the evacuation became a panicked scramble as hundreds race for the rescue helicopter *(Film shot by Yasutsune Hirashiki; courtesy ABC News)*

In March 1975, Da Nang, children wait through the cool night to see if there will be a way for them to get out before the communists arrive. *(Film shot by Yasutsune Hirashiki; courtesy ABC News)*

When "White Christmas" was played over Armed Forces Radio on April 29, 1975, the official evacuation of Americans began calmly and efficiently with US military personnel directing evacuees. The calm soon turned into chaos as desperate Vietnamese tried to escape the city. *(Film shot by Yasutsune Hirashiki; courtesy ABC News)*

In August 1975, a sailor helps a young refugee aboard a US ship in the South China Sea. Over 130,000 Vietnamese joined that exodus, and thousands of others followed in later years. *(Film shot by Yasutsune Hirashiki; courtesy ABC News)*

CHAPTER 10

SON OF A MINISTER

ABC decided to cover the 4th Infantry Division in the continuing battles of Operation *Junction City* in the highlands near Pleiku. I was sent in along with a new correspondent, a good-looking young guy named David Snell from the Chicago bureau. We went in near the end of the battle but bullets and artillery were still flying, and so it was another landing at a hot LZ.

As we jumped out of the chopper, the air was filled with smoke from the brush still smoldering from earlier air and artillery strikes. The crew chief had told us to keep our heads down and stay low. Seconds after the chopper was cleared, waiting medics began to load in the wounded, some on stretchers, and others supported on the shoulders of their comrades. The wind from the chopper blades was blowing dirt and sand in vicious blasts, and the big engines were deafening—although I could still hear the *crack* of M16s not far away and the humming *zzzip* of stray bullets.

It was a fairly typical landing on the frontlines.

Snell was already moving fast, recording the sound on his tape recorder, and then getting me to film a stand-up in the smoke and windblast of the landing zone. He was brave and cool under fire and in many ways reminded me of Roger Peterson. David did two reports from the 4th Division's battle at Kontum. Both made air, and New York sent appreciative telexes, but the real proof of quality reporting was that one ran just over three minutes—an eternity in television terms. New York said that they appreciated the human touch of showing the soldiers helping each other to safety under heavy fire.

As I've said, most ABC News correspondents in Vietnam were young: in their late twenties or early thirties. Combat coverage required endurance, physical strength, and the mental toughness to endure everything from total exhaustion to absolute horror. David Snell was one of these young guns:

> My motive for coming to Vietnam was simple enough. I wanted to work for a network and networks needed "young legs" in Vietnam. I applied for a job at ABC because I saw Peter Jennings on the air and decided if they would hire someone that young, they just might hire me. After they looked at my tape, I got a call. "Would you be willing to go to Vietnam?" I answered "Yes," and spent the next 18 weeks running every day to get in shape.
>
> When they didn't call back, I took a job at WBBM in Chicago (a CBS-owned station), and it was there that ABC caught up with me. Four weeks after starting to work at WBBM, I moved across town to the ABC Bureau where I worked from March to June before heading for 'Nam. I was excited to be going and as you will note from my journal, dumb as a stump when it came to the country and the war.
>
> I had a lot of catching up to do.[1]

In 1966, he came to Saigon for a three-month tour and proved to be a reliable reporter. In 1967, ABC gave him an 18-month assignment and he and his wife, Mary Lou, returned to Vietnam. I saw him as not only brave, charming, and good-looking—qualities necessary for a television reporter—but I also thought that he had a pure mind and an unstained heart.

★★★

I worked with him on a story about chemical warfare; the Ranch Hand program that spread "Agent Orange." The military said it was meant to thin the dense jungle cover and make it harder for the enemy to hide from air strikes.

Early in the morning, we went to Bien Hoa airbase where, in a corner of the air base, airmen were loading the chemicals into spray tanks built into C-123 cargo planes. The men worked topless or in t-shirts in the heat. Their faces and sweaty bodies were covered with the powdered chemical and quite soon, so were David and I. No one back then was worried about Agent Orange. I knew that it was like DDT but to my mind, that only harmed insects, not people.

I mention this assignment because it was the first time I worked with Snell, and he described his first impressions in his journal:

> Tony Hirashiki was cameraman … and I'd guess quite a good one, Tony had trouble with English, but he managed to express the lack of communication that exists between people as eloquently as I've ever heard… Tony was apologizing for not always understanding my wishes when as a correspondent I direct him… "I hope soon I understand the mind of the correspondent."[2]

Later he wrote me a bit more about his first impressions:

> I remember the congratulations we received after the story aired in NY and my surprise that it included praise for the sunrise that opened the story. I had no idea you had shot a sunrise, and when I asked you about it, you said "always shoot sunrise" like it if was no big thing. It WAS a big thing to me because it illustrated how much you cared about the quality of the story.[3]

Another time, I shot a stand-up with Snell at the Buddhist pagoda in Saigon and noticed that he was struggling to get it done without mistakes. In a letter, he explained that he was distracted by an off-camera interview he had just finished with a Buddhist monk:

> I remember an interview Mr. Lam (ABC News local manager) got for me with the head of the United Buddhist Church. He hadn't talked to an American journalist in 8 months and talked to me only because of Mr. Lam. The Buddhist leader was, of course, critical of the Saigon government, saying they were American puppets and that if we withdrew our support, they would fall.
>
> I asked him, "If the Communists take over the country, what will happen to your religion?"
>
> His answer surprised me; "If the Communists come, we will probably lose our religion, but that is better than losing our country. At least the Communists are Vietnamese."
>
> I was stunned. Here was a man who had dedicated his life to the Buddhist church. This was a kind of nationalism that Americans simply didn't understand. I hadn't been able to interview him on camera, but because I thought it such an important story I went back to the bureau, carefully wrote a script, and went back to the Pagoda to film stand-upper. I probably don't have to tell you, it never got used.
>
> It wasn't bang-bang.[4]

On another story, we covered a pacification program in which captured suspects, sympathizers, or ex-VC prisoners who weren't staunch enemies but still couldn't quite be trusted were kept in camps but taught skills like cutting hair and giving shaves so that so they could become barbers and make a living.

We did the story primarily with pictures and natural sound covered by a humorous script. David wrote a witty stand-upper in which he wondered if every town corner in Vietnam would have a barber and how they would compete for business. New York loved it, and the story aired for 3 minutes and 45 seconds, making it one of the longest feature pieces they aired.

Being young, tough, and a bit crazy wasn't enough to cope with the moral challenges of doing quality journalism in a war zone and the doubts that grow along with experience in the field. In his diary, he

In an aid station somewhere in the Mekong Delta, ABC News correspondent David Snell mugs for the camera in April 1967. Right before he was injured by a landmine, he'd been joking about how news stopped as soon as he arrived saying, "Premier Ky asked me to return to Vietnam so there'd be a respite from the war. I did and there was." (Courtesy Family of Terry Khoo)

wrote one of the best descriptions of what too many young journalists went through in Vietnam:

June 14, 1966—Dak To

Always before, it had been in films, not really real. But today while the movie was being shot, I was there. There as the head of a tow-headed 18- or 19-year-old came out from under the blanket which had covered his corpse. It hadn't even been too bad when, landing from a helicopter ride, I had to step over several covered bodies. For one thing, I thought they were the VC. I don't usually make individuals out as enemy or non-enemy. But in that case, it helped. But then, to find out he was an American. Now it could have been me, or a friend, now it was too close.

And then a Major, commander of a battalion, laughed as he told of a brassy young soldier (a "smartass") who "got zapped." When it was an officer friend of his, he said simply "It's a damn shame" but then went on to other subjects perhaps a dirty joke would go well here, "Have you heard the one about...."

I spent last night with a company in the field that only two nights before had been attacked by VC. Three of them had died. They had killed 110 VC. They said the enlisted men did anyway, it didn't seem real at the time. I felt like I was in a dream![5]

August 11, 1966—Pleiku

The country is still beautiful but a much different thing from the ground than from the air. The crew, Headford, Eddy and I along with Neil Hicky of TV Guide made our way for 3,000 meters with the 1st Brigade 327th Infantry 101st Airborne. We climbed some hills that weren't meant to be climbed and spent the rest of our time fording streams hip-deep in water. As we reached a resting place near the top, it started to pour down rain. I was so hot and dirty it was a privilege to just stand there and get soaked.

I wrote earlier of seeing Americans dead last Wednesday. I saw even more when we dropped in on Charlie Company of the 502. These guys had been overrun by North Vietnamese and even the living looked bad. They carried the dead on litters made by wrapping the body in a poncho and roping it to a long pole. Dead legs and arms sometimes pop out revealing ghastly wounds. My thought: I wonder if these dead men ever thought of using their ponchos in that way and being carried out so anonymously. The report reads "light casualties" but for a wife, a mother and other relatives the casualties were heavy.[6]

August 29, 1966—In Jet Heading to the States

Very good news from Saigon yesterday buoyed the spirits despite the continuous drizzle, two spots that I'd done a week ago made it on the air ... leaving only one story that I've done in the past three weeks that hasn't made it. But while that improves my disposition, it does not increase my interest in remaining here.

Part of the end of my interest came two days ago when, at a medical evacuation center, I watched as 22 American bodies were brought in from the field. One survivor of the action went from man to man saying "That's Charlie, and this one is Pete" all of which was duly recorded on a card that was attached to the dead man's shoe. Ernie Nukanen [cameraman] was disturbed when I shot stills of this gory scene, but to my thinking ... a series of slides on my coverage of the war would be incomplete without this ultimate reality. War is not glory or ideology. The basic essence of war is death.

I lay awake for some time that night thinking of the families of 22 men who would learn within the next day that what they most feared had come to pass. Jack O'Grady, former Saigon bureau chief, told me that I wasn't being realistic in insisting that the number of Americans killed in action was a significant part of a story.

"The question," he insisted "is 'Did we win or lose the battle?'" I tried to tell him, with no success, that the terms "Win" or "Lose" are probably not too meaningful. He felt that there was the significance. For me, it is measured more in personal terms. A sorrowing wife or sweetheart is more "significant," more "meaningful" than the word "Victory."

Perhaps it is I who am immature. Perhaps I should be able to see this war in larger terms than life or death of many individuals. But again and again, I'm struck by the fact that men are dying in fights over areas of land where other men have fought and died only a few months before. You drop with the first wave into a landing zone and see C-ration cans left by other troops. And you know that still more fighting will take place in this same area again.

Are we winning the war? Here are the many questions in the world today and after three months (only) I make so bold as to say...

No, we are not.

Ah, there's a strong statement. But wait, the equivocating is still to come. We aren't losing it either. Recently released figures show that while 40 thousand enemy troops have been killed or captured since January, their troop strength has gone steadily upward. Where is the victory there? While American, Vietnamese, and other "free world" 'troops have killed an average of a thousand enemies per week, they have managed to infiltrate a like number from the North and have expanded their ranks to 283,000 through a "recruitment" program in the south that has brought in some 12,000 per month.

An American general, John Norton of the 1st Cavalry, told me, "The enemy will not long be able to sustain the present level of losses." Then he paused and added, "I hope that's the voice of realism talking."

I hope so too, but I doubt it.[7]

David's second tour in Vietnam ended while covering combat in the Mekong Delta. Again, he kept a journal:

October 28, 1967—New York

I tend to start every entry with a complaint: that I hadn't written in this book for a coon's age. This time, perhaps more justification....

We had been walking all day with a company of the 9th infantry in the Delta about 20 miles south of Saigon. It had been a frustrating day: torrid hot weather (120 degrees!) the hottest I had ever experienced. We were mushing through rice paddies up to our waists in the water. Our film showed this and the efforts of the men to cool themselves off with water we found at abandoned huts along the way, but nothing else.

By four in the afternoon we had not seen our first enemy soldier. We finally got a helicopter and were headed back to Saigon, or at least so I thought, we put down after about a mile to pick up a sergeant. As the chopper was preparing to leave a captain started to tell Bob Erlenson (*Baltimore Sun*) and myself about a battle his men had been engaged in most of the afternoon. We filmed the interview.

While we listened, there was a volley of gunfire several hundred yards away. We headed towards it. We could see about a company of men spread out along a hedgerow firing into a wooded area. It took about five minutes to get within camera range. As we ran toward the shooting. I thought "At last I'm getting some action." Then as if by magic, the shooting stopped, and all was quiet. Not "deadly quiet" just "nothing."

I was disgusted. The only sure way onto ABC's air was with action film, I was missing out again. We sat with the soldiers who gave us the old line, "You should have been here an hour ago." I'd heard it too many times.

To Bob and Terry Khoo, my cameraman, I lamented the missed action, the wasted day. "It's the story of my life. When I arrive, peace descends like a dove."

I used the phrase before, but I expanded, "When I came to Vietnam last summer, the action slowed to a crawl, and all hell broke out in Chicago. I had seen some 'action' but had also gone on more than my share of 'long walk in the sun' stories. Finally, Mayor Daley asked me to return to Chicago. I did and the 'long hot summer' was over. Then, Premier Ky asked me to return to Vietnam so there'd be a respite from the war. I did and there was."

An hour later I was lying on my back, a hole through my leg, and the middle knuckle gone from my right hand.

We went through the wooded area looking for enemy troops, nothing. At 6:00 p.m. I asked a captain to get us a chopper back to Saigon. "We'll send a squad to escort you about 400 yards, the chopper can't come in here." Those words made the day for some VC who had carefully placed a claymore mine in the path we would be taking.

Ordinarily, you stay off paths figuring they would be most likely spots for land mines. For some reason, our squad leader ignored this regulation. Nobody thought anything of it. We had already punched out for the day.

Suddenly, a blast. I'd never heard a land mine, but I recognized the sound. I knew I'd been hit. "Oh my God, Oh my God, Oh my God." That's all I remember saying, but the thoughts contained in that phrase were "I'm going to die. Why am I here anyway? What a stupid thing. I'm going to die."

The blood was spurting from my hand. I felt the wound in my leg. No sooner was I on the ground than one squad member put a bandage around my hand. I was more worried about the leg I couldn't see. I might lose a finger or hand, but the leg might kill me.

When the medic came, I wouldn't let him touch the hand until he worked on my leg. When he told me the bones were intact, I was relieved, but then scared again when numbness set in in both the leg and my arm. Would I go numb all over? I didn't know. The medic answered my doubts "That's normal. You'll be OK." He was starting to leave when someone said. "Aren't you going to give him

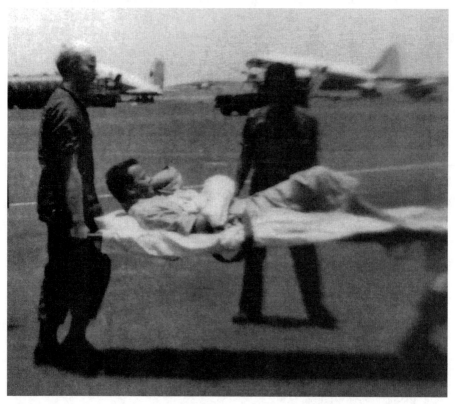

In April 1967, ABC News correspondent David Snell is taken off for medical treatment after being wounded by a landmine. Like Roger Peterson, he did a stand-up, ending with the words "This is David Snell, flat on his back in the Delta." (Courtesy Family of Terry Khoo)

a shot?" He said that he wouldn't because I wasn't in pain. I said I was, and got the shot.

Terry and soundman Hartmunt Kunz were hovering over me like mother hens. Now that I knew I would be OK (at least I'd live), I insisted they shoot the story. Then I asked for the mike and did a "lay-down stand-upper." I said something about the frustration of the day and the land mine. I then realized I didn't know how badly others were hit, so I interviewed Bob [Erlenson] who was holding the mike for me, closing out with, "This is David Snell. ABC News, flat on my back in the Delta." I've been told I said "flat on his back" but that I don't remember.

And that was that, my year in Vietnam had lasted 3 months and ten days. I was hit on Monday, on Thursday I was on a stretcher on a PanAm San Francisco-bound jet. In the Long Binh hospital I was terribly uncomfortable, but because of my fever, I slept most of the time. I had expected a number of newsmen to visit and was disappointed when only ABC types and those who were with me that day, made the effort. Perhaps it was better they didn't come. But it hurt.[8]

When David went home, he was expecting a hero's welcome, but he said that people actually didn't care that he had been in Vietnam nor that he'd been wounded. After David had recovered, his assignment was as a New York-based correspondent, but he was still struggling to adjust—with psychological wounds healing slower than physical ones. He was having problems with the Evening News staff, so he was relegated to weekend news duty. Then he did a remarkable job covering the space program and was back on the main show and succeeded as an ABC News Network correspondent for the next twelve years.

The good son of a Methodist minister turned out to be a very good broadcasting journalist.

CHAPTER 11

VETERAN

Standing between student demonstrators and the Saigon police generally guaranteed tear gas. Lots of tear gas. My eyes, nose, and throat were on fire. It was one thing to be uncomfortable—although that's really not the correct word for how I felt—the problem was that my streaming eyes made it almost impossible to focus my camera.

The Vietnamese people practiced a raucous and freeform democracy and, not that long before, Buddhist demonstrators had toppled President Ngo Dinh Diem. The autumn of 1971 was another period of political unrest because President Nguyen Van Thieu was about to be re-elected with almost 100% of the vote. Again.

On this late September afternoon, student groups, and a political party opposed to Thieu had called for a massive rally near Saigon's central market. When the police moved in and dispersed the crowd with tear gas, Lou Cioffi, one of ABC News' veteran correspondents, was in the middle of a play-by-play about the melée going on around him. Wearing a dashing tailor-made correspondent suit, he continued despite the clouds of tear gas that swept over us. He simply spoke with a microphone in his right hand and a clean white towel in his left to wipe away the tears.

At last, he signed off, then he said, "Let's get some more shots of the demonstration," and led us right into the thick of the crowd and continuing skirmishes between the students and the police. New York was quite pleased with the report and sent him a Herogram.

Lou was the bureau chief of ABC News Tokyo and, according to Teddy John, a sound engineer in Bonn who worked with Lou for years, he would introduce himself to strangers with an instruction: "It's Cioffi. C-ONE-ZERO-F-F-ONE. CIOFFI."

Lou was one of TV journalism's true pioneers beginning as a copyboy at CBS News in the late 1940s. Lou was quickly promoted to correspondent, was one of Edward R. Murrow's protégés, covered the Korean War (and was awarded a Purple Heart), and joined ABC shortly after it was formed.

At first, he was ABC's bureau chief in Paris where he was a celebrity in his own right. When I visited his office, I saw on the wall a picture of him walking side by side with France's president, Charles de Gaulle. Lou said that, while it was true that de Gaulle didn't like Americans in general, he felt that Lou was an exception.

Veteran ABC News correspondent and executive Lou Cioffi and Sho Ka Kun, a cameraman from the Tokyo bureau, recover from tear gas while covering Saigon protests in 1971. Cioffi was one of ABC's first hires and founded bureaus in Paris, Saigon, Tokyo, and Bonn. (Courtesy Sho Ka Kun)

After opening the Paris bureau, Lou set up many others including Tokyo, Saigon, and Bonn; seeking out talented local journalists and training them to become skilled in the new arts of television broadcasting. Only a few of those who began their careers with him are soundman Harry Weldon, secretary Mariko Maeda in Tokyo, secretary Lenata Gozlan in Paris, and medical student turned soundman Teddy John in Bonn. In just one case, Christel Kucharz began her career as a secretary and grew to become one of the best producers in Europe; covering stories as varied as Bosnia, Kosovo, Beirut, and Baghdad.

Since Lou worked out of Tokyo, I didn't get to shoot for him often because he would usually bring in his own crew. In the beginning, it was a Japanese crew, Rokuro Sugiuchi and Masaki Shihara, and later it would be Bob Jennings and Harry Weldon or an exceptionally creative stringer cameraman named Sho Ka Kan.

Lou was an old school foreign correspondent, speaking fluent French and Italian as well as a bit of Japanese. In those days, Humphrey Bogart's Burberry trench coat was standard for television reporters, but it was simply too hot to wear in Vietnam. There are many different stories of the invention of the lightweight and cool "correspondent suit" but I was told that Lou went to "Tailor" Minh on Tu Do street and designed a linen safari suit with four front pockets, pockets in both sleeves (one for pens and one for cigarettes), and epaulets on the shoulders to keep the "trench coat" look.

I enjoyed Lou's witty conversation filled with advice from his long experience. Once, when we were beaten by another network, Lou advised, "Don't rush to catch up. Even if you were badly beaten, don't panic. Your time will come, and it'll be a chance to beat them back."

Another time, he talked about what was essential in combat. "Don't stay too long at the frontlines. Get in quickly, cover it quickly, and get out with material. You're not soldiers so don't become a dead hero. Be a coward and stay alive so that you're able to cover a story tomorrow."

CHAPTER 12

TUCKNER'S CROUCH

It was May 19, 1970, 3 a.m. A phone was ringing in the darkness. I switched on the bedside lamp and picked up the receiver. On the other end of the line, an excited voice was speaking quickly. I had been in a deep sleep but even without dreams clouding my mind, I couldn't understand English at that speed.

After several attempts to get my caller to slow down, I finally worked out that he was my new correspondent, and I began to wake up. Something big must be happening! An attack on the hotel? Had someone lost yesterday's film? Worse yet, did I forget to ship it?

Finally, I managed to get Howard Tuckner to speak slowly, clearly, and in a surprisingly cheery tone for the middle of the night, "Tony, I'm sorry to wake you up at such an early hour. I just finished my script, and I need your help. I want to know exactly what pictures you shot yesterday and how you think they will fit into my narration. Would you mind coming to my room?"

Of course I minded. It was 3 in the morning, and I wanted to sleep. Everyone wants to sleep at 3 in the morning.

On the other hand, Tuckner was my new correspondent and widely regarded as one of the best reporters in Southeast Asia.

The decision was simple, if not easy. I mumbled something into the phone, got dressed, and went to his room.

We were in Phnom Penh, the capital of Cambodia. The Royal Hotel was an old but very classy building from the colonial period with large rooms, high ceilings, and an atmosphere of elegant decay. After the government was overthrown in 1970, a civil war had broken out and the hotel had been taken over by the international media. CBS, AP, and the BBC had all opened temporary bureaus in rooms and bungalows on the grounds. ABC had rented a three-room bungalow for an office and a ready room for the camera crews. The correspondents were in a different bungalow across the courtyard.

When I got to his room, Howard opened the door, still fully dressed. "I just finished my script. It's very good and I think we did an excellent story yesterday. Please listen carefully to my script, especially to the ending."

He read his script slowly and clearly—at least I didn't have to remind him this time.

The previous day, we had covered the Cambodian government troops advancing down Highway Three. I felt that I'd done a good job since my footage had both action scenes and human interest elements. When we got back to Phnom Penh, Howard told me that he wanted to write

In a picture taken before he joined ABC News in 1970, Howard Tuckner poses with his cameraman, In Jip Choi. Aggressive and seemingly fearless, Tuckner had the reputation as the best combat correspondent in Vietnam. (Courtesy In Jip Choi)

and wrap up this story using a slightly different angle. He seemed to be quite excited by the idea, quickly finished his dinner, and went to his room to write. That was seven hours ago which, in my experience, was an extraordinarily long time for a reporter to work on a script. It was far more usual for a script to be written on the fly so that the film could make a flight or the correspondent ad-lib a stand-up at the next location.

Cambodia was at war but after so many years of covering war in Vietnam, I found the atmosphere very strange. The tempo was slow, and the troops weren't tense, they seemed relaxed. They were troops you would never find in the South Vietnamese regular army—old men and young boys who had been sent out without much training and even less discipline.

General Lon Nol, an ally of the United States, had overthrown Prince Norodom Sihanouk and with him went his neutralist stance where he would deal with all sides in the war in neighboring Vietnam. Now the Cambodian army was being sent to extend military control over all of the country. Standing in the way were a variety of rebel groups, generally organized by the Khmer Rouge, attacking small towns and villages, and now blocking many of the main roads.

In this particular mission, the troops were being sent to open Highway Three, which had been cut only twenty miles south of the capital, and clear rebels from the local towns and villages. This was an unusually large-scale operation for the Cambodian army, and so we had driven down to cover it. The fact was that Prince Sihanhouk hadn't really ever sent his army out to fight. They were untrained and inexperienced from the regular soldiers all the way up to the officers and commanders.

In the usual Cambodian fashion, the operation was scheduled to kick off at dawn but didn't start until nearly noon because the Cambodian officer in charge had organized a cockfight, and no one was going to go anywhere until his fighting rooster had its chance for glory. This might have been the usual way for Cambodians to get into a fighting spirit. Since the commander's champion lost, it might have just been a bad omen.

When the troops finally moved out, I felt like I was watching an old World War II newsreel. The commander and the bulk of his forces advanced along the road with minesweepers out in front and the other troops fanned out on either side. The pace was slow and unhurried, and the commander was right up in the front, his officer's uniform only half-buttoned, swinging a bamboo swagger stick, shouting encouragements one moment and criticisms the next.

I have to admit, all his swagger and strutting reminded me of his rooster.

Alongside this comic commander, a young soldier was solemnly and proudly carrying an enormous Cambodian flag. He was a complete contrast to his superior, a very young man with a bright and photogenic face and a sense of pride that you could see in every step he took, the heavy flag high and proud in the tropical sun. I filmed him marching, the firm grasp he had on the thick pole in its leather brace, the flag waving in the slight breeze, and lots of close-ups of his face, so proud and serious.

During a break, Howard interviewed the young flagbearer through an interpreter. He was seventeen and had enlisted only weeks before. Before the war, he'd been studying to teach school and hoped to go back to that after the war ended. He had just been promoted to flagbearer and was quite proud of the honor. He opened the flag and showed how it was embroidered with a picture of Angkor Wat, for centuries the temples of Khmer emperors, and a source of tremendous pride for all Cambodians.

It was a sleepy, quiet, and very hot afternoon on Highway Three and the commander, a colonel, unbuttoned his uniform completely and covered his neck with a large white towel to soak up the sweat. The heat, however, had no effect on his voice, and he shouted even louder than before. The comic-opera colonel and the serious young flagbearer continued to advance side by side, like father and son.

We shot Howard standing in front of a road sign that showed how far we were from the nearest major town. He explained the reason for this march and added that we were not far from the last reported positions of the Khmer Rouge rebels. A bit further on, the whole column took a break in a small village, deserted except for an old lady who sat silently in front of her home. After a good long rest, the troops marched on, crossing over the dry bed of a stream where the bridge had been destroyed by rebels.

A good bit further on, I heard gunfire. I started rolling film, and we took cover in the roadside ditch. Around us, soldiers were firing back as bullets whined around our heads. A little way ahead, the commander was standing all alone in the middle of the road, shaking his stick, and shouting at his troops.

I focused my telephoto lens on the scene and saw the young flagbearer lying in the road with his flag crumpled in the dust. As I filmed, a medic and some other soldiers cautiously ran up, put him on a stretcher, and brought him back to the cover of the ditch. A few moments later, two other soldiers dashed out, furled the flag, and ran back into cover.

Even after the ensign's body was carried away, the colonel stood in the middle of the highway, shirtless, swinging his stick, and shouting at the top of his voice. The young soldier had been hit and killed in the first volley of gunfire but, in one of those twists of fate that happen in combat, no bullets struck the commander. Later I learned that the commander was expressing his sadness and anger at the death of his young flagbearer.

Howard turned to us and said, "We're done. Let's leave. We have enough pictures to report today's story."

When we got back to the hotel, I did a careful job on my caption sheets, describing all the details of the film I'd shot, and gave it to Howard. Now, he'd been writing for seven hours, and he wanted to read me the script to be sure that I'd gotten all the shots.

Despite my irritation about being woken up, I knew that Howard's script was excellent—a straightforward and beautiful profile of a young Cambodian, who had enlisted a few weeks ago to do his duty and was killed before he even experienced combat. It was unbelievable, but this was real life in Cambodia today. Howard asked me which pictures matched up with the last paragraph of his script.

I roughly remember how he ended the report:

A moment ago, he was only seventeen. He wanted to be a teacher when the war was over. Howard Tuckner, ABC News Highway Three in Cambodia.

I told Howard about the scene in which the flag bearer's body was evacuated from the road, and his flag was taken back by his colleagues. The footage might have been shaky because I was using a telephoto lens, but it showed his last moments in a symbolic way. Howard nodded in agreement—he had already decided to use that scene but just wanted to get my opinion. He showed me his typed script, simply titled "A Young Soldier."

I returned to my room, but I found I was so moved by the story that I wasn't sleepy. Howard had written a simple and emotional story about the death of a young kid. It wasn't significant from a military point of view. However, Howard's focus on the flagbearer symbolized all the nameless young Cambodians who were facing a war they were utterly unprepared for.

Howard Tuckner was slim, tall, and handsome—imagine Clark Gable with long sideburns. The first time I met him was in May 1966 when he was working for NBC, and we were both covering the 1st Cavalry on the central coast of Vietnam. His cameraman, Vo Huynh, was a terrific shooter with a reputation for bravery and creativity under fire.

On the battlefield, Howard and Vo Huynh were a great team, probably the best TV news team working for the nets in those years. In situations where even soldiers were keeping their heads down, Howard would stand in a half-crouch and explain the situation in a calm and cool manner while bullets zipped and whined around him.

It didn't take long for the term "Tuckner's Crouch" to become standard in both Saigon and New York.

Another great cameraman, In Jip Choi, told me how Howard's unique stand-up was born. When Choi was working with Howard at NBC, he found it tough to shoot a good stand-up because Howard was so much taller and, if they stood on level ground, Choi would be shooting up and capturing only nice calm blue sky and clouds behind Howard instead of battle. There were two choices; Choi could have moved to a higher location or even stood on a crate or something, but that would have made him an instant target.

Vietnamese cameraman, Vo Huynh, an exceptionally brave shooter who could do steady and artistic work under the worst of battle conditions. Working for NBC, he became Howard Tuckner's primary cameraman. (Courtesy Yasutsune Hirashiki)

My friend was brave but not stupid.

The other option was to lower Tuckner. Choi would motion for Howard to get lower and lower until he was in a half-crouch and the action had reappeared behind him. It can't have been very comfortable for Howard, but it was dramatic so he adopted it as a signature style and asked all his cameramen to shoot the same way. Since most of the cameramen were Asians and about the same height, this was OK with them, and thus Choi invented the "Tuckner Crouch."

Other reporters had to admit that Howard was an excellent reporter, but he was criticized for his brusque and competitive personality. In the spring of 1970, Howard left NBC and moved to ABC to become the Hong Kong correspondent and bureau chief, initially working in Cambodia. T. H. Lee and I were assigned to work with him.

Tae Hong Lee, universally known as T. H. Lee, was a veteran sound-man from South Korea, who'd begun covering Vietnam about the same time I did. When fellow Korean In Jip Choi came to work at ABC, T. H. Lee came as well—a good team took a lot of time to develop. Later, T. H. and I teamed up for a long and productive period. T. H. Lee was a very nice guy who was a high-level black belt in karate and would break bricks with his forehead to impress soldiers on the frontlines. Like me, he had a tendency to be reckless, so we made a wild team.

Eddie Chan was from Singapore where he used to work as a film censor. Terry Khoo suggested he come to Saigon and recommended him to ABC so Eddie first came to Saigon to film the Vietnam War and then was sent to open the Phnom Penh bureau where he was both local manager and cameraman.

T. H. Lee and I arrived in Phnom Penh a day before Howard Tuckner came from Hong Kong. We worked with Eddie Chan to get press cards, gather information on the military situation, shop for the needed equipment and supplies, and then enjoyed a coffee break at the fancy café in the courtyard of the Royal Hotel. Yes, we took it easy, but we knew that once Howard arrived, we would constantly be working.

According to Eddie, covering Cambodia was very different from covering Vietnam. The frontlines spread in all directions from Phnom

In Jip Choi, a native of Korea, was one of NBC News' best cameramen in Vietnam. He claimed to have invented the "Tuckner Crouch" where the reporter was so close to the frontline that he had to do his stand-up bent over. In fact, Choi was shorter than Tuckner and had to make him bend over to get the battle and not blue sky behind his head. (Courtesy In Jip Choi)

Penh and journalists either traveled by small rented sedans or larger limos with a skilled driver and enough room for all the camera gear. We picked a big Mercedes Benz limo with air-conditioning, drinks, and room for eight people. More important was the driver, a veteran named Tan, who was fluent in Khmer, Chinese, and even a bit of Vietnamese and English.

That evening, we sat over coffee in the courtyard and waited for Howard to arrive. The café at the Royal Hotel was practically a press club with dozens of reporters from all over the world meeting, drinking, and exchanging information and gossip in equal amounts.

Many were worried about the CBS crew who were late returning from the frontlines. When they finally arrived in the early evening, they said that the road they'd taken on the way out had been cut off behind them by insurgents, and they'd had to take a less-familiar road to get back to the capital. On the way, they'd been ambushed and almost captured. "The CBS team was damn lucky to make it back today," a veteran reporter told us.

They sat at a table surrounded by other journalists asking about what happened, how they managed to escape, and any other details that might help the rest of us avoid the same danger. As dangerous as Vietnam was, Cambodia was far more chaotic and perilous. The iron-clad rule for journalists was to make it back to Phnom Penh before sunset.

The crew that had just returned were cameraman Tomoharu Ishii and soundman Kojiro Sakai from the CBS Tokyo bureau. They were veterans from the newsreels who had been covering major stories in Asia for decades. We'd met several times in Vietnam, and I'd found them to be quiet and taciturn but this time, they grabbed me by the hands and spoke with urgency about how dangerous it was in Cambodia.

When men with their level of experience were frightened, it really shook those of us with much less time in the field. Both Ishii and Sakai told me about that afternoon's terrifying events and warned me that, once you'd left Phnom Penh, you were just as likely to run into rebels as government forces. They said that "Everything you've learned won't help you here. There's just no comparison." Both of them warned us not to push our luck and if we got a bad feeling, make a U-turn, and head back immediately. Finally, they shook their heads and agreed that, even if we were careful, it wouldn't guarantee that we'd come back alive.

Howard had arrived and was in the crowd listening to the CBS reporters. He spotted us, came over, and pulled us aside. "Why weren't you out there today with the CBS crew?"

It was an entirely unexpected question.

I stuttered, "We had to make arrangements to get press cards, and prepare things for covering the front while waiting for your arrival."

Howard replied in a cold manner, "Until the correspondent arrives, the cameraman has all of the responsibility. If CBS or NBC goes out to cover a story, you should assess the situation, and follow them. Today, you guys should have gone. Next time if I'm not here, you should go."

I was dumbstruck, but Howard was correct. If there had been a big story, CBS and NBC would have had it, and ABC would look like fools. Now that I look back at it, it was frightening, but it also showed the amount of trust and responsibility that all the news organizations placed on the cameramen in those days.

I bit back all my excuses and apologized.

What a terrible way to begin with the best war reporter in the business! I always wanted to impress the people I worked with, not just for ego but because that would mean that they wouldn't be looking over my shoulder all the time.

We had dinner together, and Howard was pleasant and appeared to have forgotten the scolding he'd given us earlier. He said that, when he was working at NBC, he could see that I was one of the better cameramen and that he'd specifically asked for me to be the cameraman on this trip instead of the Hong Kong crew because he felt he needed to impress New York on this first assignment for ABC News.

The next morning, we left Phnom Penh and went into the field for the first time, planning to accompany government troops as they moved out to recapture Kompong Cham, Cambodia's third-largest city. Only days ago, the city had fallen to a sudden attack by insurgents, and the government was determined to retake it quickly.

We reached the gates of Kompong Cham after hours on the road. Along the way, I'd filmed air strikes, gun fights, and bombings. Sihanouk had bought his military equipment from mostly Communist countries so the troops carried AK-47s. Anyone who had been in the field in Vietnam could instantly tell the difference between the AK-47s of the Communists and the South Vietnamese M16s but here, with both sides using the same rifles, it was virtually impossible to identify which side soldiers were on until you were far too close.

When we reached Kompong Cham, the rebels had retreated. It had taken three days, but the government forces had regained the city—or what was left of it. It was deserted, the downtown was flattened, and all the shops and houses were destroyed. The government commanders proudly displayed the first weapons they had ever captured from Communist forces, but there was little left of the city they had been sent to save.

Howard went inside the local military headquarters to check the latest news, and we waited outside in a small courtyard where some government troops were resting. Looking up, I spotted a small prop plane circling in the sky above us. At first, I thought it was dropping pamphlets as a propaganda move, but I started to film it anyway. My habit on assignment was to start rolling film on anything interesting and worry about whether it was worth shooting later.

The plane circled our position twice and then pushed over into a nose dive right towards where we were sitting. A small black object fell from the fuselage, and the plane climbed back up into the sky. An enormous explosion went off only yards away. The soldiers scattered in panic; screaming, waving, and yelling at the pilot. It didn't do any good, the little plane circled, made another bombing run, and again dropped a bomb near our position.

It was so surreal it felt like a war movie and not a real danger. I was scared, but I felt as if I was frozen so I just kept right on shooting. As the plane came in on its second bombing run, I could see by the marks on its wing that it was a T-28 Trojan, a 1950s airplane that the Americans supplied in large numbers to the South Vietnamese Air Force. The South Vietnamese were now supporting the Cambodian regime but, apparently, their communications were still faulty.

There was no way to communicate with the pilot. No one had a radio, signal flag, or even smoke signals to wave him off. There were absolutely no communications between the Cambodians and their new South Vietnamese allies much less between air and ground forces. Undoubtedly, this was an extreme example of "friendly fire" caused by the new partners' inability to communicate. I'm not sure if the pilot saw the Cambodian soldiers waving white bedsheets or if he simply ran out of ammunition but either way, he flew off to the east.

I had it all on film and Eddie Chan had shot the soldiers as they screamed at the pilot while others cared for the wounded.

The whole incident didn't last ten minutes but stayed in my mind for years. It was my first experience facing a fighter plane and filming it as it dove right at me.

I don't recommend it.

Howard ran out to join us and asked what we had shot. We told him that we had it all and filled out a dope sheet with all the scenes. The bombing run itself was only five lines, but each shot was long and extremely scary:

> Propeller fighter plane circling in the sky, nose-diving to Cambodia Army position, dropped bomb.
> Close-up of airplane and also shooting machine guns.
> Cambodian soldiers on the ground running, scattering with panic.
> Soldiers waving big bed sheets as white flags.
> Wounded soldiers evacuated (Eddie's camera).

Howard wasn't satisfied and asked, "Is that all?"

The fact was that I was still so upset that I wouldn't absolutely guarantee that I'd gotten these shots although I knew perfectly well I'd covered the entire incident. Most shooters know that it's bad luck to "guarantee" that a particular shot is on the film until it's developed and mounted on an edit table.

Howard filed several reports from Kompong Cham and the first that showed the near-miss in detail, was sensational. ABC New York sent a long cable filled with compliments and said it had been a long time since they'd seen such an exciting report—it actually looked like a Hollywood movie! Howard read the telex to us and for the first time since we started working together, I saw a smile on his face.

From then on, he started to believe in me.

Of course, it took being bombed and strafed, but it still felt worth it.

That first story started him off well with ABC and "The Flagbearer" ran only days later. In fact, we filed twenty-five stories from Cambodia in a month, and every one of them aired. The result of this streak of good

On June 21, 1971, Howard Tuckner interviews a controversial military critic of the war, US Army Colonel David Hackworth. Forced out of the military because of his analysis, in the end Hackworth was largely proven correct. (Courtesy Family of Terry Khoo)

stories was that Howard learned to trust me as his partner and knew that if I hadn't gotten a shot, it simply couldn't have been done.

Howard Tuckner covered Indochina's wars from 1965 to 1972 and was a top reporter for both ABC and NBC News. In 1980, he called me at my new station in Bonn, and we talked for an hour. He said he still had the dope sheets from our work in Cambodia, and he became quite emotional, saying how much he missed working with Terry Khoo and me.

Only weeks later, he took his own life. He was 48 years old.

He was one of the best correspondents I ever worked with—it was a tragedy that he couldn't take those talents and use them in peacetime.

PART II

BAD LUCK *OMIKUJI*

Terry Khoo (left) and Tony Hirashiki (right) sport matching goatees c. 1967. Staffers at ABC said that if they saw Terry, who was usually referred to as the "dean of the Saigon cameramen," Tony would show up within minutes. (Courtesy Yasutsune Hirashiki)

As I've said, in Japan there were Shinto shrines where you could go and find out your fortune. Written on tiny pieces of paper called *omikuji* would be written what you could expect in the future.

If you drew a paper with "bad fortune" or "very bad fortune," you could fold it and hand it on a tree branch and pray that it would change.

Even though there were bright moments, most of what follows is "very bad fortune."

CHAPTER 13

COMPETITION

In the 1960s and early 1970s when Prince Sihanouk was ruling Cambodia, it was closed to Western journalists. When Lon Nol sent the prince into exile, journalists were suddenly able to get visas, and flocked to cover the new civil war. NBC's Welles Hangen, who had been covering Asia since the early 1950s, arrived with French cameraman Roger Colne and Japanese soundman Yoshihiko Waku. ABC's team of Steve Bell, Terry Khoo, and Yuki Senzaki arrived shortly afterward and obtained a series of exclusives.

CBS News sent in two teams: George Syvertsen with cameraman Kurt Volkert and sound technician Thanong Hiransi; and Don Webster with the veteran Japanese team of Tomoharu Ishii and Kojiro Sakai along with two more shooters, Kurt Hoefle from Germany and Ramnik Lekhi from India. I had been sent in with Howard Tuckner, T. H. Lee, and Eddie Chan to extend Steve Bell's winning streak while he took a well-deserved break. All of us were friends from our time in Saigon and could usually be found in the Royal in the evenings sharing dinner and drinks.

Don Webster was a very aggressive reporter who I had run into on one battlefield or another since 1967. I thought he was a good reporter but he had a reputation for pushing crews hard and not paying enough attention to their safety. In contrast, George Syvertsen was a gentle man who reminded me of a college professor. I hadn't met him before, but he had covered Europe and Moscow as a newspaper reporter before switching to CBS and being assigned to Tokyo. He and Volkert had covered the battles for Hue and Da Nang in 1968 and came out with a solid reputation for good work.

Although Syvertsen and Webster both worked for CBS News, I was told that they were fighting to get on the air. Correspondents knew that they had to compete, even against their fellows. "You're only as good as your last story" has always been a common phrase in television news and reporters felt that no matter how many awards they had or what great stories they had done in the past if their name wasn't on the Evening News for a while, they were in trouble.

It began to get truly dangerous. Webster would take a significant risk one day and almost get captured on the highway. The next day, Syvertsen would go out on the Mekong River and come under heavy fire. The crews began to complain among themselves, saying their reporters had gone crazy, and wondering if it was still safe to follow their lead.

Yasutsune "Tony" Hirashiki shoots from the open door of a South Vietnamese Army helicopter. Cambodia was in a civil war with the Khmer Rouge and the Army of the Republic of Vietnam came in to assist. (Courtesy Yasutsune Hirashiki)

In the afternoon of May 30, 1970, Volkert had it out with his correspondent, telling Syvertsen that it simply wasn't worth pursuing such high-risk stories. Volkert wanted to leave Cambodia, but he was overruled.

Volkert describes this encounter in his book, *A Cambodian Odyssey and the deaths of 25 journalists*:

> We disagreed sharply and argued bitterly about covering the battles. In my opinion, the results of our efforts weren't worth putting our lives on the line. Usage logs showed the film reports from the Phnom Penh side of the war always played second fiddle to pieces about the US side of the incursion into Cambodia.
>
> I felt very frustrated asking George to consider the odds of survival without looking like a coward. I ran up against a brave professional journalist who made up his mind to show the bosses what he was made of, even though he had proved that already many times over. We argued for long hours, sitting with Garry Miller in the shade of a huge banyan tree near the swimming pool of the Hotel Le Royal.
>
> It was the most painful conversation I have ever had. I said I was fed up with our unappreciated but highly dangerous assignment in Cambodia and that we should go back to Vietnam and cover the American troops there. It seemed to me a fair alternative. It was part of the job to run risks but to run them for a purpose: to get stories on the air.
>
> George disagreed and strongly implied that he intended to go on following the Cambodian army on a daily basis.[1]

That evening, Yoshihiko Waku visited me in my bungalow at the Royal. I really liked Waku; on my last R&R, he invited me to his hotel in Hong Kong, and we had a great time listening to his latest Bossa Nova records. His favorite was *The Girl from Ipanema* and after hearing it a few times, I had to agree.

That night, I was surprised to see him because he'd been scheduled to fly back to Hong Kong but, as he told me, his replacement had been delayed. He was not happy about this because he wanted to stop covering Cambodia.

"It's too dangerous," he kept repeating.

I was surprised because Waku was always cool and didn't talk about his worries or fears. We talked for a while and then he left to go on his assignment. "Watch out, don't take risk."

After Waku had left, I was having coffee alone at the poolside café, and George Syvertsen came by and said, "Are you going to Highway

Three tomorrow? If you go, be careful! It's a very dangerous road, and there are lots of ambushes!"

I answered, "We have not yet decided which story to cover tomorrow. We have only one correspondent and one crew. We can't cover all, so we have to choose one."

Then our conversation turned to more pleasant topics as he said, "My wife wants to go to Chinese dinner with you guys again. How about tomorrow night?"

Syvertsen had brought his wife, Gusta, to stay with him in Phnom Penh and Eddie Chan and I had recently taken them out to a Chinese dinner. She was a Chinese scholar but still was impressed with the way Eddie would order little-known recipes depending on what was available in the kitchen that night.

After that, Gusta had asked her husband to have dinner with the ABC crew more often. I said, "It's a good idea! I'll tell Eddie Chan, and he can check what ingredients the kitchen has. Please be careful too."

Tuckner took a long time deciding which story to pursue in the morning. One choice was to go north up Highway Three where there had been a lot of fighting, and the other was to go south down Highway One to the town of Neak Luong where South Vietnamese forces were officially entering the war as allies of the Lon Nol regime.

Late that evening, Tuckner finally decided to go down Highway One. He said that, in the end, his reasoning was that Don Webster was going there, and Tuckner thought he was more likely to get a big story. "The guy is a nasty competitor," he said. "I have to watch out for him."

In the early morning of May 31, we departed Phnom Penh and drove south along the Mekong River until we reached the border between Cambodia and Vietnam. When we arrived, a large number of elite South Vietnamese troops were standing by with their armored vehicles, tanks, and heavy artillery units. The difference between an army honed by ten years of war and one which had been in the field less than two months was glaring, and the South Vietnamese were determined to make this very clear to the press.

We ran into Volkert and Thanong, and we were surprised that they were shooting for Don Webster instead of their regular correspondent. Volkert explained, "At the last moment, we swapped crews. It's better for things to cool down. George was taking too many risks."

CBS cameraman Kurt Volkert and correspondent George Syvertsen in Da Nang awaiting a flight to Saigon. (Courtesy Kurt Volkert)

George Syvertsen went north on Highway Three with cameraman Tomoharu Ishii, soundman Kojiro Sakai, silent cameraman Ramnik Lekhi, Cambodian driver Sam Leng, and producer Jerry Miller, who had just arrived to run the CBS Phnom Penh bureau. NBC correspondent Welles Hangen found out where Syvertsen was heading shortly after they left and he rounded up cameraman Roger Colne, soundman Yoshihiko Waku, their driver Chay You Leng, and followed them.

The next morning, everyone in the press corps knew that the ten journalists who had gone up Highway Three were missing, but a new government checkpoint prevented anyone from investigating. The soldiers there said rebels had just taken and now held part of the road.

For days, TV crews and reporters waited at the checkpoint in steadily diminishing hope. Others came and went, but Kurt Volkert maintained a vigil at the checkpoint. He was a big strong man, but I felt he looked almost fragile as the tears ran down his face and the grief he held inside him seemed to have hollowed him out.

He and Syvertsen had worked together every day for the past two years and were best friends as well as partners. Volkert blamed himself, saying that if he'd have been there, he might have convinced Syvertsen to turn back or take a different route. No one thought that Volkert was to blame, but survivor's guilt is a merciless form of suffering.

Two days later, Chay You Leng, the NBC driver, appeared at the checkpoint and reported that he had managed to escape from the Khmer Rouge and Viet Cong but that everyone else was almost certainly dead.

Four days later, I arrived at the checkpoint around noon and found that Kurt Volkert had been there since dawn even though he'd been out all night with the Cambodian military. The troops at the checkpoint still said the road was unsafe so Volkert went back to Phnom Penh to work on other alternatives.

Half an hour later, a villager on a motorcycle came from the direction of the enemy lines. We stopped him and asked about the area he had just traveled through. He said that the road was still cut off by the destroyed bridge, but all the insurgent forces had left the area where the NBC driver said the killings had occurred.

Newsweek photographer Denis Cameron hired a motorcycle from a villager and I paid another man to carry me on the back of his motorcycle, and we set off. It wasn't very far before we found the CBS jeep. It was flipped on its side and completely burned out.

Tony Hirashiki prepares his Auricon sound camera for a story in Cambodia after flying in on a South Vietnamese helicopter in April 1970. Note that, in Cambodia, it was dangerous for journalists to wear camouflage—it was the opposite in South Vietnam. (Courtesy Yasutsune Hirashiki)

I hadn't seen any sign of rebels, so I returned to the checkpoint, passed along the news, and then Tuckner, T. H. Lee, and I drove back slowly and cautiously in the ABC car.

We filmed the burned-out jeep, the Mercedes—which was abandoned not far away—and a shallow grave with exposed human bones. Then Tuckner did a stand-up that, in a plain and grave manner, told how this was the location where our friends and colleagues had disappeared four days ago. When we got back to Phnom Penh, he declared it "pool footage" and all the networks received a copy when it was developed in Hong Kong so they could do their own stories.

Over the next few days, Don Webster led the CBS staff in recovering those bodies and whatever personal effects were at the scene. Robert Sam Anson described the helplessness and anger that spread through the press corps back in Phnom Penh in his book, *War News*:

> Don Webster came in waving a telegram from New York. "Listen to this," he said. "Please take no unnecessary chances. Remain in Phnom Penh unless absolutely necessary. Story not worth it."
>
> Webster, a husky, usually scowling character who'd had a recent encounter with the NVA himself, balled up the cable and flung it across the room. "Little late, huh?"
>
> He heaved his bulk into a seat and helped himself to someone else's Scotch. As I watched him drink, I thought of how disdainful George had been after Webster's brush with the NVA. "That's typical of what would happen to Don," he had said. "I'm never going to get captured." George had been correct about that.
>
> "What's the fucking point of all this?" Webster asked, as much to himself, it seemed, as to anyone in the room. "You risk your neck looking for a firefight, and when you do find it, the fucking thing is two-bit. These guys fire five rounds and run. That's great if you are looking for a story on cowardice. But is it worth it? You count up the television people we've lost, and you get ten. How many minutes of combat film did we get on the air because of that? How many? How much film did George and Jerry come back with?"
>
> No one bothered to answer.[2]

ABC News producer and correspondent, Drew Pearson, used to work with Welles Hangen in Asia in the mid-1950s. Three decades later, he wrote me about the deaths:

Ah, Tony ... I always felt there was too much competition between the nets, making people do hasty things that were far too dangerous and not worth it in the end. I want some of those dead journalists back.[3]

Kurt Volkert spent weeks investigating the incident and sent a report to CBS and NBC executives in New York:

At about 10 a.m. on the 31st of May, 1970, Syvertsen, driving a Jeep with Miller in the front seat, closely followed by a CBS-hired blue Mercedes driven by Cambodian Sam Leng and occupied by Ishii, Sakai, and Lekhi, came upon the destroyed bridge at Baing Kasey. Syvertsen decided to take the Jeep around a rugged bypass and to look at what was up ahead on Highway Three. He took with him Miller, Sam Leng as an interpreter and Lekhi maybe to have a cameraman with him. Sakai and Ishii stayed behind near the blue Mercedes.

Minutes after they had heard a sharp explosion but no other firing ahead, the NBC Opel pulled up behind the Mercedes and all occupants got out. After a short talk between the two crews, a group of three Viet Cong came near them and started firing, hitting the Opel. NBC driver Leng jumped under the gray Opel and was struck by a bullet that also punctured one of the tires. A Japanese, maybe Waku, helped to pull him out. Just minutes before these events, the CBS jeep was stuck by a Viet Cong B-40 rocket, hit a mango tree and burst into flames. All in the jeep died. The NBC crew and the remaining CBS crew were taken prisoner and led for about 1 and 1/2 kilometers on a path running 300 meters east of and parallel to Highway Three, heading toward the village of Thanal Bor about 6 kilometers from the scene of the Jeep crash in the village of Baing Kasey at km 54.[4]

This search was only the beginning of nearly three decades that Volkert devoted to researching and investigating every detail of what happened on that awful day. In 1992, the remains of Kojiro Sakai, Welles Hangen, Roger Colne, and Yoshihiko Waku were found. Tomoharu Ishii's remains were never located.

I hope by finding his teammates and returning them to their families, Kurt Volkert finally closed the door on this tragedy. He has proven that he was a good and faithful friend even after death, and I'm sure that George Syvertsen would have been proud of him.

George's wife Gusta came by ABC News and said goodbye to Eddie Chan, T. H. Lee, and me, thanking us for what turned out to be far-too-few Chinese dinners. She was angry and could not understand how TV news

ABC News Phnom Penh bureau manager Eddie Chan is introduced to Cambodia's ruler, General Lon Nol. Chan was also a cameraman and has a small hand-wound camera for taking silent film slung over his shoulder. (Courtesy Eddie Chan)

had put so much pressure on her husband that this gentle man turned into a competitor so fierce that he seemed to actively seek out danger.

A memorial service was held at the Royal Hotel and executives flew all the way from New York to attend. We were told that Gusta Syvertsen refused to speak to any of them.

CHAPTER 14

CHARMING DICTATOR

Steve Bell kickstarted his career in 1959 by broadcasting Nikita Khrushchev's visit to Iowa, then he went on to report live on the death of Senator Robert Kennedy in Los Angeles, and covered the death of Martin Luther King Jr. in Memphis. By the time he joined ABC in 1967, he'd been an anchor or reporter at a number of local stations, and he soon volunteered to go to Southeast Asia for an eighteen-month tour of duty.

He was an agreeable man with a broad smile that was so charming, locals once told me that it was a "Buddha smile." Unlike a Buddha, Steve's smile wasn't ever-present. When his world was in harmony, he smiled. However, when a crewmember wasn't doing the right things or making a lot of mistakes, Steve would undergo a startling metamorphosis. His face would become as red as an Amitābha Buddha, his temper would flare up like a sudden rainstorm, and then disappear just as quickly.

He was the first ABC reporter into Cambodia which, as I've said, was far more dangerous than Vietnam in many ways. The army was badly trained and disorganized with the result that rebels could appear almost anywhere at any time. Reporters and crews knew that, regardless of the value of a story, it wasn't worth being caught outside the gates of Phnom Penh after dark.

Correspondents who took too many chances didn't last long in Cambodia. Photographers Dana Stone and Sean Flynn (son of actor Errol Flynn) posed for Steve and Terry Khoo on their rented motorcycles one afternoon, rode off down a road known to be risky, and were never seen again.

Steve, soundman Takayuki Senzaki, and my best friend, cameraman Terry Khoo, were captured by an insurgent patrol at one point but Terry managed to talk their way out. The story they were pursuing was a good distance away, so the team left the capital very early in the company of Driver Tan, who was the best of all the press drivers. He had a big dark blue Mercedes Benz limousine which fit eight people comfortably with all their gear. It even had air conditioning, something that was almost unheard of in those days.

The feeling of comfort in Tan's car was the least of the reasons he was a coveted driver that we felt we were lucky to hire. Before the war, Tan used to drive visiting dignitaries and international VIPs all over Cambodia, showing them Angkor Wat and other famous landmarks. As a result, he seemed to know every road by heart, and he was very proactive about security. He would talk to everyone he saw, asking which route was safe, where rebels had been seen, and what bridges had been destroyed. Tan was the perfect example of a local hire that international news crews depend on in a war zone. If he said a road was safe, off we went even if it was a tiny, broken backcountry lane. If he said "can't go," we turned around immediately. Even if we were returning on a road that had been safe only hours or minutes before, Tan would be checking to see if rebels had cut it in the interim. It often took a long time for him to get enough information to feel comfortable about a particular route but he made up the time by driving extremely fast.

On that day, Tan was worried. He had even insisted that the ABC crew shouldn't be the first car out that morning because the government troops were notoriously late to begin their patrols and so the rebels controlled the roads well into the morning, hoping for one more ambush before they retreated to their jungle sanctuaries. Also, the first car to traverse a stretch of road was going to be the car that hit a newly hidden landmine.

Tan was the best, but even the best were sometimes caught.

On a small road quite close to the story, Tan slowed down at a local village checkpoint and the guard waved him on, saying, "It's safe here, you can go through." Tan sped up, but they passed a dozen soldiers, maybe more, by the side of the road only minutes later. Terry Khoo was

ABC News correspondent Steve Bell was one of the first reporters to get back into Cambodia after the overthrow of Prince Sihanouk in March 1970. He and Tony got into a furious argument on a battlefield that ended with Tony calling Bell a "dictator." As the years went by, it became "Dear Dictator" and a shared joke. (Courtesy Steve Bell)

sitting up front with Tan and, even though they were going fast, both of them identified them as rebels.

A lot of insurgents would wear uniforms that looked like those worn by the Cambodian Army but usually they didn't have military boots, just sandals. What Tan and Terry had both seen was that some of these men had "Ho Chi Minh" sandals—cut from the tires of downed American planes. No government soldier would have been caught dead in them, but Viet Cong and North Vietnamese soldiers loved them as a sign of their coming victory.

In addition, they were carrying AK-47 rifles instead of the American M16s or French Fabrique National weapons the government had now begun to issue. Terry and Driver Tan talked about this but weren't entirely certain so they continued. Just a few miles on, they hit a roadblock; piles of dirt, stones, sand, and tree branches laid across the road. Since the roadblock was an excellent place to hide landmines, only a tank would be able to clear it.

Without a tank at hand, they realized that they were trapped. There was no other option but to make a U-turn and head back. They had gone by the insurgents very quickly the first time, but they would definitely get stopped on a second pass.

And they were.

The soldiers weren't lounging by the side of the road now; they were in the middle of the road with guns aimed at the blue car. In a perfect example of checkpoint etiquette, Tan opened all the windows and slowed down very gently. As he came up to the soldiers, he waved out the window to show he was going to stop.

I was told that Terry got out of the car first, picked out the leader, walked up to him, and stuck out his hand as if greeting a rebel commander was something he did every day. Taken by surprise, the leader shook hands, and Terry said later that he thought that handshake moved the situation towards talking rather than shooting.

I asked Terry how he knew who the leader was. He said, "There was only one guy with a pistol in a holster on his waist."

Despite his air of calm confidence, Terry said it was one of the scariest moments of his life. He'd decided to treat the guerrilla leader as an unthreatening equal and see if that would build a relationship of trust that might get the crew out alive. Who knows? Sometimes, if you just act as if nothing is wrong, the other side does too.

Yuki and Tan exited the car and walked up, looking unafraid and proving they were unarmed. Steve Bell stayed well back in the rear seat of the big car where it was hard to see him clearly. No one wanted the insurgents to discover that he was an American.

Terry learned that the leader was an advisor from North Vietnam and spoke Chinese and even a little English along with Vietnamese. Terry was Singapore Chinese and had lived in Saigon long enough to be fluent in Vietnamese, so they were able to converse easily. At first, the North Vietnamese advisor accused them of being spies, which was not unexpected. The rebels automatically labeled anyone who wasn't Cambodian a spy and often killed them rather than take the time to find out the truth.

Terry smiled and told the leader that of course they weren't spies. They were a TV crew out to cover the war. As a matter of fact, he hinted, they were working on a big story about ethnic Vietnamese being killed by the Cambodians. The North Vietnamese advisor was impressed when Terry told him how concerned they were over this story.

Meanwhile, Steve was beaming his best "Buddha smile" in the car, and the soldiers seemed to relax slightly. Then, Steve remembered he was a reporter and picked up his tape recorder.

Bad Idea.

The soldiers thought it was a radio and Steve was about to call in an airstrike. Hands tightened on assault rifles and muzzles rose to cover the Mercedes. Steve saw this immediately, and his smile just got bigger and more beatific. He demonstrated how harmless the recorder was, taping "One, Two, Three, Four," and then playing his voice back for the soldiers to hear. His playacting worked—even jungle rebels in those days knew the difference between a radio and a tape recorder. Since they still were unsmiling and stern, Steve just put down the recorder.

And Smiled.

Terry told me that he and the patrol leader talked for at least thirty minutes and possibly for an hour. He said it was hard to tell time because he was pretending to be completely relaxed while his stomach was tied in painful knots. Finally, he convinced the leader that they were journalists, not spies. Steve got out of the car and stood with the soldiers trying to look relaxed and comfortable.

Then came the dreaded question, "Your friend? Is he an American?"

Terry had prepared for this, and he knew that he couldn't simply lie and say that Steve was a Canadian or something because everyone had IDs, press cards, and passports and being caught in a lie would be certain death.

"Yes, he is an American but an American journalist. I'm the cameraman, and I'm from Singapore, and Yuki over there is Japanese, and he does the sound. We're an international team sent to Cambodia to cover this important news."

After a moment of thought, the guerrilla leader asked, "Can I keep your American friend with me so I can ask him more questions? It might take some more time, but I'll let him return to you later. In the meantime, you and the crew can go and get to work right now."

Terry said, "No, he has to do the broadcast live, or the world won't believe us. Why don't you keep me here for questions and let him go and finish his report?"

Terry was a brave man. He had just offered himself up as a hostage in exchange for Steve!

Was it a miracle, the "Buddha Smile," or Terry Khoo's willingness to sacrifice himself? Whatever the reason, the leader just waved his hand and said, "You can all go now."

No one wanted to wait around, but everyone shook hands with the North Vietnamese soldiers again and got back in the car pretending that they were having such a good time they didn't really want to leave. Terry said that this little bit of theater took forever and the entire time, he worried that the soldiers were just playing out an evil joke, and would shoot them all in the back.

Tan drove off slowly with everyone waving goodbye with big smiles. As soon as they were out of sight, Tan floored the accelerator and drove like a maniac all the way back to Phnom Penh.

Terry, who was my teacher in so many ways, told me that "shaking hands with the enemy" was the most important part of a negotiation. Once you'd shaken hands, maybe shared some tea or coffee, then you had turned the corner from a faceless enemy to a real person, and the odds that they would kill you had gone down.

A big smile didn't hurt.

Steve told me that on the way back to Phnom Penh, they waved down two other cars full of journalists and warned them to turn around. It seemed that the village guard was telling everyone that the road ahead was just as safe as could be. He could have been stupid, uninformed, or playing a game with journalists out of boredom. Who knows?

Cambodia was often dangerous for journalists but it was even deadlier for Cambodians. One example was the story that Terry used to get out of the ambush: the dire situation of the approximately 500,000 ethnic Vietnamese living in Cambodia. These ethnic Vietnamese had lived in towns, cities, and villages in Cambodia for decades and, in many cases, centuries, and were known as smart, hard-working people. The Khmer, as Cambodians call themselves, claimed that the Vietnamese were aggressive, greedy, and out to dominate the economy. They owned many, if not most, of the stores, worked in the gold and silver trade, and could easily be portrayed as wealthy and oppressive capitalists when it suited the government's purposes.

As General Lon Nol's incompetent and unprepared army began to suffer defeats against the rebels and their Vietnamese allies, the government used the ethnic Vietnamese as scapegoats to turn attention away from their own ineptitude and urged the local people to take their fear out on their Vietnamese neighbors. The government deliberately fanned public anger against them with protest banners that said: "All Vietnamese are Viet Cong." There had always been ethnic tensions, and the actions of the government were the lighting of a fuse. Many fled back into Vietnam, but thousands who could not or would not escape were attacked, burned alive in their own homes, hacked to death, and, thrown into the Mekong River so their corpses would float "back" into Vietnam. Since the government and the military were deeply involved, it was an extremely difficult story to cover and what was truly a genocide went on for a long time.

In April 1970, a Cambodian military spokesman reported that there had been a major battle between Cambodian and Viet Cong forces in a village along the Vietnamese border. According to the official report, ethnic Vietnamese villagers had been caught in the crossfire and many had been killed or wounded. Something about the story just didn't smell right so Steve, Terry, and Yuki drove out from Phnom Penh to check out the story along with other journalists.

As many suspected, it was clear that the villagers had not been caught in a crossfire, as officially reported, but rounded up and deliberately murdered by the Cambodian army. Terry took pictures of corpses left lying where they'd fallen, survivors, some with terrible wounds, and pools of blood where bodies had lain before they were thrown into the Mekong River. Steve Bell was able to confirm that almost 100 men, women, and children had been murdered the night before.

Robert Sam Anson was there reporting for *TIME*:

> Terry Khoi [sic], Bell's cameraman, went over to a nearby cottage where several of the less seriously injured were propped against a wall ... Terry was struggling to keep from crying, "They are my people, and they slaughtered them. Go over and take a look. There are hundreds of shell casings lying around and no holes from incoming fire. It's like they were keeping them as hostages. Soon as the VC showed up, they killed them."
>
> We found the cottage just as Terry described.[1]

Anson mistakenly wrote that Terry Khoo was Vietnamese, but Terry told me that he was simply so upset at seeing the deaths of so many of the people he had lived with and worked with for a decade, that he referred to them as "my people."

The killers probably thought their crime would never be revealed. After all, it was far from Phnom Penh, so only ABC News and a handful of other journalists had reached the village. Steve and his team headed for the Phnom Penh airport with the film hidden under Yuki's shirt and immediately put him on a plane to Hong Kong as a "pigeon" to get it to the processing lab.

Now, ABC had an exclusive that needed to be told. Unfortunately, the government had complete control of all foreign communications and demanded that all news stories had to be written in English or French and looked over by a censor. When an outgoing phone line was connected, the censor would be listening in, and he would instantly cut the line at the first deviation from the script. A story as explosive as Cambodian troops engaging in a civilian massacre would never get past the first word.

Ted Koppel, one of the smartest guys in broadcasting, was the Hong Kong bureau chief so Bell decided to take the chance that they could have an innocent-sounding conversation and Ted would get the underlying story.

Here's how Steve recalled it:

Ted: How are things going?

Steve: Terrific. Remember our old friend, Lieutenant Calley?

Ted: Sure, how the hell is he?

Steve: Great! He threw a party last night that was so wild I counted 97 men, women, and children who had such a good time they'll never go to another party.

Ted: Who was responsible, Calley's friends?

Steve: No, it was the home folks.

Ted: Who were the guests?

Steve: Locals, with ethnic ties across the border.

Ted; What else can you tell me?

Steve; Well, I counted at least 20 more party-goers with bad hangovers and some of them probably will never go to another party. There were also about dozen guests who were still in good shape.[2]

When Steve mentioned "Our Friend Lieutenant Calley," Ted immediately grasped that there was a story here because Steve was referring to the military massacre of civilians at My Lai under the command of American Lieutenant William Calley. Here's how the conversation read after Ted "decoded" it.

There was a massacre of ethnic Vietnamese by Cambodian military forces.

97 had been killed and 20 more severely wounded, some fatally.

12 others in the village seemed to have been unharmed

And that's what Ted reported from Hong Kong only moments later. What a great example of smart teamwork! The Cambodian government couldn't work out how Ted got the story and neither could the rest of the press corps. ABC was first with the complete story when Yuki arrived in Hong Kong, the film was developed, and the story sent to the States.

As satisfying as a scoop was, reporters are as human as anyone else. Steve wrote me years later about how he still replayed the decisions he made that day:

> Without a doubt, covering the massacre of nearly 100 innocent Vietnamese civilians in Cambodia ... was the most important and life-changing story I ever covered. On the one hand, our stories reported under very dangerous conditions and despite censorship, helped to create world opinion that forced the Cambodian government to stop the killing. But I have had guilt feelings ever since that we were so focused on the story (and in shock from the horror of it all), that we didn't think to take any of the wounded back to Phnom Penh for treatment.[3]

★★★

"Don't argue with me, anymore! Do what I say!"

I was having a fight with my correspondent on a Cambodian battlefield. I almost never disagreed with an order from a correspondent but I thought that what he was asking his crew to do was simply too dangerous and I felt I had to protest. Steve Bell was so angry that his face was as red as fire, and he was shouting at me as loudly as he could.

We had been following government troops all day and now we were near the town of Sprang, about 35 miles north of Phnom Penh. A vital crossroads, it had fallen to the rebels a few days ago and now the government was mounting a big push to get it back. It was a rural area, so Steve had had to drive Eddie Chan, soundman T. D. Suu from Saigon, and me in a small sedan over single-lane dirt roads just to get there. On our drive in, we had seen some big artillery guns firing steadily into the rebel positions from a new firebase and now we were filming those same shells pounding the treeline across the field.

We were waiting to film the government attack but Steve decided that he needed natural sound shots of those big guns being fired. I felt this was simply too dangerous because I would have to take the only car, make my way back to the firebase, take the pictures, and make it back. In the meantime, the rest of the crew would have no way to escape if something went wrong.

And, in Cambodia, things went wrong all the time.

I told Steve that as soon as the artillery stopped, the main attack would start, and I'd never get back in time to shoot it. Steve said that Eddie Chan could stay with the silent camera and cover the main attack. I insisted that this wasn't the right way to cover the story but Steve was just as certain that synching the shots of the big guns firing with the shells hitting the enemy positions was essential to his story.

So we were disagreeing—rather loudly. I had gone into danger with Howard Tuckner right here in Cambodia over and over again. I was one of the veteran crews and here Steve was scolding me with his loud and angry voice.

There was something else I wanted to explain but couldn't get across in my limited English. Or perhaps I felt a bit silly to bring it up. I was convinced that I possessed an extra sense which had been essential in my ability to predict a big newsworthy event, get me to the right place on a battlefield, and warned me of danger.

All I knew was that my stomach would hurt if there was danger and right then, it was cramping like crazy. I tried to explain this to Steve but I knew it just sounded like nonsense.

He finally yelled, "Don't argue with me anymore, just GO!"

Suu and I left the frontline for the firebase. As I'd feared, it took longer than expected because there was only room for a single car on the dirt road and we had to pull over and wait for other cars to get by. We arrived at the firebase, got the shots Steve wanted, and headed back. The shots were good but my stomach was really hurting.

Halfway back to the frontlines, the CBS crew and correspondent came racing toward us in their jeep. They slowed down long enough to shout, "Don't go back to the front! There was a big counterattack and the government soldiers are all running away! There's no one but the enemy back there now!" They said they'd only just had time to escape but they already had good pictures of the battle and so they kicked the jeep into gear and raced off towards the capital.

The road instantly became jammed with journalists, soldiers, and refugees in a running mob. We could only move inches at a time.

I was panicked, how would I explain losing my correspondent and cameraman? Why wasn't I there at the frontline where I could have helped them cover such a dangerous battle? Would New York think I'd been a coward and run away?

I couldn't turn and go back without them, so we kept on driving very slowly towards the battle. It was like going against the flow of a river.

There!

Steve came up, riding on the back of a villager's tiny motorcycle. He jumped off when he saw us and ran to the car.

I was glad to see him and immediately asked, "Where's Eddie?"

"I don't know, the government troops were caught by surprise and broke without even putting up a fight. In the chaos, we were separated, and I just grabbed this motorcycle and made the driver take me."

I was happy that Steve was safe but even more terrified about Eddie. The mix of emotions was just too much.

I burst into tears and shouted at Steve. "You fucking dictator! Where's Eddie? We got to find him!"

That was only a small part of what I said. I was swearing so hard that, remembering it, I can't believe so many filthy adjectives and four-letter words ever came out of my mouth and I was shouting them all at Steve. He just stood there, stunned by this calm, smiling little Japanese guy who'd turned into a screaming demon.

We were running to the front on foot when I spotted Eddie. He was covered with mud and dust but uninjured. Eddie told me that, only minutes after we had left for the firebase, the infantry began to advance across the open field, and the enemy hit them hard from behind a low hill.

We all sat in dead silence as Steve drove wildly back to Phnom Penh. At one point, he hit a big pothole, and the camera hood in my lap shot up and cut my chin. It bled a lot but I didn't make a sound. I still have a tiny scar on my chin from that bump and I swear it is the only wound I ever received in ten years of covering war in both Vietnam and Cambodia.

Laugh at my sense of danger if you like. I have proof.

Steve was a true gentleman. After we got back to Phnom Penh, he came to our bungalow and apologized. I'd cooled off so I did the same. As was typical with Steve, we were friends again in seconds and he asked how I learned such a long English word as "dictator." I was embarrassed because Steve would have been the last person I would have called a dictator. It wasn't intentional, just the wrong choice from my limited English vocabulary.

As it turned out, CBS did have footage of the battle but they got back too late to make the flight to Hong Kong so we still had a chance to catch up. The next day, the same forces were in the same positions. The government troops had regrouped and seemed to have regained the discipline they'd lost the day before.

We were following a unit down a small lane between rice fields when my stomach began to hurt. Since the camera and sound gear were connected by a thick cable, Suu and I had to jump to the same side, and seconds after we decided to go left, bullets were whizzing by. Steve did a "stand-up" lying down in the rice and a play-by-play account of what was happening as even more machine-gun bullets zipped by us. Then we crawled to get more pictures.

The battle went on for a long time but I could see the empty brass casings piling up around the machine gunners and knew they would need more ammunition soon. Steve did one more stand-up—only lying down halfway—and a bullet went right past his head. He just paused, shrugged, and continued. It was scary but I knew New York would love it.

In the end, the government won and the rebels withdrew. We made the shipment to Hong Kong and Steve's report aired the same night as CBS's. In fact, New York sent an "Attaboy" telegram that said Steve's story was far better than CBS.

It was nice to see the "Buddha Smile" return to Steve's face.

Here is how Steve remembered it, years later:

> My own recollection is as follows. We were with Cambodian troops trying to retake a town overrun by the NVA. It was getting late to make the last flight out with film that day, and when the Cambodians began lobbing artillery shells over

our heads, I insisted that you and our soundman (can't remember who) go back in the car and get bang bang.

You argued we should stay with the story, the outgoing (artillery) was not important. I insisted, saying I still had Eddie with me. You had hardly gone when all hell broke loose. I rolled into the rice paddy, but when a Cambodian courier jumped back on the road and got on a motorcycle, I ran out and jumped on behind him.

We were roaring toward the rear. When I saw you coming back toward the action, and I squeezed the poor guy until he stopped and let me off. As I got in the back with you, you said, "Where's Eddie?" I replied, "He was on the point when the firing began" and "We're going back to get him."

At that point, you—with tears in your eyes—hit me with the immortal line. "You fucking dictator!"

It was deserved then. It is cherished now, as amended, of course.[4]

That was the beginning of a friendship that has lasted through the next half a century. Every holiday season, no matter where we were, I would receive a card or letter from Steve—always signed "From xxxxing dictator with Love" and my letters back to him were begun with "Charming Dictator."

CHAPTER 15

REINFORCEMENTS

Through the first half of the 1970s, the wars in Indochina ground on. In South Vietnam, "Vietnamization" was in full swing and almost all of the fighting was being done by the Army of the Republic of Vietnam, usually with American advisors and air support. Cambodia had grown from a small rebel insurgency to an all-out civil war, a war the government was losing.

However, with fewer American troops in harm's way, getting on the Evening News became more and more challenging, and a lot of long-term war correspondents went to other bureaus or just drifted away. ABC News began to have trouble fielding enough reporters who were willing to sacrifice the time and effort to cover a war and not even be guaranteed to get on the air. ABC's answer was to encourage all of their correspondents to do a short tour in Vietnam and experience at least a "taste" of combat.

Through this period of "reinforcements," I worked with dozens of correspondents with varying levels of experience that ranged from years of intense study to days spent in-country. In general, these were veteran reporters who ABC was betting its future on, so they were smart and hard-working journalists but they all had very different ways of reporting on the war and, usually, very little time to do it in.

★★★

George Watson began at ABC Radio in 1962, one of the very first to join the fledgling network. In 1963, he was writing a Washington-based radio program for the award-winning Edward P. Morgan when the assassination of President John F. Kennedy in Dallas resulted in Morgan sharing live anchor duty with Howard K. Smith; anchor copy written by George Watson.

For most of his career, George was a Washington-based correspondent, covering the White House and eventually serving as the DC bureau chief for many years. He did more than his share of international reporting, however, taking over the Moscow bureau in the deep Cold War year of 1968, and transferring to London in 1970.

He was an experienced journalist with a reputation for his keen analysis of foreign policy, and he knew the story of Vietnam quite well; he'd watched its earliest beginnings under President Kennedy, through Lyndon Johnson's troop buildup, and now during the slow process of withdrawal under Richard Nixon. Many years later, George wrote to me about his reporting in Vietnam and how his views on the war came to change over time:

> I first went to Vietnam in 1968, just after Tet, when the bureau needed help, especially after Bill Brannigan had been wounded, not seriously, at Khe Sanh. Obviously, I felt something was wrong with the war when the V.C. were fighting inside Saigon, during my first weeks there at Cholon, the Y-bridge, and at the Phu Tho racetrack. I stayed only three months and then returned to my regular assignment in Moscow.
>
> My second tour was in 1970 when the US was withdrawing and "Vietnamization" of the war was taking place. I was there six months on this occasion, which coincided with the so-called Incursion into Cambodia... During this time, I thought that on balance progress had been made toward "winning" the war, meaning that an independent South Vietnam would be able to survive.[1]

According to the film notes on my dope sheets, one of George's most impressive reports was on land reform. George interviewed John Paul Vann, chief of the pacification program in the Mekong Delta. Vann was one of the most knowledgeable, if controversial, figures in Vietnam— he'd warned of the Tet Offensive in 1968 but was also known for leaking military missteps to his press contacts. I was impressed that George could arrange such an interview and admired him for then insisting on going to the Delta region and confirming the facts for himself. George and I drove through the region, shooting pictures of farmers plowing the fields with their water buffaloes, peasants harvesting rice, some farmers

Veteran foreign affairs correspondent and future Washington bureau chief George Watson poses with an American tank crew in 1968 during his first, rather positive, assessment of Vietnam. He returned for six months in 1970 and once again, found reason for hope in the future of South Vietnam. He wrote Tony years later that "it appeared to be good but appearances can be deceptive." (Courtesy In Jip Choi)

with modern water pumps, tractors, and motorized sampans, others still watering a rice paddy with buckets—the whole panorama of this beautiful region.

In the final report, George opened with South Vietnamese President Thieu signing the land reform bill at an elaborate ceremony. I admired how he had a positive take on the war but still checked the details for himself.

When he returned, George felt that the situation had improved and said so in a report that aired on March 29, 1970.

WHEN I WAS LAST IN SAIGON TWO YEARS AGO, THIS BRIDGE HAD BEEN THE SCENE OF MURDEROUS FIGHTING DURING THE TET OFFENSIVE. THE CITY WAS UNDER NIGHTLY ROCKET ATTACKS

AND VENTURING ACROSS THE RIVER INTO THE CHINESE SECTION OF CHOLON COULD BE SUICIDAL.

TODAY THE SITUATION IS DRAMATICALLY DIFFERENT.

SAIGON IS RELATIVELY SAFE FROM ATTACK. THE COUNTRYSIDE IS COMPARATIVELY QUIET, IF NOT PACIFIED AND AMERICAN TROOPS HAVE STARTED TO GO HOME.

...

PRESIDENT NIXON'S POLICY OF VIETNAMIZATION REMAINS MORE A GOAL THAN AN ACHIEVEMENT. SUCCESS DEPENDS ON SAIGON'S EFFORTS, WASHINGTON'S AID, AND NOT LEAST ON HANOI'S REACTION. THE OUTCOME IS UNCERTAIN BUT AFTER TWO YEARS, PROGRESS HAS UNDOUBTLY BEEN MADE.

THIS IS GEORGE WATSON. ABC NEWS SAIGON.[2]

In August, as he was approaching the end of his six-month tour, George's conclusions were still positive.

OPTIMISM IS SADLY OUT OF FASHION THESE DAYS, AND ANYONE WHO PUTS IN A GOOD WORD ABOUT INVOLVEMENT IN VIETNAM IS LIKELY TO BE DISMISSED AS A POLLYANNA OR A CRANK.

THERE IS NO CAUSE FOR UNRESTRAINED OPTIMISM. BUT AS MY PRESENT ASSIGNMENT HERE COMES TO AN END, I AM CONVINCED THAT DRAMATIC PROGRESS HAS BEEN MADE.

I FIRST SAW SAIGON IN THE BLOODY AFTERMATH OF THE TET OFFENSIVE MORE THAN TWO YEARS AGO. HALF A MILLION AMERICANS WERE FIGHTING HERE AND CASUALTIES WERE AS HIGH AS FIVE HUNDRED KILLED IN SINGLE WEEK.

TODAY, GIS ARE GOING HOME, THE MILITARY SITUATION HAS IMPROVED TREMENDOUSLY. THE COMPUTERISED STATISTICS SHOW THAT NINETY PERCENT OF THE COUNTRY IS RELATIVELY SECURE, AND YOU DO NOT NEED TO BELIEVE IN THE INFALLIBILITY OF COMPUTERS TO SEE THE STRIKING EVIDENCE OF IMPROVED SECURITY.

...

PERHAPS THE MOST THAT CAN BE SAID IS THAT SO FAR WE HAVE ACCOMPLISHED OUR GOAL. SOUTH VIETNAM HAS SURVIVED AND WITH LUCK IT MAY ENDURE

THIS IS GEORGE WATSON ABC NEWS SAIGON[3]

After the war, George was quite blunt about how these stories held up in the harsh light of hindsight:

> All this, of course, proved to be illusion, but I cannot claim to have understood the eventual outcome or predicted the collapse of the South Vietnamese forces together with the unwillingness of the US to sustain the war. So I was a "Hawk" in believing that the war could be won and that progress had been made.
>
> In my case, I guess what I learned is that appearances can be deceptive. As I have said, it looked pretty good, certainly better than the period after the Tet when I saw the war for the first time.[4]

★★★

When Sam Donaldson arrived for a three-month assignment, he was already well-known for his acerbic and probing coverage of politicians on Capitol Hill. Sam had been working for ABC since 1967 and for local news stations before that and few others in the history of TV news have had the same level of determination and drive.

Sam was probably four or five years older than me, and he reminded me of a samurai warrior with his strong eyebrows, booming voice, and stern demeanor. As I would learn, despite this tough image, he was a genuinely nice man with a warm heart. I covered several stories with him and found that he was usually interested in finding out what was going on behind the scenes.

Politics was Sam's specialty, and he taught me how to cover the inner workings of elections as we covered the duel between President Nguyen Van Thieu and General Nguyen Cao Ky. Sam also went out on the frontlines, I remember one assignment when we reported on "Fire Base Five" near Rocket Ridge in the Central Highlands. That time, we definitely had "bang bang," and I shot firefights, rockets, air strikes, wounded South Vietnamese soldiers, and a sobering picture of a black body bag.

Sam wrote about this brief taste of war in his autobiography:

Three months is not a long time. In no way could it be compared to the years that many of my colleagues spent covering the war. But it was enough for a taste. And the taste was different from what I expected.

By 1966 or 67, I was already convinced we were fighting the wrong war. By 1971, the Nixon policy was withdrawal.

Still, what I thought about policy didn't matter once I was there. I reported what I actually observed. American doctors at the 91st evacuation hospital at Chu Lai trying to save the life of a North Vietnamese lieutenant, South Vietnamese helicopter teams bravely flying into enemy fire to resupply firebases on "Rocket Ridge" near Tan Canh. And when Napalm is dropped on a nearby tree line from which rockets are being fired at you, you cheer.

Argument over, policy seems far away.[5]

Sam decided that he wanted to do a story on the influx of drugs—primarily heroin—and the effect on American troops. Jean-Claude Malet and I accompanied Sam to the white beaches of the South China Sea where Cam Rahn Bay served as the supply depot for the entire war effort. We were covering a new rehabilitation center where troops from all across the battle zone could kick their habits. The story was a success, and we stayed overnight at Cam Rahn Bay and were treated like VIPs; staying in the very comfortable officers' quarters and enjoying an excellent meal at the officers' club.

The next morning, Sam asked me to secretly film some sequences of an American officer who was the official driver for one of the generals. I asked Sam why I had to go and shoot this in such a sneaky, hidden-camera fashion. He explained that the previous night, while he was drinking with some high-ranking officers, one of them had given him the inside scoop that the general's driver was also his nephew.

"So what?" I asked.

Sam patiently explained that hiring relatives was called "nepotism" and was frowned upon in most of America and illegal in a government or military job. In this particular case, Sam had been told that the general had re-assigned his nephew to keep him out of danger. If this were true, Sam said, it would be a scandal stateside.

I still didn't understand what was so wrong about this "nepotism." In Japan and most other Asian countries, taking care of family members

In 1970, ABC Capitol Hill correspondent Sam Donaldson puts some of his trademark pointed questions to General Creighton Abrams as Ambassador Ellsworth Bunker stands nearby. Sam was asking why the military continued to say that the Cambodian incursion was a success when all the evidence was of massive failure. (Courtesy In Jip Choi)

and relatives was occasionally criticized but generally taken as a standard practice. So I balked, and Sam and I got into a pretty good argument where I forgot completely that he was a big shot from DC.

Eventually, I gave up. "I'll obey your orders, but it makes me feel dirty."

I did the shoot, but I set a condition. Before he used my shots, he had to completely confirm that the story was true. After 30 more years spent working for ABC, I now believe that Sam was absolutely right. Following a story about nepotism in the military would have been a great investigative report. At the time, I was thinking the way most

Asians would, that it would be a betrayal of the general's kindness to take these pictures.

As he promised, Sam called the general directly and confronted him with the rumor. It wasn't true and, as soon as the general sent ABC the documents that disproved it, the story was spiked. Sam wrote about this episode; mentioning the puzzling behavior of a particular oriental cameraman:

> Learning the territory in Vietnam meant learning more than how to stay alive. You were often working with a different values system.
>
> Once at Cam Rahn Bay, I got a tip that one of the commanding general's aides was actually one of the general's nephews. The position of general's aide is a highly coveted one and nepotism clearly should not be involved. I explained to my cameraman, Tony Hirashiki, why we needed to get pictures of the two men as they came out of the headquarter building, telling him that if the tip turned out be true, it would be quite a scandal and a good story for us.
>
> "I don't want to do it" said Hirashiki. "I'll feel dirty if you make me do it."
>
> I was nonplussed. What was the problem?
>
> Hirashiki explained to me that in Vietnam taking care of one's family was the right thing to do. The scandal would be if the general, having a deserving nephew in the army, did not make him his aide.
>
> I finally convinced him to shoot the film.
>
> It turned out the tip was wrong so I never used it.
>
> But the lesson—that other cultures' values are different and must be taken into consideration—has not been forgotten.[6]

In this autobiography, Sam also summed up his views on the Vietnam War and whether we had performed our proper role as journalists:

> Vietnam, as I said, was the wrong war for us. Our national interest did not require that we fight it at the loss of fifty-eight thousand Americans killed doing their duty. They were sacrificed to an obsession with fighting communism wherever we found it, regardless of whether it constituted a clear and present danger to us.
>
> Did the news media lose the war for the United States? Of course not. We reported what we found. And we reported on the gap between the optimistic official line and reality. What changed public opinion was not the press but the body bags coming home, with no end in sight.
>
> The Public was right.[7]

★★★

Irv Chapman was a soft-spoken and retiring gentleman with a pleasant smile who stood in contrast to the brash and extroverted individuals who made up the majority of the Saigon press. He was an excellent listener and, when he did have something to say, he had a subtle and witty sense of humor.

He was only a few years older than me and, better yet, he was about the same height. Irv began at Radio Press International and then joined ABC News as a radio reporter in 1963 and crossed over to the television side in 1968. Like George Watson, he was a bureau chief in Moscow during the Cold War, when Soviet bureaucrats were tight-lipped, suspicious, and uncooperative. Even worse to my thinking was the rule that he had to hire a cameraman from the Russians with the absolute certainty that the man would be a spy. It must have been a relief to transfer to Tokyo.

Irv Chapman became immersed in the culture, history, and economics of Asia and, during the time he was paired with Tokyo cameraman John Lower and soundman Masaaki Ogushi, Irv sent New York more stories than any of his predecessors. John Lower told me that Irv's stories could "stand the test of time"; they could sit on a shelf without becoming dated and John himself would be surprised when a story aired that he'd long forgotten.

While I was still a beginner in television news, a senior colleague told me that one of the most important secrets to being a good journalist, whether a cameraman, reporter or desk manager, was not to lose your sense of wonder, your curiosity about the new and different. Irv was filled with wonder—perhaps his best quality as a broadcast journalist.

In 1971, before he was officially assigned to the Tokyo bureau, he spent three months in Saigon. Through Irv's eyes, Vietnam was a treasure chest of great stories. In a recent letter, he described how Saigon appeared in contrast to the totalitarian restrictions in Moscow:

> Since I came from the Soviet Union, I found Vietnam to be a free country. Saigon had 40 newspapers, and 39 said the election was not fairly conducted. I interviewed students at university, and they gave me the same kind of response I might have heard in Berkeley California, but never in Moscow. So the issue for me regarding Vietnam was not whether it should be kept from the Communists, but whether the United States was in any way able to accomplish such a feat.[8]

In 1971, correspondent Irv Chapman records the final words of a story to a "standing room only" audience of Vietnamese refugees on Guam. (Courtesy Irv Chapman)

In August 1971, Jean-Claude Malet and I went with Irv to do a story about public attitudes leading up to the presidential election. Irv had decided to go to Ban Me Thuot, a Montagnard resettlement camp in the Central Highlands. Traditionally, the Montagnards lived as nomads, moving from one mountain to another, cultivating crops with traditional methods until the soil lost its fertility, and then moving on.

The mountain people had crossed the Vietnamese border without IDs or passports for centuries because they didn't believe that there were borders in the high mountains where they lived. I had heard that the villagers were not happy living in this new settlement with its walls and barbed wire but the South Vietnamese government wanted the Montagnard people to remain in one place for both security and purely political reasons. President Thieu's government needed the votes of these mountain people but before you could count their votes, you had to know where they were.

Dang Van Minh runs the camera and Tran Van Kha the sound as ABC News correspondent Jim Giggans interviews an American officer. One of Giggans' primary topics was increased racial tensions as the American troop drawdown continued and increased time in barracks destroyed the color-blind comradeship of battle. (Courtesy Dang Van Minh)

Irv did a report about their situation and, according to my dope sheet, the title of the story was "Village Loyalty." One line of this story has stayed with me over the years: "It's another sad example of how war and politics are the causes of the destruction of an ancient culture."

★★★

In late 1970, Jim Giggans, an American in his twenties who had graduated from the Sorbonne in Paris, joined the Saigon bureau for a long-term assignment. He was one of the first black American correspondents sent to Vietnam by ABC News. In Saigon, his home was like a French *salon*, a gathering place for artists, writers, journalists, and anyone else who seemed interesting. Jim and his wife—who was a poet—enjoyed life despite the war.

ABC News correspondent Jim Giggans rides in a military convoy in early 1971. He was the first black correspondent sent to Vietnam by ABC. (Courtesy Jim Giggans)

Again, with the American forces heading home, there wasn't much interest in New York for combat stories, but Jim always seemed able to come up with compelling feature stories. I worked with Jim for several months, covering Vietnam from Khe Sanh on the northern DMZ to the Mekong Delta in the south and across the border to Cambodia.

In Vietnam, stress and the breakdown of discipline was a big problem for American troops as they waited out the long days and weeks until they could return home. Jim and I did a piece that looked specifically at the tension between black and white soldiers.

On the frontlines, I had seen very little racism as the men relied on each other, protecting and rescuing their comrades regardless of color. Back at base, however, they tended to separate and that split—combined with the racial unrest boiling back in the United

States—unleashed resentment and rage on both sides. Earlier in 1970, Jim and I had covered the aftermath of a week-long race riot at Da Nang. By the time we arrived, the tensions had been defused but soldiers—both black and white—spoke openly to Jim of discrimination and resentment.

Our work wasn't all serious, at one point I watched as Jim was taught how to do a complex "black power" salute. I guess it wasn't taught at the Sorbonne because it took quite a long time to get it right.

The biggest morale problem was that, while American troops were headed home, those left behind were still in danger. We covered cases where American units refused orders because they didn't see the point of being "the last guy to die for a mistake."

Soldiers were listening to peace songs and they knew as much about the songs played during the "3 Days of Peace and Music" at Woodstock as anyone who actually attended. Peace symbols could be seen on helmets, tattoos, the sides of tanks, the bottoms of helicopters, and even the barrels of the big artillery guns.

Along with hard news, Jim liked to do what he called "think pieces," usually a photo essay. One day, I came into the office, and Phil Starck gave me a long list of shots that Jim had asked for:

Phil,

If you get the chance I'll need shots of GIs in the rain.... Also, if there's an outgoing flight, a shot of GIs going in with packs for the final briefing, the sign saying "freedom bird" or whatever it says, and the plane taking off. In addition, any shots you can get of crowded Saigon with a lot of Vietnamese in picture and just a couple GIs. And one more thing—a couple of shots of GIs calling the States on the phone with the sign saying stateside call or MARS call, or whatever it says. Now, if you could go over the AP and pick out ten of the "war-est" pix you can find... you know, with body bags, GIs humping through elephant grass, guy helping his wounded buddy, etc. Bring the pix over here and have Tony do some quick shots of them with zoom, or if not just several very close shots. This may sound like a lot—and it is. But when I get my award I'll share it with you...

Ciao Jim

I shot most of the images he wanted, and he put them all together under the James Taylor song, "Fire and Rain." Anchor Harry Reasoner introduced the piece by saying, "With American presence declining in

Vietnam, many United States bases look like ghost towns." and then the images and the music played for almost four minutes. Here are the tape librarian's notes on the piece:

CUT STORY: FULL COAT SOUND TRACK OF V / O GIGGANS.

HE INTVWS. GIS GOING HOME. THEY GIVE VERY SHORT SENSITIVE ANSWERS TO THE QUESTION, WHAT WILL YOU DO AT HOME?

ONE SAYS "WIN BACK LOST TIMES."

VERY APPROPRIATE, A RECORDING OF JAMES TAYLOR SINGING

"FIRE AND RAIN."

PAN SHOT OF FIRE BASE, WHERE PIECES OF TRUCKS AND TANKS LAY RUSTING IN THE SAND, OLD TIRES STACKED UP AND OTHER SOUVENIRS FROM THE US PRESENCE IN THE VIETNAM WAR.

VS OF GIS WALKING OUT OF BUILDING WHERE THEY SIGNED IN FOR DEPARTURE TO "THE WORLD."

VS OF GIS GETTING ABOARD PLANE. VS OF GIS INSIDE PLANE.

PLANE TAKES OFF.

A BLACK AND WHITE OPT. SOUND VERSION OF PREVIOUS FOOTAGE

(THE WAY IT WAS SHOWN ON THE AIR).

MOST BEAUTIFULLY PUT TOGETHER.

There is no doubt that, along with being an excellent reporter, Jim Giggans was a creative artist and television was his canvas.

★★★

Frank Mariano was unforgettable. An Army pilot and Public Information Officer, he'd had three helicopters shot out from under him. After two tours, he left the Army but stayed in Vietnam, working as a freelance radio and TV reporter, and then a staff correspondent and bureau chief at ABC News Saigon.

Correspondent Frank Mariano, who left the military and joined ABC News in September 1972 after marrying another reporter, talks to a South Vietnamese officer while cameraman Dang Van Minh listens in. (Courtesy Dang Van Minh)

Frank was married to Ann Bryan Mariano, a veteran journalist who had been in Vietnam for more than five years as a reporter and bureau chief for *Overseas Weekly*, a newspaper written for the enlisted men and specializing in stories that American officers didn't want to be told. Ann was, without a doubt, one of the toughest reporters in Saigon.

They flew to the States, got married, and returned to Saigon. Ann started working for AP and other news agencies on a freelance basis. She had adopted a Vietnamese orphan before marrying Frank and then after getting married, the couple adopted another Vietnamese girl.

Ann described Frank's appeal in her chapter of *War Torn*, a book written by nine women who reported from Vietnam:

> What drew me to him was his exuberance for life and his passionate attachment to whatever he held dear. I have always been quiet, if not shy, and I loved being in the presence of Frank's boisterous personality and marvelous sense of humor. Once when we were in the field together in Cambodia, Frank was doing a radio report, and some incoming rounds landed nearby. Without thinking, he yelled, "Honey, get down!" When friends heard the broadcast, they fervently hoped I was the "honey" in question.[9]

A bit later in the book, she described how others felt about him:

> Frank had a way of drawing people in. He was the sun in a circle of friends that orbited around him. His capacity for friendship was magical and his empathy almost boundless. When you were weak, he was strong; and if you were down, he lifted you up. Frank had a generosity of spirit that eclipsed how hard he worked and sometimes struggled in his own life.[10]

One of the first stories Frank did for ABC News was a profile of a helicopter medevac chopper that, after a fierce battle, was carrying both American and North Vietnamese wounded. An enemy soldier began to have difficulty breathing and an American soldier immediately give him mouth-to-mouth respiration.

Cameraman In Jip Choi captured the drama on film, and their report won an award for news coverage in 1972. Through his personal experience, Frank knew that American soldiers treated wounded enemy soldiers fairly up on the frontlines. Frank never lost his gung-ho attitude about the war—something he often argued about with Ann.

Later in 1972, Frank and I were assigned to check out the story of the My Lai massacre; the deliberate killing of between 307 and 504 civilians by Charlie Company of the Americal Division's 11th Infantry Brigade. The massacre happened on March 16, 1968, but hadn't been revealed in the press until Sy Hersh broke the story in November 1969.

Now that an official investigation was underway, ABC New York asked us to revisit the village, talk to the survivors, and confirm or disprove the story. First, we went to the Americal Division Headquarters in Chu Lai, but no one would talk about it. We drove south of Chu

Lai towards the capital city, Quang Ngai, to get closer to the My Lai area, which was 9 km northeast of the city. We were blocked by the South Vietnamese Army before we could reach My Lai—even the local villagers told us that it was too dangerous to go there.

We stayed in that region for the next two days, and Frank talked to the town officials and looked for any witnesses or other proof of the massacre. Although we tried, we couldn't find anything solid: no graves, specific locations, witnesses, or survivors. At least none that would talk to us. In the end, we had to give up and headed back to Saigon.

The fact was that Frank simply didn't believe—or didn't want to believe—that a massacre had occurred. He told me that American soldiers were the last people he could imagine committing such an ugly and cold-blooded act. I had respect for him because he didn't allow his feelings to interfere with his journalist's duty to pursue the story.

Later we managed to get an interview with a villager who had moved to another town. Howard Tuckner and Jim Giggans also obtained evidence that confirmed the reports of the massacre.

Contrary to Frank's desperate wishes, the story of the My Lai massacre was true.

★★★

Don Farmer became a reporter at ABC News around 1965, assigned to both domestic and foreign stories. He worked out of the Atlanta, Chicago, London, and Bonn bureaus before coming to Washington DC to cover Congress. He arrived in Saigon in 1971. One of his first stories was Operation Lam Son 719, the disastrous South Vietnamese invasion of Laos, called an "incursion" for PR reasons, although he had to endure the frustration of covering it from a supply depot back in Vietnam.

The North Vietnamese were completely prepared for the "incursion," trapped the South Vietnamese inside Laos, and hammered them mercilessly. Surrounded and outnumbered by North Vietnamese troops, the South Vietnamese became disorganized and demoralized. Don and his crew watched as overloaded American helicopters landed with soldiers holding on to the skids of the helicopters while others had lost their grip and fallen during the flight. The survivors were crying out or quietly weeping. When Don interviewed them, they said that it had been hell.

He got his story but like many other correspondents, Don was frustrated by the government's "closed door" press policy and vented his complaints during a roundtable report he did with Steve Bell, Jim Giggans, and Howard Tuckner who said, "I think a lot of the truth in Vietnam comes from correspondents who have been here for a long time. Many of them have told me that this was easily the most frustrating operation they have ever covered in Vietnam."[11]

Howard Tuckner had reported from Laos that the South Vietnamese had no way to reach their target—a suspected North Vietnamese supply base at the town of Tchepone. He said that one Vietnamese officer told him bluntly that the campaign was a disaster:

> … the lieutenant colonel's orders were to take Tchepone in three days. I went into Laos and spent two nights with this man. We talked privately for three hours the first night, and he told me he had found that the entire route—Route Nine—up ahead was mined. He said intelligence hadn't indicated that. He told me that he was seriously outgunned in firepower. They found that the North Vietnamese had about 60 tank battalions in the Laos operation area: about 600 tanks … I asked the lieutenant colonel if he would go on camera with me and say this publicly. He did. The reaction from Washington and Saigon was that he didn't have the big picture, that he was merely a local commander.[12]

Steve Bell complained that his reports, based on conversations with officers and troops as they retreated from Laos, were attacked as inaccurate by US military spokesmen who were calling the operation a major success.

Finally, Don Farmer summed it up in a line that has been quoted in many analyses of the role of the media in Vietnam:

> We were told by the Americans and the South Vietnamese that this operation was a great success, a great victory … But when they say things like, "We now have cut the Ho Chi Minh Trail," we know that's absurd. And that's the kind of statements we've been getting. They are unbelievable. Sometimes I feel we're getting slightly paranoid, that we look for lies where they may not exist. It may be partly our fault, but there's a reason for it. We've been lied to so many times that we begin to suspect that no one ever tells us the truth.[13]

CHAPTER 16

PHOTOGRAPHERS

There were a lot of Japanese journalists in Saigon and, sadly, more of them died than any other nationality. Why were we there covering a war that no Japanese was fighting? Why would anyone but an American want to face the danger and pain?

Here's a personal example that might make it clearer. I was sent to the ABC bureau in Tokyo for a period during the late 1960s and early 1970s and, to be honest, was having a tough time adjusting to peacetime. One afternoon, as I walked down the Ginza, I ran into Henri Huet—a French citizen of Vietnamese parentage who was a photographer for the Associated Press. Henri had his camera hanging around his neck and was carrying a small camera bag on his shoulder.

"Where are you going?" I asked.

"I'm going to cover a general meeting of the Rotary Club," he said, looking sheepish. He said that life in Japan was comfortable and he enjoyed his job, but it didn't compare to the adrenaline-charged camaraderie of Vietnam. I told him that I felt exactly the same and that I thought we just had to have patience, and we'd get used to a slower, more relaxed life. We shook hands and went our separate ways.

Less than six months later, we met again in a café on Tu Do Street in Saigon. We had both come back from peaceful Japan to crazy war-torn Vietnam without the slightest regret. Perhaps this applies to any country in wartime, but Vietnam just seemed to have a magnetic attraction: life was faster, the countryside brighter and more colorful, and people made friends for life in a matter of days. Once we had experienced Vietnam, one way or another, we'd always come back.

★★★

Pulitzer Prize-winning photographer Kyoichi Sawada was working in Cambodia. He was one of the greats although he was still quite young. His iconic pictures appeared across the world, the most famous was an image of a refugee family in Vietnam struggling to flee the fighting through a neck-deep canal. The mother carried a baby, another woman bore an older girl while a young boy struggled along behind; all of them desperately helping each other.

We didn't run into each other for nearly two years until one day in May 1970, when I was shooting for Howard Tuckner on the east bank of the Mekong River as dozens of refugees struggled to return to their battle-damaged homes in Kompong Cham.

I filmed a sequence where one family were at the levee on the edge of the river, one young man carrying his aging father in his arms like a baby and another son holding his mother by the hand as they carefully balanced in a tiny sampan for the trip across the river. I knew it was a heart-warming picture, and I was shooting it with care.

There was the unmistakable sound of a camera shutter going off next to my ear. I turned to see Kyoichi Sawada shooting the exact same picture. We said a brief hello and went on about our work. His picture won a "Robert Capa" award. My film of the same scene was a part of Howard Tuckner's report "The Battle of Kompong Cham." Later, I joked with my old friend about how he had such an artist's eye that his picture could be so much better than my 16-millimeter film.

Five months later, Steve Bell, Jean-Claude Malet, and I were covering a unit of Cambodian soldiers. Joining us was the new UPI bureau chief, Frank Frosh, and my friend Sawada. There was no action so we took a break in a small village where there was a small coffee shop still open. On a whim, I pulled out a little, light point-and-shoot camera I'd just bought and took photos of everyone as they relaxed. They were just snapshots, like family reunion pictures with everyone relaxed and smiling for the camera. Some thought that taking pictures of each other was a "jinx," we'd worry that each picture would be our last.

Two days later, the "jinx" became all too real. In the evening of October 29, we were at the Royal Hotel, and someone came in and

Pulitzer Prize-winning photographer Kyoichi Sawada in the field. He was close friends with Hirashiki, but was ambushed and killed in 1971 in Cambodia.

said that Sawada and Frosch hadn't returned. They'd left Phnom Penh around 3 p.m. to run down a story.

I was puzzled why they left so late—it didn't sound like something the veteran Sawada would do. I decided that Sawada must have worked it all out: how long to get there, how long to shoot the story, and how long to return before dusk. He was a total professional, and I was sure he'd be back.

The next morning, UPI sent all their reporters and stringers out to search, and they returned shortly before noon with the bodies of both men, found in a "no man's land" where neither side was in control. Malet, Eddie Chan, and I hurried to the hospital and found Frosch and Sawada lying on stretchers under the eaves of the roof, awaiting an official autopsy.

I remembered a story Sawada had told me about being captured earlier that year. Like Terry Khoo, he'd conversed with the rebel leader and after several hours convinced him to let him go. Sawada told me that as he walked away, he just kept reminding himself of the cardinal rule for a journalist in a war zone, "Don't run." It was something he had taught me when I first came to Saigon, soldiers were trained to shoot at anyone running.

That day, as I looked at his body, his legs were bent as if he'd been running when he was shot. I said to myself, "*Sawada-san*, why did you run? Once you told me not to run—you had taught me—not run in the battlefield—why you had to run?"

I was shaking and shuddering in a combination of sorrow and fear. If Sawada could be killed, could any of us survive?

Everyone in the Phnom Penh press corps attended Sawada's funeral at the largest Buddhist pagoda in the city. As we sat and grieved, I thought that the big picture of Sawada that stood at the front was soft focused—something that would have horrified the precise and meticulous Sawada. Then I realized that the picture was a cropped enlargement from the picture I'd taken with my cheap little camera—from the break at the coffee shop when we all felt so relaxed.

Since the 1971 "Incursion into Laos" was under a media blackout, it made getting across the border creatively almost irresistible and my friends found this sort of temptation a good excuse for ingenuity.

Akihiko Okamura had been banned from South Vietnam for six years after he had photographed a Viet Cong base in the jungle and interviewed one of their leaders. When his report and pictures appeared in *LIFE* magazine, he was blacklisted and sent back to Japan. He was back now and, in fact, became one of the very few journalists inside Laos.

Still on assignment for *LIFE*, he had been talking to an American officer in the Ham Nghi jumping-off point and, when a South Vietnamese truck stopped in front of him, he simply got on board. He was very confident and assured, and he rode with the unit right across the border. He was not only the first to cross the border but succeeded in getting deep into the war zone and emerged with an exclusive report and pictures. Once again, the South Vietnamese were not pleased to see his picture on the cover of *LIFE*.

★★★

In a playful moment, ABC's Terry Khoo jumps on the back of Koichiro Morita, a freelance photographer for the Associated Press. In the February 1971 Laotian Incursion, Morita simply joined a line of South Vietnamese soldiers and broke the embargo with his pictures and reporting. (Courtesy Family of Terry Khoo)

Koichiro Morita, a freelancer working for the Associated Press, walked up and began marching with a column of South Vietnamese troops heading to load on their helicopters for the flight into Laos. Like the rest of us, Morita was wearing a black market camouflage uniform so he blended right in, an effect that was enhanced when a soldier asked him to carry his M16. No one noticed that one of the soldiers was armed with cameras as well as a rifle, and he jumped on the chopper and was delivered to the frontline.

The helicopter landed inside Laos and Morita jumped down with the South Vietnamese troops in a scramble before the helicopter took off again. As they lifted off, the American door gunner caught Morita's eye and gave him a grin and a thumbs up. Morita grinned back and saluted. Maybe the American was acknowledging Morita for his impressive impersonation of

"Yellow Power." There were so many Japanese and other Asian photographers in Saigon that they talked of forming a mock political group. Waiting to make their way into Laos in February 1971 despite a government ban on coverage of the invasion are Tony Hirashiki (ABC), Syunichi Yasuda (NBC), Jean-Claude Malet (ABC), Nobuyoshi Tanaka (NHK) and, in the second row, Mutumi Iida (NHK), and Teruhiko Yashiro (NBC). (Courtesy Yasutsune Hirashiki)

a South Vietnamese soldier, or maybe he just liked anyone who had the guts to sneak into a war zone. Either way, Morita was able to get photos to the AP and written dispatches to Japanese newspapers.

Strange as it may seem, the third man into Laos was almost another Japanese. Pulitzer Prize-winning photographer Toshio Sakai was sent in by United Press International but his Japanese good looks—pale skin and handsome face—made him too conspicuous to pass as a Vietnamese. He lined up with the troops several times, but when it came to his turn, the crew chief always told him to get lost.

★★★

Someone once called this group of young Asian photographers I belonged to "a bunch of nuts." We, on the other hand, called ourselves "Yellow

Syunnsuke Akatsuka (left) and Toshio Sakai (right) were friends of Tony Hirashiki and members of the group that called itself "Yellow Power"; generally, just an excuse for the members to get together, play cards, make jokes, and critique each other's work. (Courtesy Yasutune Hirashiki and Eddie Chan)

Power." This group was made up of Shima, Koichiro Morita, Toshio Sakai, and Syunnsuke Akatsuka, who shot for UPI. We'd often gather in my apartment where we would dine, critique each other's photos, exchange the latest information on cameras, lenses, and new techniques on covering a war, and, of course, drink.

★★★

Howard Tuckner and Terry Khoo had finally persuaded a longtime friend, a South Vietnamese colonel, to allow two helicopters to accompany the colonel and his commanders as they flew in to observe the action in Laos. One would be reserved for ABC and Howard had agreed to let four photographers fly in the other.

Howard decided that Henri Huet, Shima, Larry Burrows from TIME LIFE, and Kent Potter from UPI could take the first flight since they had been waiting for two days and ABC would wait for the second. Larry,

Henri, Shima, and Kent thanked ABC for their courtesy and climbed aboard. The ABC helicopter arrived moments later, and Tuckner and his crew took off for Laos.

Award-winning photographer, Larry Burrows, who worked for LIFE *magazine, was one of the four shot down in a helicopter over Laos on February 10, 1971. Tony admired him greatly, feeling that his photos "all captured a 'decisive moment' with a compassionate touch."*

Howard and Terry spent two days and nights shooting exclusive stories for ABC. It was only when they arrived back that they found out that the first helicopter had been shot down on the way into Laos, and all four photographers were missing.

It took thirty years of work by Richard Pyle, the AP bureau chief, and fellow photographer Horst Faas to confirm their deaths. With grim determination, they finally located the crash site. The details of their long search and sad discovery is chronicled in their book, *Lost Over Laos*.

★★★

One of my favorite photography books is *Compassionate Photographer*, which contains all the masterpieces of photographer Larry Burrows, staff photojournalist for *LIFE* magazine. His many photographs are well known, especially those of the Vietnamese people and the soldiers fighting in a muddy hell.

His pictures were always well-composed, but what most impressed me was that they all captured a "decisive moment" with a compassionate touch. A few weeks before his death, Larry Burrows had been standing right next to me as we covered the chaotic war in Cambodia. Larry was twelve years older than me and a very calm and hard-working man. His trademark was a white towel worn around his neck to wipe the sweat off his face between pictures.

During a battle, he worked hard; running, crouching and often pinned down by enemy fire in rice paddies right alongside unknown newbies like me. I was always thrilled to watch him work and would try to learn what he was thinking and looking for when he set his camera and pushed the shutter button. Even if I was just watching, I always felt as if I was learning the craft from him.

★★★

Henri Huet was born to a French father and Vietnamese mother. He started out as a painter after graduating from art school in France and then became a war photographer during the first Indochina war. His photography was so beautiful and creative that he was seen as an artist among the Saigon press corps. Until the war was over, I hadn't realized what a truly great photographer he was. In particular, when you see his pictures of children you can almost feel Henri's empathetic eyes behind his camera and lens. In a picture of a scared refugee family which was taken at a low angle, the unique composition showed a kid through a GI's legs in the foreground. The kid was gazing at Henri's camera with a scared face. Another of his photo essays, "Profile of a Medic Soldier," was another example of Henri's humanism.

UPI photographer Kent Potter had just come to Saigon from Philadelphia. Kent reminded me of Kyoichi Sawada, my friend who had died in Cambodia. Both were men of few words and never showed any fear or hesitation in tough situations. I got the impression that he was too tall to keep his head down. However, his pictures were all excellent, and I thought it was just a matter of time before he would be another champion photographer.

But he never had the time.

★★★

Keizaburo Shimamoto, usually called "Shima," was another friend who couldn't quite bring himself to leave Vietnam. He'd arrived in 1965 as a reporter/photographer for PANA, a small service that only covered Indochina, Southeast Asia, and the Far East. Shima spent two years in Tokyo after that first assignment and then returned, working for Gamma and shooting freelance for *Newsweek*. In early 1971, we gathered to celebrate Shima's latest *Newsweek* photo. It showed a South Vietnamese soldier covered in sweat in the middle of an intense firefight. It wasn't a big picture, but his name was on the credit line, and that was what was important. "This is just the beginning," Shima told us with his trademark charming smile. "Even better and greater pictures are yet to come. Now it's my turn to be a great photographer." Sakai took a picture of Shima in his military camouflage with various cameras hanging around his neck and over his shoulder.

Don Farmer and I covered the death of flamboyant and influential South Vietnamese General Do Cao Tri and his close friend, legendary *Newsweek* photographer François Sully in another helicopter that crashed on its way to the frontlines. ABC's Terry Khoo and his soundman were supposed to have been on that flight but were bumped because there wasn't enough space.

Henri Huet, a photographer for the Associated Press, met Tony on the street in Tokyo and agreed that peacetime life just didn't hold much interest. They both returned to Saigon within weeks but for Henri, the attraction was fatal. (Courtesy In Jip Choi)

Keizaburo Shimamoto, generally known as "Shima," was taking photos for Gamma and freelancing for Newsweek. In early 1971, he was sure that his luck was changing for the better. (Courtesy Toshio Sakai)

I was stunned at these losses. How many more photographers would be sacrificed? A generation of talent was lost to cover the wars in Southeast Asia. All the same, I knew that there were always more young ones coming over with their single camera, ready to make their mark, dazzle all of us with their skills, and replace those who were lost.

CHAPTER 17

AMERICAN GUY

On July 1, 1971, ABC gave Ron Miller his first assignment as a network correspondent—a year in Saigon. Miller was slim, about three years younger than I was, and stood around 6 feet 2 inches tall. He was gentle and friendly with kind eyes, the sort of all-American guy who reminded me of the movie star Jimmy Stewart.

The Saigon press corps was composed of men and women who were tough, assertive, competitive, and egocentric. Many of us dreamed that war reporting would find us fame and recognition within our profession.

I will admit that this is why I came and perhaps why I kept coming back.

In the heat of competition, we often forgot to treat others with gentleness or kindness because we simply had to win and were using every fiber of our being to do so. Into this jungle came Ron Miller, a man who embraced the world with gentle good humor and since he didn't care about competition, he usually thought of others before himself.

I have to tell you; this was a new approach for me. I had been told to beat the other guy at all costs: get there first, stay until the last, and think and move and search out new angles, exclusive viewpoints, and an element of beauty and human feeling.

Since Ron didn't seem to have this competitive mindset, I worried about whether he would be able to survive Vietnam. Well, not on the battlefields as much as in the merciless competition in Saigon and New York.

Ron explained to me that it wasn't necessary to do what our competition did nor to work in the same way. As a matter of fact, he felt we should be unique and thus out of the contest altogether. That way, we could simply do good stories and the hell with the competition.

I found this all fascinating but it didn't make me any less concerned. Whenever we covered big stories with all the other nets, I would push Ron into moving faster and going further. Usually, correspondents were the crazy ones who pushed their crews.

In our case, this wasn't true.

I was the crazy one.

Our first assignment together was a demonstration by South Vietnamese veterans on the streets of Saigon. I had covered so many protests since 1966; some organized by students, others by Buddhists or by opponents of the Thieu government, but this was new.

This march was made up of disabled veterans, war widows, pensioned soldiers, and their families. Usually, the Saigon police responded aggressively when called in to stop a demonstration but on this day, the police were watching from a little distance away. It was hard to tell if this was due to respect or fear.

The leaders were disabled soldiers—some were walking with an artificial leg or using a cane—others had lost an arm. Some of them had knives, and others were carrying live grenades with their fingers right on the pin—ready to prime and throw if the police or military tried to interfere. They said that they had already faced death on the battlefield, and now they were dying from the government's neglect. They had nothing to lose.

Ron and I, with the rest of the media, were following them, but we were afraid to get too close because of the hand grenades. Rumors swept through the media that the protesters were preparing to set fire to themselves. I could smell gasoline in the air, and it reminded me of when Buddhist monks and their followers used self-immolation as a form of protest.

This demonstration, already unpredictable, could get out of hand very quickly. I was afraid of the hand grenades, the knives, and now the threat of fire. We were simply too close to these angry soldiers. While I was thinking all this, Ron calmly walked up to the leaders of the

ABC News correspondent Ron Miller arrived in the Saigon bureau in July 1971 and wasted no time establishing the type of stories he wanted to do—exhaustive interviews, real people, and a touch of humor. (Courtesy Ron Miller)

demonstration and began to ask them questions through an interpreter. Why did they organize this? What did they want from the government?

Ron was the first newsman to talk to the veterans, and I was right by his side to get the interviews on camera. I wasn't thrilled about it, but I was right there.

Ron, however, was a great listener and soon he had the organizers agreeing to talk and bring in some of the other veterans as well. It seemed to me that they appreciated Ron's fearlessness as he walked up despite the grenades, bush knives, and all the other threats of violence. Ron just spoke like a trustworthy journalist and people felt that he could be relied on to tell their story honestly.

The leaders of the march began to talk about their problems. As the American combat troops pulled out and the Vietnamese Army had to take their places, casualties had skyrocketed. Instead of caring for them, the South Vietnamese government proclaimed that they couldn't afford to pay for so many disabled soldiers, war widows, orphaned children, and pensioned retirees. These demonstrators were just asking for a little more rice so that they and their families could survive.

They set off again and arrived at the Ministry for Veterans and handed in their demands without setting off grenades or setting themselves on fire. It really was sad and even pitiful—these brave men and women asking only for what they deserved.

After we had finished filming, I asked Ron if he was afraid. He thought a second and said, "I don't like hand grenades, but I didn't think they were going to throw them at us. We're newsmen."

Indeed, the fact that Ron had simply gone right up to these desperate people and listened to their story with respect and a sincere attempt to understand might have made them a little less angry and violent. Right then, I really thought he was like Jimmy Stewart in *It's a Wonderful Life* when he convinces the town not to create a run on the bank.

★★★

In October, the Thieu regime called for a presidential election; universally seen as a fraud. Ron, Tran Van Kha, and I were sent to cover the balloting in Da Nang. As it had been back in 1966 when I covered the rebels in the pagoda, Da Nang was overwhelmingly Buddhist and vehemently opposed Thieu. Demonstrations against the election had been going on for weeks and when we were there, the opposition filled the streets with protesters all day long.

On voting day, all the main roads into the city were filled with roadblocks of burning tires and the stinking black smoke from the tires covered the entire city. Buddhist leaders had asked people to abstain from voting, and very few people lined up at the polling places. In the early morning, we had gone to several villages and military barracks to see how the voting was going but very few villagers were daring to vote, and the soldiers all came in together and voted as one.

ABC's Ron Miller, on the right, enjoyed talking to people and translating their stories to the world. One of his first stories was with military families and wounded Vietnamese veterans, a group that looked extraordinarily dangerous until Miller stepped in. (Courtesy Ron Miller)

Government troops tried to open up the roadblocks with armored vehicles and break up the crowds. Demonstrators were throwing stones, bricks, and homemade firebombs. When the South Vietnamese soldiers began to shoot, mostly into the sky, the crowd broke apart but at each roadblock, there would be more demonstrators and a larger skirmish.

Ron and I followed the action through the smoke and the clouds of tear gas. Ron did his radio report even though he was crying. Although I used every curse word I knew in English, Vietnamese, Japanese, and Chinese, it didn't stop my tears and pain. Ron never got angry and even smiled at me with tears in his eyes as he completed a weeping stand-upper to finish the story.

New York praised Ron's "Da Nang Election" report and said that we had better content and more exciting pictures and sound than our competition. Ron had covered the story his own way and still managed to beat the other team. I started to like his way of working.

★★★

In this period, we often went to cover the final moments as American units departed Vietnam. In 1971, we covered the 23rd Infantry Division ("Americal") as they left from Chu Lai on the Central Coast. I thought about the day in 1967 when I had filmed the same division as they arrived in Vietnam—also at Chu Lai.

In 1967, there had been a ceremony with young Vietnamese girls wearing beautiful local dresses welcoming the soldiers with smiles and garlands of fragrant white jasmine flowers. The band had played Glenn Miller songs, and General Westmoreland made a welcome speech saying how proud he was to see them. The soldiers all looked tough and proud and marched in formation off to their camps.

Four years later, they were back at the Chu Lai airfield; heading home. More journalists were there than grateful Vietnamese, and the ceremony was very simple. There were no flower girls, no colorful gestures, and only one speech of thanks. General Creighton Abrams pinned medals on their jackets and made a short speech. A soldier played a solo tune as they folded the American flag and began to board a "freedom bird," as the planes headed back home were called.

A few soldiers looked back and then they were gone.

In 1972, Ron Miller with Dang Van Minh as cameraman and Jean-Claude Malet doing sound were pinned down by rockets on Highway One, near Quang Tri—the northern end of the road the French had named the "Street Without Joy" so many years ago. Fortunately, they all managed to escape without any injury.

After he had come back to Saigon, Ron Miller greeted me with a big smile, and I gave him a hug because he was one of my favorite correspondents; a man who always treated me as another journalist and not just a technician. After we had finished exclaiming over his good luck, he said he needed to ask me a favor. I immediately said I would do anything for him.

Then he asked the favor, and I was stunned and felt that he had blindsided me.

He had decided to get married, and he wanted me to be his best man. "No way!" I said. "I shouldn't be the best man! I'm just a cameraman. Ask the bureau chief or some top correspondent."

Ron told me that it wasn't necessary to have some VIP as best man and usually it was a good friend or a brother. He said that I was the most faithful cameraman he'd ever known, and I showed the trust, loyalty, and camaraderie that was essential between a correspondent and his crew. He said that I was as close as a brother, and he wanted me by his side.

I thought that was very nice, but I really didn't want all that responsibility. Anyway, who was Ron going to marry? Ron brought *Trisha-san* with him to live in Saigon, and they were happy and sweet with each other. Did he suddenly fall in love with someone new? War makes people do crazy things, but Ron wasn't that kind of guy.

"With whom you want married?" I asked.

"Whom? Of course with Trisha!" Ron laughed, then he explained that he and Trisha had been living together for nearly ten years, but they hadn't gotten around to getting married.

I was puzzled: "Why did you suddenly decide to get married now?"

He told me that when they were attacked on Highway One, RPGs had exploded all around them—very close, and there had been almost no cover. Ron thought he might be finished at that moment. He described more details of it many years later in a letter:

> We were going up Highway One from Quang Tri to the DMZ. The NVA was moving south in South Vietnam at the time, and we went to see. As we went north on Highway One, we came upon a helluva firefight off to our right in a very sandy area. We could see soldiers fighting no more than 75 yards away, and we moved toward them slowly on the highway. Finally, we stopped the jeep and went on foot for a bit more. Now we could see figures moving and fighting—great footage—we moved closer until the men we had seen fighting began shooting rockets toward us—they were NVA regulars—the ARVN were on the other side of the NVA line.
>
> We were proceeding toward the enemy without knowing it. The crew jumped to the left off the terraced road, and I jumped off to the right. The rockets kept

During a particularly close rocket attack, ABC's Ron Miller promised to marry his long-time girlfriend if he lived through it. He did and they did, on June 24, 1971 in the Continental Hotel. Tony was best man. (Courtesy Ron Miller)

Tony Hirashiki thought that Ron Miller's marriage was a great idea, until he found out to his complete horror, that he was expected to be the best man. Here, in June 1971, he celebrates speaking English all the way through his toast to the new Mr. and Mrs. Miller. (Courtesy Ron Miller)

coming in, but the shrapnel went over our heads as it hit the road—just then Cobra gunships came in and tore up the NVA. I remember going to the site of the fight and seeing grotesquely broken bodies of both sides. It was truly awful. The dead NVA were buried there. As we proceeded back to the jeep I picked up a still warm rocket tail that still remains on my desk. I don't remember if the story ever got on the air. I do remember enormous fear and gratitude for the Cobras—a few more minutes of shelling and I think we would have been gone.[1]

Back in Saigon, Ron told me it had been so bad that he prayed hard and promised if he survived, he would do something good. The last shell landed murderously close, but miraculously it didn't explode.

His prayer had been heard!

When he got back to Saigon, Ron asked *Trisha-san* to marry him, and she agreed. I suppose the matchmaker was a B-40 rocket-propelled grenade that didn't go off.

They both agreed that the best man should be combat cameraman Tony Hirashiki.

Well, after I heard the story, I could not refuse him. I was still nervous, but it would be good practice since I expected to be the best man at my friend Terry Khoo's wedding a few months later.

On June 24, 1971, Ron and Trisha got married in the beautiful courtyard of the Continental Hotel. Trisha was so beautiful, a mixture of joy, tears, and laughter. Ron was so happy and charming, and people told me I did my job well. I even managed to give a toast in English without any mistakes.

However, there was one unfortunate moment. As we proceeded into the ceremony, I escorted the maid of honor. She was Trisha's best friend and was the tallest woman I've ever seen! Everyone burst into laughter and cheers at the sight of her on the arm of the extremely short best man. The well-mannered guests became silent, but some of the most ill-mannered (who were generally friends of mine) kept on laughing and making jokes.

Despite this, it was a beautiful wedding; joy, happiness, and simple peace for a short moment. All of us shared this with Ron and *Trisha-san* and Quang Tri, An Loc, and all the other battles were forgotten for a little while.

CHAPTER 18

DOCUMENTARIAN

In the early spring of 1972, I teamed up with Drew Pearson, a longtime producer who had just been made a correspondent. Drew's father, Leon Pearson, had been a foreign correspondent for the International News Service and their Paris bureau chief right after World War II and then worked for NBC Radio. Drew's uncle, also called Drew Pearson, rose to fame as a syndicated columnist whose column, "The Washington Merry-Go-Round," lampooned politicians and uncovered scandals for decades.

Drew did not want to be compared to his father or famous uncle, so he chose to make his own way. He joined the Army in 1959 and after two months of basic training, he was sent to combat photography school. Drew was one of a new breed of broadcasting journalists; those who learned their trade as they traveled the world. Drew produced, filmed, reported, and edited his own documentaries for distribution on public television. During the early 1960s, Drew covered stories as a stringer cameraman and radio reporter in Africa and Asia for NBC, ABC, and the BBC.

He joined ABC News as a producer, reporter, and occasional cameraman with the "ABC Scope" documentary unit—a weekly 30-minute show that was anchored by Howard K. Smith. By the time I arrived, Drew was fluent in Vietnamese and was already seen as an expert on Vietnamese culture and, inevitably, on the war. Drew would battle New York when there was resistance to his stories. He was soft-spoken and gentle but had a core belief in justice and an independent mind. At one point, he clashed with legendary journalist, John Scali. In a letter, Drew recalled:

> One of the programs, about "nation building" created a stir in NYC when the host, John Scali, refused to narrate it because he thought my script was too negative, Bill Sheehan stuck with me though and told me to record the narration in Saigon, with an open and close. The conclusion was that "nation building" was a failure. I did the program in An Giang, an easy province to be successful in because it was "Hoa Hao," [fervently Buddhist and pacifist] but even there, the program was corrupt and not helping the people who needed it. I said if it can't succeed here, it can't succeed anywhere else in Vietnam where the war makes everything more difficult.[1]

Drew covered stories all over South Vietnam and since I was Drew's cameraman, I was kept quite busy following him. What was odd to me was that after almost a month, not one of our stories had aired on the Evening News. I had to wonder why: the content was accurate and unbiased, and Drew was admired as an excellent journalist with a solid knowledge of Vietnam. Why weren't his stories being shown?

It wasn't only those of us on his crew, other friends in Saigon worried about the same things. Some said that his reports were too long to be television spots—a common problem. Every reporter had to struggle to condense a day's work into less than two minutes or fight even harder to get the producers in New York to give the story more time. Every second was precious and sometimes the arguments were quite ... loud.

Since the Evening News included the most important stories from America first and international stories second, unless the foreign stories were exceptional, there was generally room for one and perhaps two stories a night. Drew's stories were long, but they had depth and combined many details from every part of Vietnam. It was much more the style of a documentary producer who would take the time to focus and explain the facts.

Another factor that could have caused his stories to hit the shelf was President Nixon's continual insistence that Vietnamization was working. The American people wanted their sons back from this war and having the Vietnamese take a bigger and bigger role in the fighting resulted in more and more soldiers boarding airplanes for home.

Drew felt that, despite all the assurances of the South Vietnamese and American governments, Vietnamization simply wasn't working.

Consequently, every night, you would have the reporters of two networks sending in dispatches on how well Vietnamization was going and Drew stubbornly shipping stories that showed a very different picture.

A few years earlier, Drew had produced an hour-long documentary with Ted Koppel saying that Vietnamization was a hoax and a mirage. Drew had to fight tooth and nail with ABC's lawyers to get the show on the air, but it ended up winning the Overseas Press Club Award for Best Interpretation of a Foreign Story.

At this time, the spring of 1972, fighting had died down in Vietnam, the last major battle had been the disastrous "incursion" into Laos almost a year ago where the South Vietnamese were driven back in complete disarray. Nevertheless, the fact that most of the fighting had died down convinced many in the media that Vietnamization was succeeding, and that peace was drawing near. Drew, on the contrary, interpreted this as the "quiet before a storm" and felt that the North was regrouping and rearming for an enormous attack. For weeks, he spent a good deal of our time attempting to prove this but, even though they couldn't find a problem with his reporting, New York hesitated to be the lonely voice of caution on the airwaves.

As Drew's cameraman, I was worried about his way of covering the news, but I still believed that he would be recognized eventually. In the end, I chose to follow him without saying anything.

On March 30, 1972, we left Da Nang in the early morning to go up to the dividing line between North and South Vietnam. We were planning to drive up to the Ben Hai River, where, if we stood on the south bank, we could see North Vietnam just across the river. Since this was literally the frontline of the war, there were nearly a dozen firebases that commanded the entire length of the DMZ. As American troops withdrew, most of these bases were being transferred to the South Vietnamese Army although American forces still manned a few of the biggest with their 105-millimeter and 155-millimeter artillery pieces.

It was a long distance from Da Nang to the DMZ so we left early in the morning. We drove along the Hai Van Pass—which connects Da Nang and Hue—and enjoyed a short period of tranquility as our old and battered jeep struggled to climb the mountains and manage the endless hairpin curves, and we soaked in the beautiful scenery. We even had time to stop for a quick breakfast at a local tea shop at the top of the pass. We arrived at the ancient capital of Hue, not too far from the last border town of Dong Ha, and continued driving north on National Highway One.

After entering Quang Tri province, not far from our destination, our way was blocked by a wave of refugees. I had never seen so many fleeing people: men, women, children, the elderly, soldiers, mothers carrying babies, fathers with kids strapped to their chests and backs, trucks and cars overflowing with people, farm carts fully loaded with belongings and small furniture, chickens, ducks, pigs, and water buffaloes, all headed south as fast as possible.

We continued going north, but it was slow and difficult moving against such a tide of humanity. Everywhere we looked, the roads and the ditches on the sides of the road, were filled with people, people, people. I was filming, and Drew began to record radio reports and descriptions on his tape recorder. My partner, Kha, would talk to the refugees, collect information, and tell it to Drew so he could work it into his reports.

According to the soldiers Kha spoke to, the North Vietnamese had crossed the 17th Parallel and the Demilitarized Zone in great force. Soviet-made 130-millimeter artillery fired more than 12,000 shells into the South Vietnamese military bases and firebases. According to military records, Camp Carroll, the biggest and strongest base, took the brunt of two thousand rounds from the North Vietnamese big guns during the first few hours of attack. Camp Carroll lasted another day and fell—reportedly without firing a shot.

Coming right behind the bombardment were thirty thousand North Vietnamese regulars backed by Russian and Chinese tanks. It's estimated that a total of 100 tanks hit the battered bases. The South Vietnamese Army had been engaged in a major rotation of troops when the attacks hit and as a result, communications, transport, and command structure were all badly disrupted even before the attack and most of the troops were inexperienced and poorly led.

All the mighty firebases along the DMZ fell within the first five days, and half of Quang Tri province was taken over by the North. Because of when it had started, this offensive became known as the Easter Offensive.

What you can't see behind ABC News Correspondent Drew Pearson (left) is the battle of Loc Ninh where thousands of North Vietnamese soldiers and tanks are driving towards Saigon during the Easter Offensive of April 1972. Pearson recalled the moment in an email, "There was small arms fire around our heads; we could hear the rounds going through the air, doing their whoosh, past us; there was recoilless rifle fire too. I remember thinking, "So this is how it is, just before you get killed." (Courtesy Drew Pearson)

It wasn't a small attack, but a full-scale armored offensive, much more powerful than the small-arms attacks conducted during the Tet offensive in 1968.

We were stunned to see such large numbers of refugees. Drew wanted to go further north to check out the firebases, but it was impossible to get there in the jeep so he decided to wrap up the story and to send it in as the first report of the new North Vietnamese offensive. We were the first TV crew on the scene and had even beaten out the still photographers. Of course, we knew that the rest of the media was surely on their way now, rushing from Da Nang and Saigon. But we didn't see any other press crews even after Drew wrapped his first report so this was an exclusive and the ABC News team was at least a half day ahead of its competitors.

It really was Drew's big scoop, he had stuck to his belief that there was something coming, and he was right! The North Vietnamese had been building up their forces, and now we were facing an enormous attack.

For once, Drew was told that his script was too short and in the Hong Kong bureau, producer Dave Jayne, who was in charge of editing, complained that he had to use part of Drew's radio report to fill out the television narration. When we heard about this, Drew smiled wryly because one of the usual criticisms was that his narration was always too long. That day Drew could have written fifteen minutes if he had wanted to.

I was told that New York sent a cable to Drew congratulating him for the exciting content of his report and for beating out the competition. This was the first of Drew's news stories to air, and it cheered up the whole crew.

★★★

The Easter Offensive was massive. Not only did the North Vietnamese roll south across the DMZ and hit Quang Tri, but they also attacked from Laos into the Kontum area in Central Vietnam and came from bases in Cambodia to hit Loc Ninh and An Loc and other strongpoints very close to Saigon.

The second day, we went north again to try to reach Quang Tri City where the fighting was said to be fierce. Outnumbered but supported by continuous American air attacks, South Vietnamese soldiers were still defending Quang Tri City. We reached the outskirts of the city, where we could see smoke rising and hear guns firing, but we could not get any closer.

We turned back and drove to a small military base on the side of the highway where we'd seen a US flag flying near the gate. Just as we reached the base, shells began to come in, and several American soldiers came out of their compound, rushed to the flagpole, lowered the flag, and folded it carefully. I filmed the scene as other soldiers saluted crisply even as more shells exploded nearby. Then a helicopter appeared, landed in the fast maneuvers used for a hot LZ, the remaining soldiers loaded up, and took off. I thought it was very symbolic and kept rolling my camera.

Drew wrapped up his second report, including the footage of the last American soldiers evacuating with the American flag. The next ten days passed by very quickly as New York became more and more impressed

ABC reporter Drew Pearson was a documentary producer for most of the time Tony Hirashiki knew him in Vietnam, working for the ABC Scope program. He had covered Indochina for years and Vietnam since the 1960s. While many others were proclaiming victory and Vietnamization, he was convinced that North Vietnam hadn't given up. The Easter Offensive of April 1972 proved him right. Once they began to work together in 1972, Tony realized how his brash and honest style often got him in trouble with the executives in New York. (Courtesy Drew Pearson)

with the high quality of Drew's reporting. The fact was that ABC News was leading the other networks because of Drew. As far as I can remember, Drew made air for fourteen straight days on TV and radio during the morning, evening and weekend programs. It was satisfying to hear that the stories that had been sitting on the shelf of some edit room in New York were pulled out and broadcast as well.

One afternoon on our way back from the northern front, we spotted a small elementary school that had been turned into an emergency field hospital. One of the soldiers greeted us in Vietnamese. Kha translated, and we discovered that only days before, this soldier had proudly shown us his new American tank. He'd even allowed me to film while riding inside and on top of the tank. It was supposed to beat the latest in Soviet weaponry but only two days after we had filmed his tank unit, they were defeated in a bitter battle. All the tanks had been destroyed, and most of the soldiers were killed and wounded. The tank driver was one of the few survivors, and he was severely wounded.

The reason this bandaged soldier started talking to us was that he wanted to know what was happening at the front and all over his country. He also asked if there was any chance that we could drop off a letter to his family at the post office. Kha gave all the newspapers he had to the wounded soldier and his colleagues so that they might get a picture of what was happening. They were all very appreciative, so Kha said that we would mail home any letters they wanted to send and bring more newspapers the next day.

The next day, Kha kept his promise and bought ten copies of each of the four or five big newspapers, and we collected all their letters. It became a new routine, as our camera team became postmen and newspaper delivery boys to even the most dangerous parts of the frontlines. One day we even delivered newspapers during a heavy firefight. The soldiers were amazed.

Within just a few days, we were quite popular on the front. The soldiers liked us, trusted us, and shared their food with us. The officers even allowed us to stay and film them in combat. We didn't do the newspapers and mail to get anything, it was just sharing something they couldn't get and we could. Sadly, the fighting at Quang Tri was so heavy that the soldiers who read the newspapers in the morning might be killed that evening.

Two days before we were scheduled to go back to Saigon, Kha and I delivered a bucket of fresh crabs to one platoon near the defense line because they had shared their lunch with us the previous day. When we arrived, the platoon was fighting so the soldiers would not let us near the commander's position. The platoon leader asked us over the field radio why we had come, and we answered that we were delivering fresh crabs, and he said "OK." Much to the soldiers' amazement, we carried the crabs to the command position even though we were crawling at times to avoid the gunfire.

The following day we could not find them, the platoon had been annihilated in a heavy battle. I would like to believe they had the chance to taste their fresh crabs.

Drew, Kha, and I at that point were one of the best teams at ABC. Drew regained his charming smile—the same smile I used to see when he was a documentary producer. When a new team came up to replace us, we went back to Saigon, and the first thing we did was to check the telex files at the Bureau. As expected, there were nearly ten nice Herograms or "Attaboys" for us.

As he was reading the cables, Kha suddenly raised his voice and said, "Look at this. It's not a Herogram. It just says 'thanks.'"

DREW, USED YOUR QUANG TRI'S TANK STORY 1:30, THANKS
DREW, USED YOUR SOUTH VIETNAMESE ARMY DEFENSE LINE, THANKS

Kha showed us a cable sent to our replacement crew, Ron Miller with Minh and Malet:

RON, YOUR HIGHWAY ONE REPORT WAS SUPERB AND VERY POWERFUL. DON'T TAKE RISKS, WATCH YOURSELF, THANK YOU

Kha was right. There was definitely a difference in tone between the telexes. Our cables were business-like, even though Drew's stories had aired on the show every day. On the other hand, the telex to Ron was warm, sincere, and compassionate.

Although we were grown men, in our line of work we still had boyish hearts and rather simple emotions. Words of praise, respect, love, and care are appreciated more than awards. I tried to calm Kha down, but he was very upset. A Vietnamese who enjoyed playing cards and chess, Kha was very competitive about his job. He hated to lose to a competitor in a game but he really hated losing a competition on how well he did his job. Everyone in our bureau tried to calm Kha down, and finally, bureau chief Kevin Delany had to call us together and assure us that New York knew we had beaten all the other networks.

This finally appeased Kha.

As the war came closer and closer to Saigon, An Loc was the key to the South Vietnamese defense. With no resupply by air because the Americans were gone, that left Highway Thirteen as the last remaining supply line. Drew, Kha, and I headed to the town of Chong Tanh next to Highway Thirteen.

On the way there, Drew briefed me on the history of the highway. Lined with rubber and tea plantations, it went straight from the Cambodia border to Saigon. Many significant battles had taken place in the towns along this road including Operation *Junction City*. Drew even told me that the first American soldier had been killed on this highway.

Before working with Drew, I was a simple combat cameraman who cared about getting exciting pictures. Ever since teaming up with Drew, I saw things differently and became a better journalist as my interest in Vietnam expanded and extended beyond the war.

Along the edge of Highway Thirteen, elite Vietnamese Airborne soldiers were ready to fight—positioned in foxholes about the size of manholes spaced twenty feet apart from each other. We arrived during a lull in the fighting and so we started to take some pictures of the soldiers in their foxholes. When the fighting resumed again, we didn't have time to make our own foxholes so we stayed down by the shoulder of the road, hiding from incoming bullets while filming the fighting. Everyone in our team was fairly short which, as usual, is quite convenient on a battlefield.

The battle started to get more intense with incoming bullets whizzing by our heads while Skyraiders were dropping bombs on the enemy. We could see smoke rising from behind the enemy lines.

Not far from my position, a young soldier in his foxhole was giving instructions to the Skyraider pilot by radio. With his upper body exposed outside of the foxhole, I saw that his arm had a tattoo of the English words "Never Sad." The young soldier's face was so photogenic that I panned my camera down from his face to a close up of his tattooed arm and then panned up again.

Then I tried to get Drew to do a lying-down stand-upper in the middle of all this combat. He took the mic and I rolled film, but I didn't find out what he said until years later:

> When we were doing the on-camera piece, with rifle rounds whooshing just overhead, I was saying, "Tony, get down, get down!" But of course, you didn't get down because you couldn't—and also shoot me with that bulky Auricon.

The following night the story titled "The Battle of Highway Thirteen" was aired on the evening news. Next morning, bureau secretaries Miss Loi and Miss Thuan excitedly informed us that New York sent a Herogram telex addressed to Drew and the crew. Kha and I saw it first. It said:

DEAR DREW! EXCELLENT REPORT ON HIGHWAY THIRTEEN. IT WAS THE BEST REPORT WE EVER GOT.
ALL NEW YORK STAFF TAKE OUR HATS OFF AND SALUTE YOU.
THANK YOU FOR YOUR GREAT WORK THE LAST TWO WEEKS.

It had been sent by Executive Producer Av Westin himself, and it was warm, personal, and encouraging. When Drew showed up at the bureau, we all applauded him loudly and then handed him the telex. As he started reading the telex file, we all waited for his reaction. He was calm, but his cheeks turned a little reddish. After he had finished reading it, he put his hand on my shoulder and quietly said, "Thank you."

The moment I heard those words, I lost control of my emotions and burst into tears of joy. It wasn't only me. Many members of ABC had tears in their eyes. We all celebrated that our big boss in New York had finally recognized what a great correspondent Drew was.

While I was working at the Quang Tri front with recovered and rehabilitated Roger Peterson, Drew suddenly left Saigon. I didn't have the chance to ask him why. I wished he stayed much longer so I could learn more from him. Decades later, he revealed to me why he left Saigon at the height of his victory as a TV correspondent:

> During these days, Sibylle (later Mrs. Pearson) was very upset every morning when I left our apartment on Tu Do, just at dawn. She would cry every morning because she thought I wouldn't come back. That was the reason I wrote to Nick Archer asking to be re-assigned to work on documentaries in NY. He refused and fired me.[3]

Drew had chosen to leave for love just as his professional career and reputation were reaching its highest point. He left me a short memo that I read when I got back from the frontline:

> Tony—leaving today—wish you the best—been hearing about your last film story in Quang Tri—would like to hear about it from you—see you some place, sometime in the future—Thanks for your fine professional companionship these last months—and your friendship too—Hope we can work together again—I like the way you work—
> best.
> Drew

I liked the way Drew worked. A good documentary producer can be a great combat correspondent!

CHAPTER 19

QUIET IN KONTUM

The second front of the Easter Offensive drove into the central mountainous region of Kontum Province and the central coastal area of Binh Dinh Province. The purpose of this attack was to cut South Vietnam in half. By mid-May, the enemy had advanced and surrounded Kontum City, the provincial capital. A loss here would mean that South Vietnam was cut in two so the government proclaimed it the last line of defense and prepared to hold it with everything they had.

My new correspondent at the time was Dick Shoemaker, who had come from the Los Angeles bureau. Kontum was my first assignment working with the young, slim, and quiet reporter. I remember that he wore a cowboy hat made out of camouflage fabric rather than a helmet.

My partner and soundman was my old friend, Jean-Claude Malet. Malet was an excellent journalist as well as a sound technician—he'd worked as an ABC freelance reporter and cameraman before we became a team.

Dick, Malet, and I followed South Vietnamese soldiers to the edge of Kontum City—which was the closest to the frontlines. We could see heavy house-to-house fighting and were told that the North Vietnamese had succeeded in breaking through and holding a small part of Kontum City but, in the past few days, the tide of battle had changed. The South Vietnamese soldiers were fighting hard and making the enemy pay for every foot of ground. The units were holding, fresh troops had arrived from Saigon, and air support from US B-52s, close-in air defense, and bombardments from the Seventh Fleet off the coast were inflicting heavy casualties on the attacking forces. It was a slow and painful process, but, the South Vietnamese were forcing the enemy onto the defensive.

Street battles were continuing in the close-packed houses that surrounded Kontum City. The government troops were using 106-millimeter M40 recoilless rifles, antitank weapons which were like small rockets in a tube. We got too interested in what we were filming and forgot basic safety rules and, as a result, almost got blown away by the blast coming out of the rear. We were covered with black powder but luckily uninjured. The only "loss" was Dick's cowboy hat.

As we filmed, the South Vietnamese soldiers began to move forward, crouching and firing, then charging and throwing hand grenades. They went with a lot of courage and determination from house to house, street to street, corner to corner, driving back the enemy troops. It reminded me of the old newsreels of the German and American armies as Patton and Montgomery drove the Nazis out of Europe.

Dick Shoemaker's "Battle of Kontum City" aired on the ABC Evening News. Of course, this report had lots of exciting footage of men firing, antitank guns, and grenades which, I'm sure, helped the New York executives decide to air it. Dick got a Herogram for the coverage and Malet and I were thanked for the footage.

The next day, Jean-Claude Malet and I went out by ourselves to see if we could get into Kontum City. After a series of misadventures, we wound up in a South Vietnamese Army compound right on the frontlines where they had knocked out three of the brand-new Soviet tanks. As we walked in, a US advisor approached us with a friendly smile. He introduced himself as Major Wade B. Lovings which I thought was an excellent name.

Since we didn't have our correspondent with us, Malet became the reporter and recorded himself asking the advisor to explain the situation they were dealing with while I got it on camera. Just as we completed the interview, another firefight broke out.

In this battle, the two forces were closer than I'd ever seen before— only a matter of yards separated them. In the middle of a field next to the compound, two of the ruined Soviet tanks were providing cover for a troop of South Vietnamese soldiers who were getting ready to try and take out the fourth tank. The North Vietnamese troops were on the far side of the third ruined tank. They were so near each other that the government forces were carrying hand grenades instead of rifles.

The South Vietnamese charged—heading straight for the enemy positions—but when they were about half-way and totally without cover, the enemy made a direct hit with a B-40 rocket and then opened up with small arms.

Several of the South Vietnamese soldiers dropped instantly, and the others began to withdraw but were hit by another RPG. Now there were more than a half-dozen severely wounded soldiers lying in the middle of the battlefield; some crawling slowly back to their lines and others crying out for help.

Major Lovings ran straight into this screaming chaos, disregarding the bullets *zipping* around him. When he reached his troops, he picked two up by their belts in the back and carried them back to the safety of

Tony Hirashiki and Jean-Claude Malet relax outside the city of Kontum where, in May 1972, North Vietnamese forces had surrounded the city. The two-man team went in to see the real situation. (Courtesy Jean-Claude Malet)

sandbags piled up in the compound like a set of luggage. After he dropped them out of the line of fire, he went back and picked up more.

I kept filming Major Lovings' crazy acts of bravery. The big American was completely unprotected and should have been an easy target, but the enemy soldiers actually held their fire as he dashed back and forth in his insane rescue mission; bringing back soldier after soldier.

Were they showing respect for Major Lovings' bravery and humanity or just caught by surprise? I'll never know.

It was surreal, and I almost thought I'd wandered into an old war movie. But it wasn't a movie, it was very real, very dangerous, and one of the most authentic, brave acts I've ever witnessed.

I interviewed the major about how well his Vietnamese troops had fought and how proud he was of them. He said he was on his third tour of duty in Vietnam but had never seen anything like these South Vietnamese troops. He bragged that his men had been called weak and inexperienced when they took up their places on the defense line, but they never gave up, fought hard, and defended their position.

I could see through the lens that the major's eyes were wet with tears as he talked about these men and he had to stop talking when he choked up with emotion.

We walked towards the center of Kontum City. It was eerily empty—a no man's land. At the intersection of the main streets, I found an abandoned helmet which had belonged to a South Vietnamese soldier—it had a large hole in the middle made by a machine-gun bullet or a piece of shrapnel. I filmed it from a low angle, with the close-up of the hole in the helmet revealing the now-empty main street in the ghost town of Kontum City. (For footage see plate section.)

Then we kept walking.

Not far from the center of the city, we came to a small park where refugees had gathered, waiting to be evacuated by helicopter. A small square had been cleared for a landing zone, and the park had been made into a staging area to get people into groups to load. The majority of the refugees were Montagnards, elderly people, women, children, babies and some wounded soldiers.

There were only a few American troops coordinating helicopter takeoffs and landings and organizing the boarding. In the beginning, the refugees obeyed the orders of the American soldiers, letting women, children, and the elderly board first but, even though they were using big Chinook transportation helicopters, space was limited, and every takeoff meant some refugees were left behind to wait for the next Chinook. To make things worse, each time an American helicopter landed or took off, North Vietnamese gunners would aim their rockets at the landing zone area and make the people run. It was chaos.

After more shells started landing nearby, strong men—soldiers who should have been in the fighting units—were pushing, pulling, and yelling to get on board. They didn't care about anyone else in their panic to get away. It was living hell. Nobody could really be blamed; it was the only way that anyone could escape from this destroyed town. Increasingly, shells were crashing into the city and people ran through the smoke-filled streets. (See footage in plate section.)

Happily, there were enough helicopters that everyone made it on. We boarded with the last load and headed back to their base. The next day, President Thieu proudly announced that Kontum City had held, and South Vietnam was still one country.

When we got back, we found Dick and told him of the scenes we had shot; the destroyed Soviet tanks, Major Lovings' heroism, and the ugly scenes at the evacuation. I typed up all the notes and realized that I had shot 800 feet of film—about 20 minutes of good material. Malet had been the perfect correspondent, and we had recorded the name, rank, and hometown of every American soldier we'd met—both at the South Vietnamese base, at the evacuation zone, and on the helicopter. Dick read my dope sheet carefully and started to write his script. After finishing, he read it to us and recorded his narration on camera.

Dick ran down the day's events as they had unfolded: the captured tanks, the battle between the North and South Vietnamese forces, the American advisor rescuing his wounded, the comradeship between the soldiers, the helmet with the hole in it, the ghost town of Kontum City, and the refugees fighting to getting on board during the shelling.

We had witnessed so much action that day but when Dick checked with Saigon to find out what the military briefer had said about Kontum at the "Five O'clock Follies," he hung up the phone and wrote his final line:

> HOWEVER, MILITARY SPOKESMEN IN SAIGON SAID THAT THE KONTUM FRONT WAS RELATIVELY QUIET TODAY.
> DICK SHOEMAKER. KONTUM, SOUTH VIETNAM.[1]

CHAPTER 20

ROGER RETURNS

Roger Peterson, the correspondent who was my first teacher and so very dear to me, came back to Vietnam, assigned to Saigon for three months as one of the many reinforcements that ABC was sending. His injured right arm and hand were much better but still not completely recovered. He would hold two tiny metal balls in his palm and roll them around as part of the rehabilitation. He'd also been lifting weights to build up the wounded muscles so he was stronger than ever.

When I was a rookie, Roger had taught me a lot; how to survive in the field and how to shoot footage that would make a great story. Now I felt it was my turn to pay him back with great footage, and I wanted to show him how much I had improved as a cameraman during the last three years.

At the end of June 1972, Roger and I finally worked together again. He had decided to follow Vietnamese Marines on an operation. The Marines were one of the elite forces in the South Vietnamese Army and they were usually sent into the toughest battles and performed the most important missions.

Quang Tri City had been the first major city to fall in the Easter Offensive and the North Vietnamese had used its surrender for a considerable amount of propaganda. Now, the government was determined to take back the city and, eventually, all of Quang Tri province. The Marines we were following were supposed to be the "tip of the spear" in this massive attack. Their plan was to break through enemy lines and drive deep into Quang Tri; an area that the North Vietnamese had controlled for over two months.

As usual, the American forces would provide choppers and air cover so Roger, Kha, and I were going in with these troops in a US Marine Sea Knight helicopter. The landing zone was "hot," so everyone scrambled out the back ramp as quickly as possible, the big twin rotor chopper pulled out, and the Marines were immediately in a furious firefight with North Vietnamese regulars.

My camera was rolling before our helicopter even touched the ground, and I continued to shoot almost continually until we reached the first rendezvous point. Roger had done a quick stand-up at the landing zone with the South Vietnamese Marines racing out of several Sea Knights and heading for combat.

Roger hadn't changed a bit, he was still just as brave and quick as he'd been three years ago. Just like before, he would be writing in his small notebook, with two canteens on his belt. As I followed him, I couldn't remember which canteen held the Jack Daniel's—the right or the left. Another thing that hadn't changed was his concern for his crew: he was always looking to check that we were right behind him and following in his footsteps so that we wouldn't hit a land mine. I still couldn't pronounce his name, but he didn't complain. I felt as if we gone back in time, an enormous correspondent with a tiny cameraman, once again a team just like in *Of Mice and Men*.

The Vietnamese Marines' mission was to slip around the North Vietnamese defenses and move as deep into enemy territory as they could. What I learned was that they were not only "the spearhead" of the attack but a diversion as well. The commanders wanted the enemy to worry about soldiers behind their lines who could strike at any moment.

This was only the first stage of the offensive so we soon arrived at a small village and took a long break. We had had to really hustle to keep up with the tough South Vietnamese Marines, and I was exhausted. Luckily there was nothing to film so I stretched out on the ground under the bamboo and went to sleep. Like every good soldier, I knew to sleep every time I had the chance and here, the sounds of bamboo fronds rustling in the breeze were as peaceful as a lullaby. If I were a great *haiku* poet, I could have made a poem about the bamboo trees in the gentle breeze.

Luckily, I was not a great poet, so I took a nap instead.

Suddenly, the Marines around us whispered warnings, saying, "Be quiet! Don't make any noise! Stop talking!"

The soldier next to me put his finger to his lips and then cautiously pointed the same finger past the bamboo trees to some rice fields.

Only yards away, over a dozen North Vietnamese soldiers were moving right to left across the field. I rolled over and began to film. They weren't running but marching quickly along the narrow raised path that ran between the fields. Most were wearing khaki uniforms, but some were wearing the farmers' usual black work clothes that the GIs called "black pajamas."

I used a big tree root to steady my camera like a tripod and went to my maximum telephoto lens. When I zoomed all the way to the 120mm setting, I could shoot pictures so close that there were only four or five soldiers in the frame. I could clearly see them smiling, talking, and laughing as they marched along with their guns resting on their shoulders. Usually, pictures of the enemy were shot from far away and were very fuzzy; this was a chance to really see them as people and not just dots in the distance.

Roger was holding the microphone to his mouth and barely whispering as he recorded a description of the scene. The Marines lying around me were literally holding their breath as they watched the enemy march past.

I worried that the noise of the camera rolling might be loud enough for the enemy to hear but the Auricon was built to be quiet, and no one noticed the sound. When the last soldier disappeared from view, I heard a big sigh of relief from Roger.

I had been shooting combat pictures for seven years now, and I had never gotten such good shots of enemy soldiers in the field. Well, I did get shots of North Vietnamese when they were captured or killed, but this was different—these men were vivid and totally alive.

The Marines were going to dig in and set up a field headquarters here, but we had good material and wanted to get it back to Saigon. We were told that it was too dangerous for a helicopter to land, but they would probably send one in to take out the wounded tomorrow. We would just have to sit and wait—which was normal for a field shoot.

It was an unusual location; we were in the middle of the battlefield and could hear artillery firing from both sides with the shells going over our heads. First, you would hear the gun firing with a sound like *Pon!* then the shell going *shuru shururu* overhead, and finally the *Bung! Do Kan!* of the explosion.

Roger's report was going to be powerful, and I was glad that I could reward my teacher with the results of all I had learned. Roger sat with his back to the big tree and worked on his script as Kha and I tried to get some sleep.

At midnight, a commander's aide came over to our bedrolls and said that one helicopter was on the way, we should move to the landing zone, and be ready to get on as soon as it touched down. It was a pitch-black night with no moon and no stars so a Marine had to guide us.

I wondered, how can the helicopter find the landing zone with no light? Then, when we heard the beat of the twin rotors, one of the soldiers, who was hidden from sight in the tall grass, began to flash instructions with a pair of flashlights.

Above us, the medevac chopper turned on their searchlight, found the landing zone, and touched down perfectly. The wounded were loaded first, and there was just enough room left for our crew. All the lights went out, and the South Vietnamese medevac chopper carried us through the night out of enemy territory. All the way back to base, I lay on the floor of the chopper and repeated, "It's too good to be true! It's just too good to be true!"

A couple of weeks later, we learned that the troops we had traveled with had been discovered by the North Vietnamese and were outnumbered and wiped out. Roger's report "ARVN Marine Assault" was praised as one of the great news pieces of the war and New York ran it at over three minutes in length as the first story in the Evening News. Herograms came in from New York for both Roger and the crew:

DELANY PLEASE PASS ON TO PETERSON, HIRASHIKI, KHA OUR HIGHEST PRAISE FOR TONIGHT EXCELLENT COVERAGE WHICH LED SHOW FOR THREE MINUTES STOP REGARDS
SHEEHAN/ARCHER

DELANY FOR PETERSON SATELLITED FOR YOUR ARVN ASSAULT WHICH OUTSTANDING WORK BY ALL CONCERNED STOP SPECIAL THANKS TO YOU COMMA HIRASHIKI AND TEAM. CHEERS.
RICHTER

I heard from one of the CBS cameramen that CBS News in New York sent a Rocket to their Saigon bureau:

REGARDING COVERAGE OF NORTHERN FRONT. WHY NUMBER ONE NETWORK WAS BEATEN BY NUMBER THREE NETWORK?

I was hoping that Roger would tell me how well I had done and how much I'd learned since he'd left but Roger told me later that he knew I was expecting praise, but he was afraid if he made too much of my good work, I would take even more chances and put myself in more danger.

Instead, he told me very seriously, "Tony, you had better think of leaving Vietnam. You took too many risks out there, and your luck can't continue forever. There are only so many jokers in a deck, and you've already used most of yours."

Decades later, Roger added one more thought in his letter:

> What did concern me was your eagerness. I really thought I'd end up carrying you back sooner or later. How you ever managed to get out of the mess in one piece still amazes me.[1]

CHAPTER 21

BATTLE OF AN LOC

The Easter Offensive had failed, and South Vietnamese soldiers were steadily pushing back and retaking town after town. One of the key strongpoints of the defense had been the city of An Loc, only 80 miles north of Saigon. It had been surrounded completely by the enemy for months, but the defenders refused to quit. They were resupplied by air drops of food and ammunition while thousands of rockets and artillery shells hammered the town from all sides.

The South Vietnamese troops knew that they were the last defense for Saigon. With all this fighting, it was almost impossible for journalists and camera teams to get into An Loc and very dangerous to work once they were inside. Veteran journalists said it was tougher than the infamous siege of the US Marines at Khe Sanh back in 1968.

One day in early June 1972, Terry called me over, and I could tell he was very upset. He said he was going into An Loc to shoot news stories. I wondered if he had a death wish because it was so totally unlike him. I was praying that the Assignment Desk wouldn't ask me to go, and so far my prayers had been answered. Of course, staff crews had the right to refuse an assignment if they felt it was simply too dangerous. No staffers were going into An Loc.

The assignment desk managers knew they couldn't force a staffer to go, but freelancers were another matter. We were hearing of news organizations offering as much as $300 or $500 for film and similar amounts for photos.

Terry didn't think it was fair. Freelancers all operated on a very slim margin, so eventually they were going to have to take the chance and go in. He said, "How dare they pay a freelancer 500 bucks and no insurance and send him into a place where there's no guarantee they could get out alive!"

So, Terry had decided to go into An Loc, without any extra money, to show that a freelancer's life was as valuable as a staffer's life. He was going there because of his duty as a journalist and a sense that the news operations weren't playing fair.

Howard Tuckner, perhaps the bravest of the correspondents, had a strong connection with a South Vietnamese colonel in An Loc so he volunteered to go in with Terry. The colonel had arranged to have a fast helicopter with volunteer pilots on call to try and sneak them in and out.

Howard and Terry were the first network television journalists inside An Loc since it had been surrounded back in April. Terry said it was a hell that he would never be able to forget. An Loc had been shelled constantly for nearly two months, and the streets were littered with dead bodies just left to rot because it was too dangerous to crawl out and pull them back. In some place, bodies were piled in heaps the size of small hills. Under the incessant shelling, there wasn't any way that they could be brought out and returned to their families, it wasn't even possible to bury them within the city.

The stink of death covered the entire town like an awful fog. Wounded soldiers would wait at the landing zones until a chopper made it in; but the North Vietnamese gunners had pinpointed where they waited and would drop shells right on top of them.

It was a town of death, and the only living things were South Vietnamese soldiers, battered and starving, who refused to give up.

Howard and Terry spent a whole day in An Loc and shot enough for a story which would, of course, be an ABC News exclusive. They went back to the landing zone to meet the special helicopter in the late afternoon. The wounded soldiers who surrounded the airfield had been waiting for a medevac for two days and they swarmed the chopper, pushing and fighting to get on board.

Howard and Terry managed to get seats with the help of the aircrew, but they both looked at the ugly scene of despairing men, not cowards but seriously wounded, in a desperate mob with the strong trampling the weak. The chopper was about to take off when they both watched one man simply lose his strength and fall to the ground.

Howard looked at Terry and said, "Forget it."

Terry nodded, and they unfastened their seat belts and jumped to the ground. They helped the wounded up to take their place, especially the badly wounded man they had watched fall and then they just walked away.

Howard had the red, white, and blue ABC News shipping bag with the first film of An Loc in his hand and now it would just have to wait until another helicopter made it in to get them out.

It could have been a long wait.

But nearly twenty injured soldiers lifted off in their place. In an extreme circumstance, both Howard and Terry made a moral decision and risked their lives for the lives of others. I admired their decision and the quick way they acted. To be totally honest, I am not sure I would have made the same decision.

Terry and Howard had to find a place to sleep that would be safe from shelling. Howard said that they were so thirsty that, at one point, Terry lay down and sipped water from a puddle right next to some dead bodies and then almost fainted. It was a bad night, but they did manage to fly out the next day, and their story was still exclusive.

In the middle of June, after ninety days of fighting and thousands of losses, the North Vietnamese had had enough. They pulled back having lost nearly half their troops and accomplished almost nothing.

CHAPTER 22

QUANG TRI

As I said at the very beginning of this book, I didn't really think much about luck until I came to Vietnam. When I first arrived, I thought any good luck or misfortune I encountered was due to my own actions. After six years on the battlefields of Vietnam, I had changed my mind. I paid attention to my instincts for good stories and used my sixth sense to avoid dangerous situations. Many of my colleagues and friends came to believe that luck, both good and bad, was far too important to ignore.

For a cameraman in a war zone, good luck is finding dramatic situations and the great film footage of danger, death, and even beauty that can exist right on a battlefield. Finding those situations and that footage inevitably meant taking risks, walking right next to death and injury without any protection and still staying just on the right side of the line so that you and your teammates came back safe. Luck was essential.

I had enjoyed three streaks of good luck *omikuji* since I came to Vietnam. The first was during the spring of 1966 when I first arrived in Saigon as a greenie without a clue and landed a staff job at ABC News, met some amazing people who taught me how to stay safe and still get good pictures, and was in the right place at the right time for some major stories.

The second streak of good luck started in the spring of 1970 and continued until the end of the year as I worked with Howard Tuckner and Steve Bell in the confusing and dangerous civil war in Cambodia.

The third lucky period began in the late spring of 1972 during the Easter Offensive as I worked with Drew Pearson, Roger Peterson, and

Ron Miller. In all these times, I had good reporters, we did important stories and some exclusives, and all of us managed to make it back safely.

But good luck doesn't last forever.

I was well aware of this but I was young, aggressive, and eager so I ran out my streaks of luck as if I was playing poker; challenging myself to go further, shoot better, and improve my skills as a war photographer. Brash and overconfident, I only worried about developing my abilities and didn't worry about the bigger picture.

★★★

As the Easter Offensive wore on, people I respected and friends in the business said that they had noticed an improvement in my work and praised many of the stories I had filmed. When I started at ABC News, my nickname was "two left hands" because of all the camera gear I'd broken, I was so short that I had to practically run to keep up with troops on the march and, despite the efforts of my bosses, I simply couldn't learn to speak proper English.

Because of all these shortcomings, I always felt that I had to work harder than all my colleagues to get good pictures, find the important stories, and simply survive. Now, six years after I'd started out, I believed that my time had finally arrived, and I thought that I would do really great work in the next few years.

Now, my friend and teacher, Roger Peterson, was so worried about me that he'd told me to think about leaving Vietnam. I believe he saw something in my future that I just couldn't see and even after he returned to Washington, he would write me and warn me to take care of myself.

Roger wasn't the only friend who was increasingly worried about my thoughtless approach. Terence Khoo was considered by everyone in the press corps to be one of the best in the business. He was from Singapore and of Chinese descent so we were both foreigners in Vietnam and he was the first friend I made in Saigon. Terry, as he was always called, was not much taller than me and only two years older, but he was an English aristocrat—very calm and self-possessed at all times. With his long beard and a neat mustache, Terry looked a lot like the ancient Chinese philosophers you see in classic paintings, a paragon of nobility and wisdom.

Terry Khoo does last-minute light checks before an interview with South Vietnamese President Nguyen Van Thieu in 1967. ABC soundman Frank Eddy stands directly behind him. Khoo was the "go-to" person for important shoots and anytime it was absolutely vital to get the shot. (Courtesy Family of Terry Khoo)

The correspondents found him exceptional, and he was usually the cameraman that they would request first. One of the reasons was his language skills; raised in the polyglot culture of Singapore, he spoke English, Vietnamese, French, Malaysian, and several Chinese dialects. Even the local Vietnamese staffers, who normally distrusted foreigners, accepted Terry as a friend. Former bureau secretary Miss Hien Boase wrote to me about Terry:

> I began working for ABC News mid-1965. One morning at the office Mr. Lam introduced me to Terry Khoo. A man with a full black beard stood before me with very sad eyes and very aloof. I had the feeling he was someone very cold

and distant. He had a tough exterior and swore all the time. So initially I did not warm to him. I had the impression of someone very cold, tough and full of swear words.

As time went by, I learned that he was someone tough like a bear on the outside but soft like cotton on the inside. At one point in talking with him I found out he was Fukien Chinese. Most of my best Chinese friends were Fukien Chinese so I had a special feeling for them. For me the Fukien have very good qualities such as a strong fidelity and a complete dedication to their friends. If you become friends with a Fukien, you are their friend for life. People say that friendship between a man and a woman does not exist. But with Terry, I had a true friendship. I could trust him like my brother and could tell him everything. I used to call him "Khoo da ge" or "Big Brother." Terry was all or nothing in his friendships. He either supported you 100% as a friend or he did not want to have anything to do with you.

When Terry went out to dinner or to a party with us, he always wore his Mao champagne-toned Thai silk suit. He looked like a prince from a noble family. Tony Hirashiki became Terry's and my friend at around the same time. I was always happy to see Terry and Tony together. They were so close that if one came to the office, the other was either with him or would appear within minutes.[1]

Terry began covering Vietnam in late 1962, when I was still at a television station in Osaka, just learning my way around a film camera, and probably unable to point to Vietnam on a map. *The New York Times'* David Halberstam, UPI's Neil Sheehan, AP's Malcolm Browne, and historian Bernard Fall; these were the people who served as Terry's professors in the war zones that were his classroom and he received a superb education in the nature of war in Southeast Asia.

When I got to know him, I found that most people were impressed by his character, behavior, and consideration for others. More than just a technician, he was a leader and mentor to many of the young Asian journalists who came to Saigon with a dream but not a lot of experience. Terry was as competitive as anyone, but he spent the time to share his judgment and keep both colleagues and competitors safe.

Terry had a house on the same street as the Presidential Palace, and it was known as "Terry's Villa" or "Terry's Salon." Everyone was always welcome, from his oldest friend to a freelancer who had just gotten off the plane. No invitations were necessary, and food and drink were always available—especially to the young kids who were struggling to get by until they got their "big break." Terry supplied them with delicious French and Vietnamese dishes prepared by his in-house cook, Chi Bay, and even advanced them money when a freelancer was hitting rock-bottom. One freelancer had been a street orphan before Terry discovered he was talented. Terry not only taught him the skills of a still photographer but supported him financially until he could get by on his own. Years later, the kid became a well-known staff photographer whose pictures were used around the world.

In the six years since we'd met, Terry had also completely changed my life ... not just how to be a better cameraman but a better person.

For instance, he encouraged me to say "no." Terry thought that I was far too willing to go along with whatever my reporter or other colleagues wanted, even when I figured it was dangerous or simply the wrong way to cover a story. He said that I now knew my job as a photojournalist, and I had to speak my mind firmly and clearly—say "no" and stick with it, not bowing to the will of others. It wasn't just the act of refusing but making sure that the refusal was clear and definite. Terry said that was a mark of a grown man and, in our jobs, it could also be the difference between life and death.

Terry was my mentor, but he was also competitive so we continually challenged each other to get the best footage and, far too often, went into peril to get it.

These days, Terry had begun to tell me that my film was really good and, especially, he praised my coverage of the Easter Offensive. He told me that the cameramen at the other networks were impressed as well and that he was very proud of me.

"Now, you are one of the best," was how he wrapped it up.

Terry had begun his career as a still photographer before he took up the 16-millimeter film camera and he would still carry an old Leica M2 with him everywhere he went. It was so old and battered that the paint was peeling off to reveal rusted metal, but that only proved that its owner was a veteran and in fact, many of the photos Terry took with it appeared in magazines and newspapers across Asia. He specialized in profiles of ordinary people and the faces of children.

Sam Kai Faye was also from Singapore and, in fact, had taught Terry Khoo how to be a photographer. Terry had convinced him to come to Saigon and he soon became one of ABC's best. (Courtesy Chin Kah Chong)

Terry had first learned how to shoot from Sam Kai Faye, a photographer in Singapore who had won the British Commonwealth Photo Contest in both 1958 and 1959. Sam was working at his brother's photo shop in Singapore when his old friend and pupil, Terry, convinced him to take up a news camera and come to Vietnam and work for ABC News. Terry, who had been the student, became the teacher and Sam soon became an excellent film cameraman and got a freelance job with ABC in Saigon.

Sam was an older man, but he and Terry were close friends despite the difference in their ages. Sam had a gentle and sincere manner and people always felt relaxed around him. Even though Terry was a dozen years younger, he acted as if he was Sam's older brother and constantly worked to take care of him and keep him safe.

I met Sam for the first time when I visited Singapore in 1967, and he treated me like family simply because I was one of Terry's friends. No questions asked. I felt I owed Sam for his kindness, and I finally got a chance to repay him years later when he came to visit Japan. I was there on R&R, and I showed him the sights and then we went to see *Hair*, the new American musical that had just opened with an all-Japanese cast. If you were around during the 70s you'd remember that during the finale, the whole cast would dance in and out of the audience half-naked. If you weren't around back then, trust me, it was an experience.

I had a friend in the show so I arranged for Sam to be pulled up out of the audience and taken to center stage like a VIP. At first, he was surprised and perhaps embarrassed but soon he was dancing as wildly as the cast to the song "Let the Sunshine In." He had a huge smile and afterward he told me that he had never had such a great time in his entire life and that he would cherish the memory forever.

As confident and attractive as he was, Terry was not lucky in love.

Back in Singapore, before he came to Vietnam, Terry dated a woman named Yung Mei. She was the daughter of the well-known author Elizabeth Matilda Chou, who, under the pen name Han Suyin, wrote the book that was the basis for the Oscar-winning 1955 movie *Love Is a Many-Splendored Thing*, a love story about two foreign correspondents who meet during the Korean War.

Terry and Yung Mei drifted apart, but they remained close friends even after their romance was over. I didn't know anything about her until I was spending some R&R in Singapore with Terry and he took me waterskiing. On the stern of his new speedboat was painted "Mei." I asked Terry what the name of the boat meant, and he just smiled and talked about other things. Later Sam told me who "Mei" was and I met her when she and her husband, a Broadway producer, visited Terry in Saigon.

Mei was a bittersweet memory but his second love story was sad. One day, Terry asked me if he should send flowers to a girl named Betty as congratulations for winning an international beauty contest. He said that he was almost ready to marry her, but he knew that if Betty kept on winning pageants, she would have to travel and represent the pageant organization as the reigning beauty queen and would not have time to see him.

Betty loved Terry, but she loved beauty pageants more. One day, he got the news that she had won the Miss Pacific pageant and would tour all over Asia and Australia for a year. Terry sent her a large bouquet of flowers and never mentioned her name again.

It took many years but finally Terry found his true love. He was a very private man, but I noticed that for two vacations in a row, he went home to Singapore on flights with a stop in Hong Kong. Many people take flights with a layover, but Hong Kong and Singapore are in completely opposite directions from Saigon.

A bit of investigation and the mystery was solved: his new love was an ABC bureau secretary named Winnie Ng. Terry told me that she was beautiful, smart, charming, and passionate. After all that, he didn't need to tell me that he was crazy about her.

We were all excited to hear the good news; everyone wanted Terry to be happy. The love affair moved very quickly and, within months, Terry

Winnie Ng (left) and Anhue Hirashiki (right). Shortly before his death, Terry Khoo had decided to ask Winnie, who worked in the ABC Hong Kong bureau, to marry him. (Courtesy of Yasutsune Hirashiki)

had decided to propose to her and get married as soon as possible. I was nominated to be the best man for their wedding which was frightening but, since I'd already survived the job once, I agreed.

Just seeing them sitting together is one of my happiest memories. It was clear that Winnie was totally in love with Terry, she kept saying "This is just too good to be true."

I didn't drink so most of my off-hours were spent reading, gambling, playing chess, or talking. Usually talking with Terry. We would often discuss what we would do once the war was over, plans for the next stage in our lives; usually fanciful daydreams as much as anything realistic.

Face it, people who really think about their future don't become war journalists.

Late in 1972, we were both in Saigon, and we had a long talk over dinner. Terry told me that he had just made a very important decision about his future. Surprisingly, he said he'd also made decisions about my future and our future together.

He said that the war was about to end and that it was no longer meaningful to either of us. We knew the story and could predict the ending. The fighting was still heavy, but it was more to influence the agreements being signed at the peace talks and not about winning or losing anymore. If we kept on covering the war as aggressively as we were used to doing, the probability of injury or death would still be high but we would die covering a story that simply wasn't worth it. In many ways, what Terry was saying was very similar to the feeling that the remaining American troops had, "Who wants to be the last to die for a mistake?"

Terry had apparently been thinking quite hard about all this, and he had decided to take a job that ABC had just opened as a staff cameraman in the Bonn bureau in West Germany. He told me that I absolutely had to come with him, and then we could both keep working for ABC.

His reasoning showed the essential character of Terry Khoo. He'd taken the job because he knew that I wouldn't leave Vietnam until he'd already gone. The fact was that Terry was taking this job in West Germany to save my life because he, like Roger Peterson, felt that I had taken so many risks that my luck simply had to run out. He made me promise to take any job that New York offered—whether it was in Hong Kong, Tokyo, or even in the United States.

Terry knew that the reason I hesitated to take a job away from the war wasn't that I was having a streak of good luck but that I had become addicted to the war itself—recording the scenes of madness, ugliness, sadness, and hopelessness and always on the lookout for the brief moments of bravery, happiness, and true glory. I had already given up a job in the ABC Tokyo bureau because I couldn't adjust to a peacetime life after the continuous adrenaline rush of Vietnam.

Terry understood all that because he'd been caught by war's appeal for years longer than I had. However, he was grimly certain that our time was up and if we didn't get out now, it would be too late. We would die for a story that was simply no longer worth the sacrifice.

Terry sat and waited for my decision. I knew he wouldn't take the job in West Germany if I stayed in Vietnam, so I promised to follow him as soon as a new job opened up. "I'll leave Vietnam right after you."

To be honest, I wasn't sure if I was telling the truth or pleasing a friend. I'm still not sure, forty years later.

In early July, Terry went for an R & R in Hong Kong. The plan was that he would come back, pack up, and move to Bonn. He sent me a telex from Hong Kong, asking if I wanted him to bring me anything back.

I responded that I wanted a new portable typewriter that would type in cursive and a long-playing record of a work by Bach. At the end of the telex, I added,

SEE YOU IN QUANG TRI.

The next day he telexed back that he had bought everything I asked for and ended with the line,

CONFIRMING YOUR 10107.– SEE YOU QUANG TRI REGARDS TERRY

The next day, I went up to Hue as the duty crew on the frontlines of the South Vietnamese counterattack. The North Vietnamese were being pushed back, but it was so slow that it was as if nothing was happening at all. I was there for two weeks and didn't shoot a single worthwhile story.

A week before Terry Khoo, Sam Kai Faye, and military cameraman Tran Van Nghia were killed in a North Vietnamese ambush, Khoo posed with a group of friends and competitors for what would be his final photo. From left, Hoang Dinh De who worked sound for ABC and Phan Bach Dang *who worked sound for NBC, cameramen Vo Huynh (NBC), Terry Khoo (ABC), and Joe Lee (ABC), and AP photographer Koichiro Morita. (Courtesy Yasutsune Hirashiki)*

In mid-July, Terry wrapped up his vacation and returned to Vietnam. We met up in Hue, and he gave me the Olivetti portable typewriter I'd asked for and the recording of Bach. He was supposed to be on his way to Bonn, but he'd told Saigon bureau chief Kevin Delany that he needed a few more pictures to finish a feature story so Kevin finally let him go.

The plan was that In Jip Choi or Sam Kai Faye would replace Terry and then there would be a day when the crews would overlap so that Terry could pass on any tips or notes the new cameraman might need. It always helped a new cameraman to get the "lay of the land" from his predecessor. I was happy because I would get to work with Terry for a couple more days before he left.

Terry and his soundman, T. H. Lee, arrived in Hue in the late morning of July 15. Just before noon, there was a barrage of incoming shells not far from the hotel; the North Vietnamese were shooting directly into the city, and there was a rumor that they might try for a counterattack on Hue along with a renewed offensive from the Laotian border to the west. It was only a rumor, but often that was all we had to work with.

Terry and I went out with our cameras as more shells landed on the streets. Some civilians were injured, and a government soldier had been hit and was lying lifeless in the street. We assumed that the enemy was trying to unnerve the city because the shells weren't aimed at the center but at the residential areas south of the Perfume River where our hotel was located.

When the shelling ceased, Terry and I took a break and sat on a bench in a park by the river to catch our breath. For a time, we just relaxed and watched the river flow past and then Terry said, "If we had been hit by one of those shells today, nobody would give us any sympathy. They would just laugh at us, saying what stupid guys we were. Let's not waste our lives."

He might have been correct. The shelling wasn't a big story, there wasn't going to be any change in the military or political situation. People had been hurt and killed but, sadly, that wasn't news, it was just another day in a war.

We went back to our hotel, and there we met up with a number of other journalists—many of whom were Terry's best friends in the press corps. Most of them were Asian: AP photographer Koichiro Morita, CBS sound technician Thanong Hiransi, ABC soundman Jean-Claude Malet, and NBC cameraman Le Phuc Dinh. That night, we all got together in Terry's hotel room to celebrate his new job and his future with Winnie Ng. Unsurprisingly, everyone said that he'd made a good choice and that she was pretty, cute, smart, pleasant, and everything else we could think of. Then we peppered him with questions, beginning with "How much do you like her? Are you in love with her?"

For the first time, Terry wasn't reserved but came right out and said, "I love her lots. I've totally surrendered." We all laughed at him and with him. It was a great night, we were all happy for Terry and Winnie, and happy to be together.

I stayed after the others had left. Terry had always been the older man who listened to my youthful enthusiasms and complaints. That night, it was my turn to listen.

Terry talked about his plans for the future; he and Winnie would get married and then wait a short time before they had a baby. She would continue in her business administration courses while Terry worked on his still photography so he'd be ready to get a job at the *National Geographic*. We discussed the wedding and all the things I'd have to take care of as the best man.

Sometimes, we would drift off into stories of good times we'd shared over the years, but Terry was mainly focused on the future. Over and over, he reminded me of my promise to leave Vietnam and forget the war.

I promised I would.

We talked most of the night and the next day I traveled back to Saigon, groggy with lack of sleep.

Two days later, on July 18, Terry slipped a short memo to me inside the bag with the undeveloped film from a story in Quang Tri:

> Yesterday, we faced a little dangerous situation, but we did a good story. Jim Bennett received a good telegram about his report. That's good for him. He is a very nice guy, and we need to support him. I'll try to do a better job for him while I'm here.

Jim Bennett had only recently joined ABC but was a veteran journalist. He'd served in World War II, worked as a newspaper reporter, and had been in Vietnam longer than any other television correspondent—most recently working for NBC. Off duty, he was a charming guy who loved jokes and drinking with other members of the press corps.

He did have a problem controlling his temper. We had all heard that NBC had let him go after an incident where his Vietnamese crew had been treated unfairly while covering a story in a war zone and Jim really let the Marine press officer at the Da Nang press center know how he felt about it. What we'd heard was that he got so angry that he punched the guy and, even though many thought his anger was justified, the military pressured NBC to let him go.

A relative newcomer to ABC, Correspondent Jim Bennett had possibly done more reporting from Vietnam than anyone else. Here, he does what he says could well be "the last report from Da Nang" as enemy troops close in during the final advance in 1975. (Film shot by Yasutsune Hirashiki; courtesy ABC News)

The Asians who worked in the press corps had heard of Jim's explosion and heartily approved of the way he'd fought for the rights of minority journalists. Joseph Lee, Terry, and I had agreed that we would back him up as best we could.

When the news came that he'd gotten a staff job at ABC; Jim Bennett, Terry, and I were all in Phnom Penh, and we stopped by to congratulate him. Jim was, unsurprisingly, in a good mood and said, with his trademark charming smile, "I'd be very honored to work with you. But you guys are Kamikazes. I'm not sure I could follow you all the time, taking such risks. Please take it easy, your lives are more important than these stories."

Jim's tone was half joking, half serious. We took his words as proof that Jim was more concerned about the safety of his crew than any shots he might miss. That was more proof that Bennett was worth our best efforts and Terry and I promised each other right then that we would work hard for him whenever we had the chance.

Sometimes people's good intentions take a wrong turn and end up bringing about the opposite result. Jim's primary concern was for his crew's safety. We crew members appreciated that, and so we tried to repay him by making an extra effort, which meant taking more chances.

Over the years, Jim Bennett has spoken very little about his experience in Vietnam and Cambodia, especially regarding his assignment with Terry and Sam in Quang Tri. He did address it decades later in a long interview he gave to writer Larry Engelmann:

> I lost a cameraman in Vietnam. He was killed. His name was Terry Khoo. He was a Singaporean Chinese. And the other young fellow that was with him that day—that was during the Easter offensive in I CORPS—was Sam Kai Faye—and that was a strange set of circumstances. Both were Chinese. Both from Singapore.
>
> ... Terry Khoo was one of the top cameramen, in the world for that matter, but one of the top cameramen in the country, and had been with ABC over there for years, to the extent that he was being transferred to Rome to get him out of there, he had done enough, had been there for years and years. This was his last day...
>
> The night before that Terry and I had had a big fight. He wanted to take Sam up the next day and I said, "No," he was supposed to leave the country, to fly back to Saigon and leave the country and I didn't want him to go. And we had an argument over it and I said, "No, you're not going out. We're going to make this transition as easy as possible and you're going to get back to Saigon and you're going out. They don't want you doing anything more."[2]

The next day, July 19, In Jip Choi, was preparing to go to Hue to replace Terry but he'd caught a nasty cold, That evening, Sam Kai Faye called and said, "Please let me change the schedule, I'll go to Hue first, and then you can come up to replace me."

At first, Choi refused, "No, it's already been assigned to me. I'll go."

Sam was the kind of man who would always insist on taking care of his friends and colleagues. Apparently, he went and volunteered to go to Hue because the next phone call Choi received was from Kevin Delany, the bureau chief. He pointed out that Choi sounded terrible, "You are seriously sick. I've changed the Hue assignment to Sam. He told me he was eager to go anyway."

Choi was an excellent cameraman, one of the best. He was Korean and had had a tough time for all the years he'd worked in Vietnam because he was only able to see his family in Seoul for a few weeks every three months.

Now all that was going to change. He found out that he'd been transferred to Hong Kong and was told that he could move his family down as part of the move. What he didn't know until later was that it was Terry who had sat down with Hong Kong bureau chief Dave Jayne and recommended that Choi should be allowed to bring his family to Hong Kong. This surprised Choi a bit because he and Terry had never been close, not that there was a disagreement, but Choi just didn't hang out with Terry's crowd.

Early in the morning of July 20, NBC cameraman Le Phuc Dinh was driving north on Highway One to the Quang Tri front. The assignment desk at the NBC Saigon bureau had told him that ABC News had gotten good footage the previous night and Le Phuc Dinh, like everyone else, knew that getting beaten to stories was a good way to be out of work. So Dinh, who was an excellent shooter and was in the running to be considered NBC's ace cameraman, left in the pre-dawn hours to get to the frontlines and try to get better footage for his network.

Despite the fact that they were competitors, Dinh was one of Terry's friends and, like many others among the crews looked up to him as a mentor. I'd been warned that many Vietnamese disliked and distrusted the Chinese—a relic of centuries of warfare between the two neighbors—but this certainly didn't apply to Dinh, who was an exceptional young Vietnamese just as Terry was an exceptional Chinese.

In fact, Dinh hadn't had any sleep at all because he had been talking to Terry at the hotel until 5 a.m. and then headed straight out to shoot. During their conversation, Dinh recalls that he told Terry repeatedly not to go back to the front. Like me, Dinh believed in luck and jinxes and thought that on your last day in a warzone, you shouldn't push your luck. Soldiers had the same beliefs, someone who was "short" (scheduled to go home in a few days) would be the last guy you'd ask to walk point on a patrol.

Terry suggested that Dinh go for the position that he would be leaving open at ABC News, and told him that he had already spoken to the managers about the younger man's skill and recommended they hired him.

Arnold Collins was coming in to replace Jim Bennett on the day in July 1972 that Terry Khoo and Sam Kai Faye made the fatal decision to go out and see if they could shoot any "bang bang" footage. (Courtesy Arnold Collins)

Later that morning, the ABC crew were relaxing at the hotel in Hue. Jim Bennett was briefing Arnie Collins, a correspondent so new that he was still wearing sandals. He needed to visit the black market and buy boots, ponchos, and all the other gear needed for work in the field. He'd tried to get it in Saigon but an almost unheard-of event—a raid on Saigon's thriving black market—had made that impossible:

On Wednesday, July 19th in Saigon, fate or luck intervened in an aborted trip to buy military camouflage. I was now equipped for the field with an ABC flak jacket and helmet but needed to buy a set of Camies and GI boots for the days to come up the road.

I was taken to Saigon's booming open-air Dan Sinh market, a black market where military clothing and equipment miraculously reappeared for sale, openly displayed in stacks along the many narrow covered aisles. We had just arrived there when, with a wail of sirens and screeching of tires, the police descended on the market in an apparent raid, and we backed our way out and returned to the bureau.

Though seemingly inconsequential, it was my lack of field gear the following day in the field that may in some way have changed lives—or had no importance at all.

But here's what happened.

On a brilliant sunny July 20th, bureau driver Mr. Thiep drove me back to Tan Son Nhut airbase together with my cameraman Sam Kai Faye and soundman Tran Van Kha. Poor Sam had only hours to live.

We boarded a chartered Beechcraft Baron two-engine executive aircraft piloted by an American civilian in unknown employ and climbed quickly to fly north over lush green hills and jungle to Phu Bai airport serving the ancient imperial capital of Hue, which was to be our base of operations for a regular ten-day deployment. Hue was at the time the jumping-off place for coverage of Quang Tri City, a city south of the DMZ that was still contested and had already been pounded into rubble.

With this crew, I was to relieve correspondent Jim Bennett, cameraman Terry Khoo, and soundman T. H. Lee. Picked up in the usual white news crew jeep with "TV" emblazoned in large taped letters across the windshield, we drove to the Huong Giang Hotel, a busy though not yet fully constructed newsman's hangout named for Hue's Perfume River. As we pulled into Huong Giang's large gravel driveway and parking area, we saw just a few other vehicles and a lone man sitting cross-legged on the large circular dirt and rock base that surrounded and protected a parking lot tree.

Decades later—I can still see him seated there. Terry Khoo jumped down and came to greet us.

"I wanted to meet the new correspondent," he told me pleasantly.[3]

Le Phuc Dinh had had good luck. Even before he reached the Quang Tri front, he saw the North and South Vietnamese in a skirmish close to Highway One near the My Chanh River. It wasn't a large-scale battle, but there were some airstrikes, and he got good footage. So good, that he thought it would make a story so he went back to Hue to get it shipped

In July 1972, Terry Khoo poses with soundman T. H. Lee. Lee, a black-belt martial artist, was the only journalist to escape the North Vietnamese ambush in Quang Tri. (Courtesy Yasutsune Hirashiki)

back to Saigon right away. He arrived at the Huong Giang Hotel before noon and met the two ABC crews at lunch in the dining room.

Later, Dinh told me that he actually didn't want Terry to see him that day. He knew that Terry would ask him what he had shot and might go after the story. Which is exactly what happened. Terry asked Dinh where he'd been and even though Dinh tried to minimize the action, NBC reporter Tom Streithorst and the NBC film shipper were excited about how good the footage was and that made Terry curious.

Arnie Collins picks up the story again:

> We had been sitting for perhaps ten minutes when Terry approached us and said he had just heard a rumor that a North Vietnamese tank had been seen to the west of Highway One, between Hue and Quang Tri City. He wanted to go up the road and check it out.
>
> You should understand that we were relieving Terry of his last Vietnam assignment, and he had been re-based to Germany and ABC's Bonn bureau. He had essentially shot his last footage of the war and with Jim and T. H. Lee was returning to Saigon where he would pack up and leave.
>
> Jim did not believe the rumor and had no intention of going back up the road—or of having his crew do so. He said "No" emphatically and argued that there was no tank and that he and they were flying back on our aircraft that afternoon. They would not be chasing any rumors.
>
> But twice more Terry approached our table, anxious to see for himself, never one to miss a story. On that third time, Jim said, "Oh, all right, go ahead but we're staying here. Arnie doesn't have any field gear."
>
> Terry was pleased and the two crews left together. Terry's last words that day after Jim had warned him to be careful were "It's all fate anyway, baby, so play it cool!"[4]

Dinh checked into his room and took a shower. When he returned to the dining room, Terry and Sam had left.

Terry's partner, soundman T. H. Lee, had gone to his room during lunch to take a nap and was woken by Terry and told that they were going up Highway One to see what was happening. He quickly got up, gathered his sound gear, and left Hue with Sam and Terry. There was a seat free in their jeep so South Vietnamese military cameraman Tran Van Nghia came as well.

When the ABC jeep arrived at the area near the My Chanh River that Dinh had mentioned, the skirmish was over. There were no houses in that area, just empty fields covered with high grass, small boulders, and small trees on both sides of the road. The crews stopped the jeep, surveyed the area, and spotted a line of South Vietnamese soldiers moving away from them about two hundred meters to the west. The end of the line was on a small path that ran parallel to the highway.

They parked the jeep and decided to take a short cut through the field, catch up to the soldiers, and shoot some footage. According to T. H. Lee, the field looked smooth and empty but actually high grass, trees, and rocks made it slow going. What was worse, the growth was high enough to hide a North Vietnamese ambush.

The first shots came from soldiers hidden in the thick brush until the South Vietnamese line had passed them by and was now moving toward the road. After the first volley of gunfire, the crews all dove to the ground and Lee, who was uninjured, called out to Terry, asking if he and Sam were all right.

Terry answered, "I'm OK, but Sam's been hit."

At the sound of their voices, more bullets were fired in the direction where they were pinned down, and Lee heard Terry moan in pain. Lee was a martial artist and in excellent condition so he rolled along the ground until he was near the road and then ran.

He hid by the jeep and waited for over 30 minutes, but no one else came out of the field. He drove quickly back to Hue, told the other ABC people what had happened, and asked for help rescuing Terry, Sam, and Nghia.

Arnie Collins recalled when he heard the news:

T. H. Lee burst back into the restaurant, wild and in tears. "Mr. Terry's dead," he told us, "Mr. Terry's dead." and he could barely get the story out.

Some ten or fifteen minutes north up the road you cross a tiny stream at a place called My Chanh and some hundred yards beyond, there to the west of the highway, our crews had spotted a large contingent of ARVN soldiers who had moved off the roadway and across the field toward a dominating ridge line. As the crews followed them, they came upon a slight decline, perhaps a bomb crater in the open field, and started to walk down through it when an enemy soldier—NVA or Viet Cong—fired on them at close range from a hiding place within that little bowl of sunken terrain.

Sam was struck in the stomach. Tran Van Nghia, an ARVN cameraman who freelanced for ABC, was killed outright, struck in the head, I was told. Terry, initially unwounded, stayed behind with Sam, both pinned down while the Korean soundman T. H. Lee, who was probably the toughest and most fit of the ABC news staff, escaped uninjured.

Jim and I jumped into a jeep and raced up the highway to the point just beyond the little stream where we saw an Australian reporter-cameraman, Neil Davis, standing on the edge of the road with an ARVN mortar man, behind an embankment of sandbags. Neil was a highly accomplished veteran newsman and was later to lose his own life in Southeast Asia while shooting another story. He had arrived on the scene some minutes before us.

Terry and Sam were pinned down less than 50 yards from where we stood but their attacker was still in there with them. When we called their names, he answered repeatedly with AK fire.

Our friends were silent.

The ARVN soldier who was with us had no orders to do anything but hold his position and the large contingent of ARVN soldiers who had preceded and drawn our crews into that field had reportedly split into two groups when they heard shots fired behind them. Skirting the ambush site on both sides, they had returned to the highway, posted the lone soldier, and returned to their base.

With no response from Terry and Sam, Jim and I and Neil jumped back into our jeeps, and raced back to Hue and to the US Military Command.

Some hours later they responded to the area, treating Terry and Sam as US nationals because of their ABC affiliation. But they turned us away when we tried to follow them back up the road. Jim returned to Saigon, and I reported the story.

That night I conducted a little remembrance service in the Huong Giang dining room where we all had lunched such a short time before.

A three-day battle with very real and present North Vietnamese units ensued over the bodies of our crew members, and the area was eventually bombed by US aircraft.[5]

ABC News contacted the regional South Vietnamese military and soldiers attempted a rescue mission but were driven off by heavy North Vietnamese fire from their hidden position in the center of the field. No one could reach the area where the three men could be lying wounded.

Kevin Delany and I went to Hue early next morning, July 21, on a chartered flight. We reached the location on the side of Highway One before noon and joined in the rescue operation until dusk. The situation only became worse as the quiet field had become the site of an extensive battle. As Arnie said in his letter, it turned out that there were quite a large number of North Vietnamese soldiers hidden in the shrubbery in the field where our men had been shot and, even though South Vietnamese soldiers and medics tried to reach them several times, the enemy would counterattack, and they were driven off under heavy fire.

Finally, the South Vietnamese had to call in artillery fire and bombard the exact position where Terry, Sam, and Nghia lay. A light reconnaissance plane flew over and reported that Terry and Sam were lying side by side but the pilot couldn't tell if they were alive or dead.

I wanted to go into the field with a white flag and beg the soldiers to release the men as an act of mercy. Kevin stayed next to me the entire time, partly to keep my spirits up, and partly to keep me from doing just such a desperate and dangerous act. Kevin, who was both a brave and gentle man, was as upset as I was but he knew that another crew member getting injured or killed would only make a disaster even worse.

This barren dip in the field is where the ambush occurred that killed Terry Khoo, Sam Kai Faye, and Tran Van Nghia. After the three were shot, a major battle erupted and air strikes and artillery were poured into this area. (Courtesy Koichiro Morita)

When night fell, we went back to the hotel without Terry and Sam. In the hotel that night, I ran into AP's Koichiro Morita and completely lost control of the emotion I had been holding tight inside my heart. I broke down and cried loudly like a child with stomach pains. I knew how loud I was, but I simply couldn't stop. The only other time I'd ever cried that hard was when I was eight years old and my father passed away.

Morita tried to calm me down, assuring me that there was still a possibility that they were injured but alive. Even as he tried to comfort me, his own face was covered with tears.

I said, "Terry would never come back by himself without a wounded Sam! If he was alive, he would already be carrying Sam, and they would have come out together a long time ago!"

I imagined Terry lying beside a wounded Sam, comforting and caring for him. If Sam was already dead, then Terry would have decided to die with him. That's how closely bound they were. As close as brothers. They would either come back together or die together. From the moment the first fatal shot was fired, their destiny had been decided.

I was told that the Saigon bureau had informed Winnie of the situation as she was on her way into Saigon from Hong Kong. I begged Kevin not to let her come up to Hue, and although she wanted to join us, she listened to Kevin's advice and remained in Saigon. That night, I used the new cursive typewriter that Terry had brought me from Hong Kong to write her a letter:

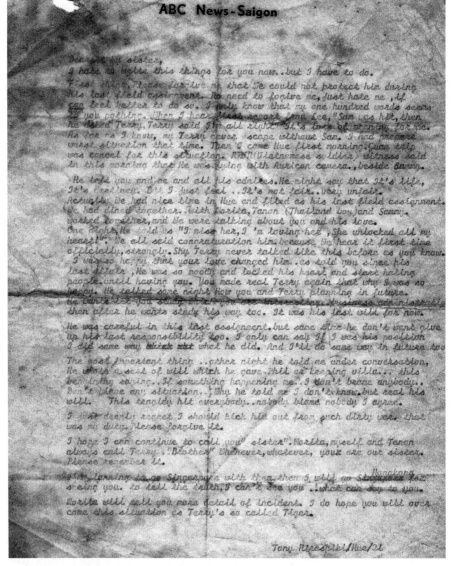

Initial letter to Winnie Ng by Tony Hirashiki using the typewriter that Terry Khoo had just brought from Hong Kong. Full transcript is on page 356. (Courtesy Yasutsune Hirashiki)[1]

It was written in childish English, and it was an awful letter. I couldn't even express my feelings. I just lined up a bunch of empty words.

On the third day after the shooting, the bodies of Terry, Sam, and Nghia were recovered from the battlefield and brought to a nearby military base. As the first reconnaissance had reported, Terry, Sam, and Nghia were lying side by side. Terry's camera was covered with mud, but it was right next to him. During the three-day battle, nearly three thousand shells had landed on that location, and we expected to find the bodies damaged from the bombing, but they were almost undamaged except by the heat. At least that's what I thought at the time, but I was too upset to really understand or remember almost anything.

At the base, a American officer asked Kevin and me to identify Terry and Sam. As we started to check the bodies, I lost control of my emotions again and burst into tears. I couldn't stop crying, and I couldn't even see the bodies clearly so it took a long time for me to identify them. I just felt weak and fragile and was crying like a little child.

Kevin remembered that day far more clearly than I did:

> Again your memory for detail is remarkable. But in the Quang Tri account there are several things that I recall somewhat differently.
>
> Yes, after Sam and Terry were hit, heavy fighting continued in that area and I recall that the day after they were hit, the ARVN tried very hard to drive the NVA from the field in which they were hit so they could be reached and evacuated. At that point, we did not know but believed that one or both were wounded but possibly still alive. My recollection is the ARVN took some wounded and maybe even had one or two killed in the attempt to try and evacuate Terry and Sam. I recall feeling badly that our concern for them—which we made known to both the ARVN and American military—had resulted in further casualties. Because the NVA was so hard to drive out of the area.
>
> I remember that MACV [US military command] ordered air strikes and the strikes repeatedly continued for two days—until on the third day the area was cleared of the enemy and it was possible to evacuate the bodies of Sam and Terry and ARVN cameraman Nghia.
>
> I recall that the bodies were brought to an ARVN base not too far from the fighting scene and you and I went to identify the remains. They were in an open-sided structure that looked something like a stable.
>
> Tony, here is a point where I think our recollections are somewhat different. I recall the bodies were quite scorched from having been out in the open field

during lots of shelling, bright sun and heat, and most particularly, many air strikes. (It was the poor condition of the bodies that prompted the decision to recommend the coffins remain closed when they arrived in Singapore. We were sure it would be too hard on the family.)

Yes, I recall you being quite emotional at the ARVN base as would be expected under the circumstances—and I was doing the best I could to keep my emotions in check.

My most vivid recollection is that you were on your knees and said, "This is Terry," And I looked and finally said quietly, "No Tony, I believe this is Sam."[6]

At this point, I had anger building in the bottom of my heart and felt as if I was going mad. I hated the soldiers who had killed Terry and Sam. Since it was the North Vietnamese who had done it, the North Vietnamese were now my enemy.

Even though I had been covering the war for so many years, I had always kept a distance from it, trying to be neutral and unbiased. I had never touched a weapon, not even a small pistol. I seldom used the word "enemy" on my caption sheet. Instead of saying Viet Cong or VC, I tried to write NLF (National Liberation Front) because it was not my war.

That day, it became my war. Whoever had killed my brothers, Terry and Sam, was my enemy. I shouted and cried out for the loss of my best friends and cursed at the top of my lungs those who had taken away my hopes and dreams of the future. More than the North Vietnamese soldiers, I hated myself because I had not protected my best friends, my brothers, from tragedy.

After we had confirmed their deaths, Morita, some soldiers who were colleagues of Nghia, and I went to the site. It was still too dangerous to go into the field so we stayed near the road. There we put up wooden crosses that said "Terry, Sam, Nghia's Hill." It was a temporary memorial, and I came back a few months later with Jean-Claude Malet and used local marble to build another memorial in the field where they'd died.

After their bodies had been recovered, and we had confirmed their deaths, Arnie Collins held a memorial service at the hotel. This is his recollection of that service:

"Terry and Sam Hill," the handmade memorial built by Tony Hirashiki and friends near the road. Fierce fighting and bombing prevented anyone from getting to the spot where Terry and Sam died until several days later. (Courtesy Koichiro Morita)

The next evening I conducted a memorial service in the restaurant of the Huong Giang hotel attended by some dozen or more correspondents, photographers, and camera crew members where everyone retold their Terry and Sam stories.

Terry was everyone's hero and was particularly remembered. Several Asian colleagues now believed that not only had Terry died as he would have wanted but that foreseeing some future "less noble" death, he had actually chosen to meet death on that field in Vietnam. My colleagues who had covered Vietnam and Cambodia for years with Terry Khoo and seen him emerge unscathed from every sort of violent encounter were shaken to the core by his death.[7]

Later, Arnie did a TV story about the continued fighting and the fact that Terence Khoo and Sam Kai Faye were the first ABC News cameramen to be killed in the Vietnam War. At the end of the piece, he made a point of saying how this particular location would be remembered:

```
                                          Cameramen TERRY KHOO and SAM KAI FAI
                                                  here
                                          went down in a hail of north
     body                                 vietnamese automatic rifle fire.
                                          South vietnamese medics tried to
     wounded ARVN                         get them out and were themselves
                          TWO              wounded.  TERRY and SAM lay out
                          TAKES            in the open and died while the
     GS fighting                          two sides exchanged fire.
                                          Arnold Collins ABC NEWS at MEE-CHON
```

The end of Arnold Collins' first script about the deaths of two of his friends and co-workers. Recorded on the first day after they were shot in July 1972, it was made to be altered if anyone was found alive. (Courtesy Arnold Collins)

ABC News broadcast Terry's unfinished feature piece—the one he had wanted to go to Quang Tri to complete. During a previous assignment, Terry had found a young North Vietnamese soldier's body and read his diary and looked at the pictures of his family. Terry had been trying to finish a profile of this young man when, ironically, he was killed by the man's North Vietnamese comrades.

The ABC office had arranged to send the bodies of Terry and Sam to Saigon by military airplane to be re-examined by medical experts before they were brought back to their homes in Singapore. When Kevin and I returned to the Saigon bureau, Winnie was waiting there. We hugged, but I didn't have any words to say to her. I just repeated, "I'm sorry" while we were hugging. I was unable to look her in the eyes.

It was once again convenient to be a non–English speaker, unable to say the right things to offer comfort or condolences to a person in such pain. Even if I had been able to speak English or Chinese fluently, I couldn't have found any words to comfort Winnie.

Before the bodies were flown back to Singapore, a memorial service was held at a prestigious sports club in Saigon. It was a large and crowded event attended by colleagues, well-known journalists, unknown young reporters, cameramen, high-ranking officers, common soldiers, UN forces, local folk show actresses, and Vietnamese singers. It showed how popular Terry and Sam were. They were both great journalists and professionals and Terry Khoo was simply one of those people you are lucky to meet once in your life.

ABC executives Bill Sheehan and Jack Bush, were flying directly to Singapore to attend the funerals and Kevin Delany asked me to accompany the caskets, make sure the families were taken care of, and stay until the burials. Jean-Claude Malet, T. H. Lee, and Morita came as well, and I was sure that Kevin had asked Morita to go to Singapore with us because I was simply too emotionally broken to handle the details.

At the airport in Singapore, there was some confusion with the baggage handlers and, after waiting a short time, journalists, executives, and technicians simply carried Terry's and Sam's caskets out.

Kevin had given us strict orders to make sure that the caskets remained closed no matter if the families requested that they be opened. As he said in his letter, the condition of the bodies was simply too much to expect them to bear, and he didn't want them to hurt anymore than they already were.

Although that was a simple order, it turned out to be the hardest part of the mission. Every family member wanted to see Terry and Sam—to be certain in their hearts that their loved ones were dead and say a final farewell.

Just before the funeral service was held, Terry's mother told me that she wanted to change Terry's clothes before his burial. For me, that was the hardest moment because, as his mother, she had the right but I believed that it would be painful for her to see Terry in his condition so I told her, "Mother, I'll change the clothes. I'm his brother, I'm your son, I'm a member of your family, so let me do this."

For over six years, she had treated me as another son so she allowed me to take over this task. Morita, Malet, and I changed Terry into new clothes. Sam Fai Kaye's family opened the casket despite our request, and his favorite niece fainted and was ill for several days after she saw him.

Before the burials, we asked both families if it was possible to bury Terry and Sam side by side—the way they had died. But Sam was a Buddhist and Terry was a Christian so they were given separate funeral services and buried in different cemeteries.

When it came time to bury Terry, his mother grabbed on the corner of the casket and wouldn't let go. She just held on and wept, crying out her son's name over and over.

"Terry. Terry."

It was a heart-rending voice. Finally, I held her tiny shoulders and pulled her hands from the casket, hugged her shoulders tightly, and began to cry out as loudly as she did. It was the only way I knew to comfort Terry's mother—crying with her from the bottom of my heart.

A few days after the memorial service in Singapore, I wrote several letters to the people who were closest to Terry. Some of them were life-long friends, others had on many occasions worked closely with Terry. It was tough to write the details of the tragedy. I got back very few responses. I knew that they also didn't have words to express their feelings.

Yung Mei, Terry's best friend, wrote me back half a year later:

> I was extremely upset when my friend from Singapore cabled me in Peking. And even now, I find tears when Joey and I remember his visit. Further, I miss being able to write to him. It was always such a pleasure to hear from him—He was truly one of the very few people I've known and do know who was so utterly selfless and full of warmth for others—His loss is everybody's loss.

David Snell—Terry's favorite correspondent and a close friend—wrote me in January 1993, twenty-one years later:

> Dear Tony,
>
> It was great to hear from you after so many years. Mary Lou and I have thought of you often over the years and reread your kind letter about Terry. For many years his picture (taken in our New York apartment) has been on the wall of my study along with the cover picture from ASIA Magazine 1968. The picture is of a village elder who seems to be crying for his country. Printed across the picture are the words "Vietnam 1968. How much longer?"
>
> After all these years we still feel the pain of his death. But increasingly, we also feel so very lucky to have known him and loved him.[8]
>
> I don't know if we told you that I was in Chicago when Mary Lou called to say she'd heard the news about Terry on NBC's Today Show. They didn't know whether he was alive or dead at the time, but Mary Lou, nursing our new baby—Christopher—was so upset she couldn't go on.
>
> I was scheduled to stay in Chicago for another week, but called the assignment desk saying, "I'm going home." They didn't understand and tried to talk me out of it, but I said, "I'm going." All weekend long we kept telling each other, if anyone can make it out of that situation, Terry could. We pictured him pretending to be

dead until the fighting subsided and prayed for the miracle you talk about. When word finally came, we were devastated.

Your story brings it all back. The tragedy of his death but also the wonderful person he was.

Another Terry story: Before his last trip to New York, he called from Hong Kong to ask if there was anything he could buy for us there. I was in Mississippi when his call came to me. It was in the middle of the night and I couldn't get my head on straight. Finally, I said, "My father-in-law would like a Pentax camera like the one I have." Terry brought it as well as a 130 mm lens he thought I needed, but when I went to pay him he said, "You can't repay a friend."

That has been my definition of "friendship" ever since. What a privilege it was to know him. Thanks for the reminder of that.

Your friend, David[9]

Mrs. Hien Boase—Terry's best friend and colleague at the ABC bureau:

I was very lucky to have Terry as a friend but sadly it did not last long because he was gone so soon.

But sometimes you have to believe in fate. I remember in 1967 Terry disappeared on mission in Cambodia. We thought something terrible had happened but somehow he escaped and was welcomed like a hero back in Saigon. He was interviewed and sent to the US to explain his experience. (Do you remember this incident Tony?)

The second time, in early 1971, Terry was almost killed when he was refused permission at the last minute to board a helicopter with Francois Sully and General Do Cao Tri. The helicopter crashed and Sully and General were killed, Then another helicopter, four famous photographers were killed in Laos. Terry sent a letter to me dated April 25, 1971 of this incident in which he wrote "Spent harrowing days in Laos, fearing against fear. That's something one cannot explain in words. I was very lucky, indeed very lucky. Poor Henri, Larry, Ken and Shima—all good friends and exemplary in their own respective fields. I was supposed to have got onto the same helicopter instead and learnt of the tragedy the next day when I got out of Laos. I hate to think about it; it makes me sick. I am thinking of getting out."

Unfortunately, he was not able to do so. Poor Terry was able to avoid death three times but not the fourth one—.[10]

Sam's elder brother Sam Kai Yee was very upset and blamed us for persuading Sam to get involved in the Vietnam War. He was particularly angry towards Terry, who first introduced his brother to Vietnam. I understood the anger and sadness of Sam's brother and his need to blame someone for his pain. He and his family all loved Sam Kai Faye so much.

Three years later, on the anniversary of their deaths, after receiving my cable dedicated to Sam's memory, he responded in a very warm letter that he finally recognized his younger brother Sam Kai Faye had found good friends and enjoyed our friendship until the moment his fate came. I felt forgiven, although only a little bit.

Sam was cremated, and his ashes interred at Mandai Columbarium.

The marble and gold face of the memorial that holds the ashes of Sam Kai Faye in a Singapore cemetery. (Courtesy Chin Kah Chong)

Terry's mother made a beautiful tombstone for her son. She had ordered the best marble from Italy.

The inscription on his tombstone reads:

A FINE AND COURAGEOUS JOURNALIST WHO DIED AS HE HAD LIVED. TENACIOUS YET COMPASSIONATE, HIS SELFLESS CONCERN FOR OTHERS PUT HIM IN DANGER'S PATH MANY A TIME. ON THE BATTLEFIELD HE WENT BEYOND HIS DUTIES AS JOURNALIST, RISKING HIS LIFE FOR US AND SOUTH VIETNAMESE FORCES TO EVACUATE WOUNDED CIVILIANS. HE DIED IN ACTION IN A WAR-TORN BATTLEFIELD IN QUANG TRI. TRULY A MAN WITH COURAGE OF SOUL.

Sam and Terry were always together, helping each other as real brothers. Then they died in Vietnam together and went back home together. I have often imagined what kind of conversation Terry and Sam had in the last moments before they died. While taking care of a wounded Sam, Terry might have said, "Don't worry Sam, I will go with you. We'll always be together no matter where we go."

Somewhere, Terry and Sam might be taking beautiful pictures for the Heaven edition of *National Geographic*.

The elegant marble memorial to Terry Khoo erected by his family in Singapore. He bequeathed enough of his life insurance that, fifty years later, medical students are still receiving scholarships. (Courtesy Chin Kah Chong)

CHAPTER 23

SURVIVOR'S GUILT

I came back from Singapore grief-stricken and exhausted. Those ten days had been the cruelest nightmare I had suffered in my entire life. The first person to call when I returned to Saigon was bureau chief Kevin Delany. Under stress and in total chaos, Kevin had handled the aftermath of the tragedy like a true professional, but he was also hurting inside. He had lost a good friend who had also been the most valuable man on his staff.

We talked, and Kevin told me not to be bothered by anything anyone said about me. I asked, "What were people saying? Was I too emotional? Too unreliable?"

Kevin told me that several people had decided that I was partly responsible for the deaths because, they said, Tony and Terry were always competing on the job and taking risks to do better than the other guy. Eventually, our robust competition and my aggressiveness had indirectly led to the tragedy.

I was shocked.

It was true that Terry and I had challenged each other every day since we first met six years before. We were the best of friends, and I told anyone who asked that Terry was the best, and it was my goal to be as good as he was. I wanted to be like him, not only as a journalist but as a good man. It was something that transcended competition. I had my eyes set on Terry because he was my mentor and life-long friend.

Now people were saying that my competitive spirit had forced Terry to take unnecessary risks, push that one step too far, and had resulted in tragedy. I thought for a long time about that accusation. Was it my desire to be as good as Terry that brought about his death?

After much thought, I realized that I could not deny my responsibility.

I'd seen Terry as invulnerable and iron-willed. I didn't think he would ever die or even be wounded. Look at how he had survived in An Loc, a town where death reigned supreme.

But I had to recognize how careless I had been. If I had loved and cared for him in the same way that he did for me, I guess I should have stopped him from going on that last trip. Instead, our final telex exchange kept repeating in my mind. I'd sent him the glib words, "SEE YOU IN QUANG TRI" to which he had written back, "SEE YOU IN QUANG TRI. REGARDS TERRY"

The fact was, it had bothered me even before I heard that I was being blamed. Had I invited Terry to a city of death and he had gone because of me? I should have known it was too dangerous, and I should have stopped him from coming up to Quang Tri.

It was hard to admit my guilt, but I could have prevented the tragedy if I had just listened when Roger and Terry tried to warn me to slow down.

The next day, I went to see Kevin and said that I wanted to have all the stories I'd shot removed from competition for awards and that I never wanted to have my work submitted for awards, particularly if it was coverage of war.

I had several great stories submitted for awards that year: "Kontum Battle" with Dick Shoemaker, "Highway Thirteen" with Drew Pearson and "ARVN Marines Assault" with Roger Peterson. I had thought that this was finally going to be my year, but it should not come at the price of my best friend's death.

Kevin approved my request and told New York to withdraw all Hirashiki stories from participation in any film contests. I didn't regret it at all. I felt less weighed down by my survivor's guilt.

Getting an award for taking war pictures and filming the suffering of humankind was wrong. It's an important and honorable job to cover war and tragedy as a news cameraman, but it is a serious thing and not something to do just for a statue or a plaque. I continued this practice for the rest of my career. After the Vietnam War, I covered dozens of other wars and tragedies, including 9/11, and never submitted my work for an award.

Thirty-five years later, after he read this recollection, Kevin Delany wrote me his point of view regarding the tragedy. His compassion and genuine care for his cameramen had never changed:

> First, I must tell you, Tony, that I did not look forward to reading this chapter because, of course, I knew how it ended. It was painful for me to recall the events though I know it must have been much more difficult for you to write about them. You had to re-live so many difficult memories and tell how the events unfolded every step of the way.
>
> At any rate, I don't pretend to be a psychologist, but I think you had to write about Terry and Sam's fate to exorcise their ghosts from your system. Just to get it off your chest after all these years. By that, I don't mean that you had any responsibility for what happened to them—because I don't believe that for a minute—nor would any reasonable person.
>
> It was essentially just bad luck that brought on their very sad deaths. Anyone can second guess things ... if I only had done this or that. But that is hindsight and no one could guess what would take place in that field that day. For that matter, after the fact, I could blame myself for allowing Terry to go to Hue at all. But Terry was a strong personality and once he made up his mind it was very hard to dissuade him that he should not go and none of us envisioned him getting into a combat situation like that on the trip as he was just supposed to provide orientation about the area to Sam and nothing more.
>
> I can understand why Jim Bennett might feel that he should have stopped Terry from going up Highway One. But after saying "no" to him twice, strong-willed Terry persuaded Jim the third time he asked. Jim could never imagine what would happen to Terry and Sam and cannot be blamed for what occurred.[1]

I didn't realize it until years later, but Jim Bennett indeed was tortured by many of the same doubts and pains that I was suffering. Decades after the war. Jim gave a single interview on the event and when I read it I realized how much the incident had hurt him. The only difference was that it was the memory of Sam Kai Faye and not Terry Khoo that was only a "blink away." Larry Engelmann began the interview with a description of Jim Bennett:

> He can't stop thinking about the war. Not a day goes by, not one, when he doesn't find himself thinking about it again, remembering things that happened on particular days, words that passed between men walking down a jungle path,

Jim Bennett poses with fellow correspondent Charles Burke at a Saigon bureau party. (Courtesy Ip Jim Choi)

the beautiful faces of children, the laughter of the young soldiers, the taste of "33" beer at the end of an exhausting day, the last moments and last words between close friends.

Then he wonders why he remembers these things, why he's been unable to tuck them safely away in some remote compartment of the memory where a special effort must be made to pull them out. But it hasn't happened. And when he tries to forget, he only remembers more vividly. Nothing seems to work.

So, over time, he's learned to live with the past always just a blink away.

Jim Bennett:

"I had gotten kind of close to Sam and I was close to Terry too, but when Sam first came into country which was about six months before I had kind of taken him under my wing."

"He and I had been up in Hue before. And we did a marvelous story that I kind of thought more or less typified what was happening during that particular offensive, which was a losing proposition. We were coming back, having been up to the front, so to speak, and here was this long funeral procession with two or three caskets being carried and the wailing families were trailing behind and they were going down the road and they started to cut across the open field. And it was a very dismal dim drizzly day, cold and dank and death was in the air, about the only way I can characterize it."

"They were three ARVN soldiers who had been killed in one of the recent battles. It had to be recent because they believe in burying the dead on the same day. It was a Catholic ceremony too. The priest with the altar boys were trailing behind in this procession."

"And I said, "Let's shoot this Sam. I think this story tells a hell of a lot, because there were three of them.""

"Well, we went over, he grabbed the hand camera, with the three lenses on the front, Bell & Howell, and I was going to wide track it, get the wide sound. I wasn't going to do any interview, but we did need natural sound. It was great sound with the wailing and so forth going on."

"So we followed them over and they were going through the liturgy there at the grave site and they started to lower the caskets into the hole in the ground. And I'm standing on the opposite side from where Sam was filming, and I looked up at Sam, and my God, he had his lens cap on."

"And Jesus I just came apart. And I just screamed at him, jerked him around and really landed on him terribly. He felt so bad."

"Well he managed to recoup. He got his lens cap off. There was enough of the ceremony going on that I got it. It did make a marvelous story. It typified what I was trying to show of what was happening. The lost cause and the look on these people's faces and the entire atmosphere was so symbolic of what was actually happening in those days. And I did manage to get an excellent story. One of the best ones I think I did."

"Sam felt so bad about it and I really just couldn't get over the fact he had his lens cap on. And then, when he went like that, I never had a chance to even say I'm sorry."

"So I quit. I quit and moved my family to the island of Penang off the coast of Malaysia. I put my kids in school there. I stayed down for about three months. I just had to have time off I guess."

"But I literally had quit."[2]

I can assure you from personal experience that there is no cure for survivor's guilt, even time only dulls the pain. Kevin Delany tried to tell me a great deal of what caused this tragedy was simply part of what made up a good war journalist:

Finally, all good cameramen and correspondents have a strong competitive instinct, and that is what makes them so good. But to say that competitiveness pushed other cameramen or correspondents into dangerous situations and somehow made them responsible for unexpected circumstances on a battlefield is just absolute nonsense.

I say this, Tony, because you should not in any way blame yourself for what took place in Quang Tri. Terry and Sam did not plan or want to get into that dangerous situation but unfortunately it happened.

Before I go further I want to digress a bit. I know you recall how Mrs. Khoo came to Saigon about three or four months (?) after his death and insisted that she had to go to the location in Quang Tri where Terry died. She said that according to her Buddhist faith, she had to do so or Terry's soul would wander endlessly without rest. So she did go there and complete her mission. I forget, but didn't you go with her?[3]

In fact, Terry's mother came to Vietnam accompanied by Winnie and her daughter-in-law, Polly, intending to visit the Quang Tri frontline to comfort Terry's soul. We dissuaded her from going up Highway One and instead, Malet and I took her and her family all over Saigon to the places that Terry had loved going to. She was satisfied. Maybe she felt that Terry's soul was not at Quang Tri, but decided to stay with me and all of Terry's many friends in Saigon so she let it be.

CHAPTER 24

CEASEFIRE

Even though it became apparent that the peace negotiations were in the home stretch, both sides still fought furiously to gain and hold every square mile of territory before a treaty tranformed what had been won in battle into a legal fact on paper. Only six months after Terry Khoo had predicted the end of the war, a treaty was signed mandating that a ceasefire would go into effect on January 28.

I was in Alice Springs, Australia when President Nixon announced the ceasefire and peace treaty. Irv Chapman and I were doing feature stories, including one of the treatment of the Aborigines but I begged Irv and the New York desk to allow me to go back to Saigon and cover the end of the war I had lived with for so long.

The months since the deaths of Terry and Sam had been terrible. I believed that I had not only lost mentors and friends but my luck as well. In my own eyes, I had become once again, a less-than-average cameraman with "two left hands."

On the day that the ceasefire came into effect, I was sent with camera and tripod to the Catholic church that stood next to the central post office: a major Saigon landmark. I had my camera locked on the clock tower ready for the moment that the clock would click over to 8 a.m. and the bells would ring.

My correspondent was Ted Koppel, the young ace of ABC News who had been covering Vietnam and Hong Kong for years and was now a respected expert on the region and the workings of diplomacy. Ted was standing with the church behind him so that I could begin with a close-up of the church clock and then slowly pull back and pan down to Ted as the bells rang. In the meantime, he would be talking about the meaning of this moment—peace finally after the long and painful war.

I was practicing the camera move so that it would be perfect when the bell began to ring.

Early.

Several minutes early.

There was no choice—I had to begin the move and reveal Ted. In the streets around the church, all sorts of vehicles—buses, jeeps, cars, trucks, rickshaws, motorcycles—were blowing their horns and making as much noise as they could. Ted was, as usual, calm and steady and did the stand-up perfectly even though the church clock hadn't done its job. It was a fitting ending to the Vietnam War where so little had gone as planned.

I worked that entire day, but I couldn't stop wishing that Terry and Sam were there to see this, and I thought of them everywhere I went.

I went out on the streets to see what changed on this first day of peace. There was a tiny tourist agent who had opened an office near the Majestic Hotel and workers were pasting up posters that said "Welcome to Beautiful Vietnam" and "Visit Peaceful Vietnam." The Vietnamese are sensible people so they were already hoping to make money in the new postwar Vietnam.

I took a picture of a policeman on a street corner taking a nap under the shade of a big tree. It's something you wouldn't have seen in the days when guerrillas could attack at any time.

There was a final briefing by the Military Assistance Command, Vietnam, an event that, for seven years, had been known as the "Five O'clock Follies." Over the years, the briefings had become more like extended arguments than real briefings, but everyone still covered them for the official take on the day's events.

On this last day, American military spokesman Major J. Faubus gave the report. It was short, there had been a few dead and wounded over the previous day and, for once, the briefing was quiet—no arguments or harsh questions and angry answers. Major Faubus made a short comment to the press and closed with "Thank you and goodbye, ladies and gentlemen."

My notes show that Ted Koppel was there, but I don't remember that he said anything or asked a question.

Early in the afternoon, Arnie Collins, Malet, and I drove up Highway One to Tay Ninh, northwest of Saigon. Before he arrived in Vietnam, Collins had been based in Cairo, Egypt and he said that he'd done more stories in his first three months in Vietnam than he had in three years in Cairo. He was 37 years old with red hair and was a quiet and pleasant man to work with.

We were going to Tay Ninh because we'd been told that there had been fighting around the city for the past few days, and we wanted to see what had happened now that the ceasefire was in effect. I guess we were expecting to see peaceful scenes of the countryside where farmers would be celebrating the new peaceful Vietnam.

We were stopped at a checkpoint about fifty kilometers from Saigon and told that the highway had been cut up ahead. Local guerrillas had attacked the road yesterday, and now government troops were moving up the road in armored personnel carriers and tanks, intent on opening the road.

They were advancing through a densely populated area, and it had been tough house-to-house fighting for the troops accompanying the armor. Some of the houses were burning, and bullets were flying everywhere—including right over our heads. This wasn't the peaceful celebration we had seen that morning in Saigon.

This was business as usual.

When we heard the bullets *zip* over, we ducked and took cover in the courtyard of a house. It stank of chicken shit. Arnie was holding his helmet with one hand to keep it from flying off. I looked at my watch and saw that it was 2 p.m., only six hours since peace had been declared and here we were, lying next to each other like sardines in a can with all of us face down in chicken shit.

On the other hand, it was a great place for a stand-upper, so I motioned Malet to hand Arnie the microphone. Arnie looked surprised, and he mumbled something like "idiot cameraman." I made a rolling gesture with my hand to let him know the camera was recording, and he began to ad-lib the situation as bullets and shells went off in the background.

He was very natural and quick thinking, and it reminded me of how Howard Tuckner used to work in his famous crouching style. I couldn't hear what Arnie was saying in what he described as a "lay-downer" but here is what he wrote in that night's story for ABC:

(open; Collins lie-downer in road way)

THIS IS ARNOLD COLLINS SOUTHEAST OF TAY NINH CITY … AND MANY HOURS AFTER THE CEASEFIRE WAS TO HAVE GONE INTO EFFECT. THIS IS THE WAY IT'S BEING OBSERVED.

BUT AS THE CEASEFIRE CAME INTO EFFECT AT THE ROADBLOCK … IT ALSO ENDED.

(Chopper

ARVN watch or Talk radio)

NORTH VIETNAMESE SOLDIERS JUST IN FRONT OF THE TREELINE OPENED UP ON ARMORED PERSONEL CARRIERS SENT IN TO CHECK THE ROAD … THE TIME WAS TWO MINUTES AFTER 8 IN THE MORNING … WHILE SAIGON'S PEACE BELLS WERE STILL RINGING.

(Heavy fighting)

…

(Lie-down closer in firefights)

FROM ALL THIS, IT SEEMS THAT THE CEASEFIRE WILL BE LATE ARRIVING HERE, DAMPENING PROSPECTS FOR A NEGOTIATED PEACE.

THIS IS ARNOLD COLLINS, ABC NEWS NEAR TAY NINH CITY.[1]

CHAPTER 25

FALL OF CAMBODIA

The Vietnam War had ended, or at least paused, but in Cambodia, war was raging. The government's troops were still poorly trained and badly equipped, and had been mauled by tough North Vietnamese regulars for years. Now, most of the fighting was against Cambodian Khmer Rouge forces—well-equipped, fresh fighters, supported completely by North Vietnam.

Many large cities, including the capital, Phnom Penh, were surrounded by insurgent forces, but that didn't stop refugees from flooding into the city as fighting spread across the countryside. In the beginning, the government helped the war refugees, even going as far as opening the national stadium and the grounds of the royal palace for emergency housing but now there was simply no more space.

By the spring of 1973, the Khmer Rouge were so close that they could shell and rocket anywhere in Phnom Penh. Since they couldn't avoid civilian areas, or didn't bother to try, there were mass funerals throughout the city with Buddhist monks leading long processions through the streets.

Inevitably, as Cambodia's situation worsened, news executives thought the story was better, and we began to see photographers, reporters, TV correspondents, and crews arriving at the press hotel. These were old friends regardless of who they worked for or against. The conversations would stop when we thought of all those who were gone and then begin again with a sigh. Yes, it was a terrible story to cover, but it was still good to see old friends again—especially after so many had been lost.

In those days, it seemed as if every member of the press in Phnom Penh had experienced the reality of how close the line is between life and death in war journalism. Some were recovering from injuries, some had been almost killed, some had been captured and either escaped or talked their way free, others had been ambushed or had shrapnel from a bombardment just miss them even as others were killed.

In many ways, we all felt that we were pushing our luck every time we tried to cover a story. We didn't tend to get depressed or afraid but we would get pretty wild and crazy once the job was done and we were safe in the hotel. Most people drank or smoked marijuana—which was legal in Cambodia—and we would all talk and talk, remember people and places and just try to keep from being alone with our thoughts.

As always, there were new faces, young reporters and kids with single cameras around their necks looking for a lift to the front. One Cambodian photographer was nicknamed "Moon Face" because his face was almost perfectly round. His real name was Tim Kim Heang, and he was working as a freelance photographer, but he was also a well-known comedian and had appeared in several Cambodian movies. Of course, once the war began, no one was making any movies and especially not comedies, so he couldn't find any acting jobs and began to take pictures with an old Pentax camera that somebody had given to him.

In 1971, Moon Face, UPI reporter Kate Webb, and a group of journalists, had been captured by insurgent troops—a combination of Khmer Rouge and North Vietnamese forces. After 24 days, they were all released and, according to Kate Webb, it was Moon Face who saved her life.

When they were captured, one of the soldiers pointed his gun at her and shouted, "My?" which means "American?"

Moon Face quickly answered "Anglais! Anglais!" meaning British. Kate was actually a New Zealander, but she had no doubt that his quick reaction had saved her from being killed or taken off into captivity.

Once he was known as "Moon Face" a comedian on Cambodian movies, but in 1973, Tim Kim Heang was a freelance photographer and "fixer" for the networks. When the UPI staff was kidnapped by the Khmer Rouge in 1971, they credited "Moon Face" for their release. (Courtesy Yasutsune Hirashiki)

Moon Face and I became close colleagues, and he would often stay in my room at the Hotel Monorom on those days we didn't go out on a story. He didn't speak much English, but he knew some French and Vietnamese. I didn't speak the Khmer language, but somehow we communicated well without using any proper language at all. It was a crazy quilt of English, Vietnamese, Khmer, and lots of body language. Moon Face was particularly good at it from his training as a comedian. Only weeks later, he would send one last roll of film out with a friend and be swept under the genocidal rule of the Khmer Rouge.

Before the Vietnam War ended, Korean cameraman Joseph Lee had settled in Phnom Penh as a staffer for ABC News. At one point, he was captured and held by Khmer Rouge troops for almost a month. He told me the story on one of those long nights in Phnom Penh. He was following Cambodian government forces on a small operation when the unit he was with went up against a stronger Khmer Rouge force and fled. Joe was positioned too close to the front to run, and instead hid in a rice field with his face in the dirt.

After an hour, he thought the insurgents had left, so he crawled out of the rice paddy, and immediately was captured by a small unit of Khmer Rouge. As they marched him back to their base camp, Joe secretly tore up all of his IDs and press passes. The 300,000 Korean troops who fought alongside the Americans in Vietnam were known as fierce fighters and hated by the enemy.

When Joe was young, Korea had been under Japanese occupation, and he had been given the Japanese name Ichiro Shimizu so that was the name he gave to his captors. He spoke Japanese fluently and had learned Vietnamese in Saigon.

Then Joe had a stroke of luck. The troops that captured him were under the command of North Vietnamese officers. As soon as he reached the base camp, Joe talked to them in a mix of English and Vietnamese and explained that he was a journalist and cameraman. Again, he was cautious; he actually spoke Vietnamese quite well but he didn't want the officers to know that he'd lived in South Vietnam, so he mashed up his words to seem like a Japanese—by and large, no one hated the Japanese.

ABC cameraman Joseph Lee had moved to Phnom Penh permanently and still was captured by a rebel unit. For a month, he hid his Korean identity, and developed a rapport with his captors. In 1973 Cambodia, the line between war and crime was vague and extremely dangerous. (Courtesy Yasutsune Hirashiki)

In time, he became friendly with one of the North Vietnamese advisers and was treated as a guest more than as a prisoner. He wasn't handcuffed or tied up since he didn't attempt to escape. The adviser showed him pictures of his wife and family back in Hanoi. Joe said he seemed to be very lonely and enjoyed talking to someone besides the Khmer Rouge soldiers he led. Joe pretended to be learning Vietnamese from the officer in long conversations about many things—anything, in fact, except the war.

The most dangerous moment came on the day he was released. Just before he was to be let go, the North Vietnamese officer returned all of his belongings, spreading them all out on a table. He would carefully note down each item and Joe would sign for it. The danger came when the officer came to his ID holder.

Joe was terrified. What if the man looked at the almost-empty wallet and realized there were no IDs? Instead, the officer handed it back with a smile and said, "Your wife is very beautiful."

Joe's relief was short-lived. His wife was smiling at him in a traditional Korean outfit instead of a Japanese kimono. Joe was frozen; had the North Vietnamese officer known all along that he'd lied about his nationality? Why didn't he accuse Joe of lying? Why hadn't he been punished or killed if the man realized he really was Korean? Would he really release him or was this just a final trick and they would shoot him as he walked away, just as he thought he was free?

Joe told me that this was the most frightening moment of all the weeks he'd been in captivity. His mind was racing through every scenario and every possibility. After the paperwork had been completed, the officer shook Joe's hand and assigned a young Khmer Rouge soldier to escort Joe to a road that led to a government-controlled area. Even as he walked along the jungle trails, Joe was worried that the soldier might have orders to shoot him in the back so he tried to walk side-by-side as he would with a friend. When the man waved him forward to the road, Joe said "Thanks" in Khmer and walked rather quickly to freedom.

At this point, we weren't going out into the field much because, with Khmer Rouge shells and rockets falling every day in every part of Phnom Penh, there were enough stories right there in the city.

Shells fell anywhere at any time, hitting hospitals, schools, markets, anything. In those days, ABC News was based on the third floor of the modern Monorom Hotel on Monivong Street, Phnom Penh's main street. As was the usual custom, other news outlets stayed in the same hotel so they could get news and rumors quickly.

United Press International's Pulitzer Prize-winning photographer Toshio Sakai was staying in a room on the fourth floor. Sakai had won his Pulitzer in 1967 with a photo of American soldiers in a monsoon rain—one man on guard and the other taking a nap under a poncho. It was titled "Dreams of Better Times." One day on a shoot, Sakai's foxhole was much deeper than mine but he said that if it got bad, I could jump in his shelter. Now that's a good friend.

Now Sakai was assigned to cover Cambodia for UPI. When rockets and shells began to strike quite near our hotel, he decided that the safest place to sleep was in the bath tub. Indeed, a steel tub was safe even if it was a bit reminiscent of a coffin so it wasn't long before several of us were sleeping fully clothed in our dry bath tubs: we even kept our shoes on.

It was like being a fireman.

There would be an explosion.

First, we would check to see if we were still alive and then we would climb out of our tubs to film the story.

One evening, Jean-Claude Malet and I were relaxing in his room after a good dinner. We weren't really doing anything, just chatting. Malet was lying on his bed and I was sitting in a big hotel chair.

Suddenly, the sound of an incoming shell, *shyurururu* and then the enormous *BANG!*

We both went to the balcony to see where the shell had hit. I don't recommend this since most artillery crews don't bother to re-aim and one shell is generally followed by a second. The second round hit trees less than twenty feet from where we were standing. It was so close, it wasn't even like a sound, it was more like a flash of lightning. We were covered with dirt, dust, and branches and quickly retreated into the bath tub.

After a few nervous moments, we realized that our luck had held. Neither of us had even been scratched. Several shells had exploded close to me in Vietnam but this was the closest ever.

Phnom Penh was surrounded by the Khmer Rouge by January 1975 and rockets dropped into every area of the city. As Tony said, "You would hear an explosion, check to see if you were still alive, and run to cover the story." After all the time Jean-Claude Malet and Tony Hirashiki had spent on the frontlines, the closest call was in 1975 while they were talking in a Phnom Penh hotel room. Artillery struck right outside and they went out to watch. The second shell hit the balcony and Malet found a red-hot piece of shrapnel sunk deep in the pillow where his head had rested a moment before. (Courtesy Jean-Claude Malet)

After several more rounds didn't quite reach the hotel and landed in the buildings across the street, Malet got out of our bath tub foxhole to see how much his room had been damaged.

I heard him scream and ran out. Malet was a cool and calm guy and had been in combat many many times. I'd never heard him scream and now he was pale and shaking as he pointed at his bed.

There was a sharp, fist-sized piece of metal sticking right out of the pillow where his head had rested only moments before. The metal was still too hot to touch—it was shrapnel from the second shell that had gone past us as we stood on the balcony. It would have killed him had it had struck only seconds earlier.

In early March, a delegation of American congressmen visited Phnom Penh on a "fact-finding" mission. After two days they announced that Cambodia would get no more aid or military assistance and left.

The Khmer Rouge had held their fire while the delegation was in the city but the bombardment began again at dawn. The first wave of shells landed in the middle of the central market. Frank Mariano and I ran from place to place and filmed the civilian casualties. By late morning, we had our story shot and went back to the hotel.

Just before noon, shells began to drop right outside my window again. I got my camera and went out to shoot. Right outside the hotel, the street was a scene from hell. Among the dead, dozens of wounded people were crawling, screaming, or just collapsed on the pavement.

I remember one woman holding her dead baby in her arms and crying in Khmer, "Why did you kill my baby? What for? It's enough. Just stop! Why do you continue to fight?"

One of our hotel security guards had been killed instantly and the doorman was badly wounded. Frank Mariano stopped a passing bicycle rickshaw and tried to get the doorman into the back to get him to a hospital but he died in Frank's arms.

Suddenly, I realized this wasn't just a dead body, it was a man I'd talked to and shared cigarettes with. He was a nice man and now he was dead. Also injured was a cyclo driver who always seemed to be available when I needed to go somewhere. Today, he was wounded but I couldn't help him.

I suppose I could have comforted him but I think I went a bit crazy and just filmed pictures of the hell around me: dying people, close-ups of suffering faces, terrified faces, people in agony. I was all combat cameraman: ugly, heartless, and cold-blooded. It seemed as if when I put that camera on my shoulder, I changed into someone else. I had noticed it and several of my colleagues had mentioned it to me. I'm a nice guy and I always have been, but when that camera goes up, I turn into a monster.

Frank continued to try and help people and when Malet handed him a microphone to do his stand-up, his hand and arm were covered with blood along with most of his shirt. It wasn't his blood, he was uninjured. He was still completely shaken by the violence and to begin with he couldn't say anything. He was unable to describe the scene. The first takes were shaky and halting and he would stop and have to start over. It took a while before he finished a single stand-up.

In the evening, when I had time to think, I hated myself. It's not unusual, many war photographers say they feel the same way. Even Robert Capa, perhaps the greatest photojournalist ever, wrote to a friend after he recorded the first Japanese attacks on the Chinese civilians of Hankow in 1938, that he felt like a "hyena."

> Even if you know the value of your work, it gets on your nerves. Everybody suspects that you are a spy or that you want to make money at the expense of other people's skins.[1]

New York hadn't shown much interest in Cambodia but that night Frank's story did run and showed the very real, very ugly, very savage war that was still happening. The fact that I could make people acknowledge this reality is why I became a cameraman but, that night, it didn't make me feel like a good person.

When General Lon Nol left for Hawaii, we all knew the fall of Phnom Penh was near. The US Embassy told the non-Americans in the press in no uncertain terms that they should be out of Cambodia a week before the scheduled evacuation. After that, it was "American nationality only" and only American citizens could remain to cover the story and know that they could have seats on the last flights out. I left Cambodia and was replaced by John Lower.

In the final days, all third-country nationals were ordered to leave Phnom Penh; only Americans would get out on the final flights. In early 1975, John Lower—seen here with long-time soundman Masaaki Ogushi—was sent in alone and he and Frank Mariano watched the flag being lowered at the US Embassy and then took the last flight out—along with the ambassador. (Courtesy Masaaki Ogushi)

John remembers those final days in Phnom Penh:

I was frightened for my life … I was taking R & R back in Japan and got a 2 a.m. call asking me to get on the first flight to Bangkok and then on to Phnom Penh. Ogushi couldn't go with me. So, I had to pack up everything—all the sound gear with all those damn cables—and off I went to Bangkok. Norman met me and told me there was no way to get in commercially but perhaps a relief flight was going in.

Indeed, an old weathered American flyer was airlifting powdered milk to a Cambodian relief agency. He agreed to take me. The plane, an Electra, had no seats. The entire fuselage was packed with bags of powdered milk. I stacked my gear on top of it and off we went. About halfway through the flight, I walked up to the cockpit to chat with the pilot about the conditions at the airport.

The news was grim—the Khmer Rouge had rocketed it just few hours earlier. The pilot had not been able to contact the tower. So, I asked if he was going to take the plane over to Saigon if the Communist forces were still rocketing and he said, "Sonny, this is a one-way trip. We'll make a corkscrew landing if we have to."

I remember feeling totally helpless, like my life was not in my own hands, that I wasn't in control. I was plain scared.

We made a fast approach and hit the tarmac hard. I had all my gear strapped to my body, slung over my shoulder, ready to jump off the plane, and run for cover. The plane came to a halt and I raced to the door but it was jammed.

I thought, "Shit! We're wasting time. I want out of this trap."

The old pilot reached for the fire ax and bashed the handle open. I scrambled down off the plane, wondering where I was going to find shelter.

Then I suddenly realized. All was quiet. Not even the crack of gunfire. In fact, Cambodian families were lounging around the boundary of the airstrip, out apparently to watch planes landing, like people do on Sundays back home.[2]

After the scramble to arrive, John spent several days waiting for something to happen.

Frank Mariano was my correspondent. He woke me up early on the morning of April 16th and told me to pack up. The evacuation was on. We got our stuff together and headed toward the US Embassy.

The US choppers were flying in over the palm trees heading for an athletic field behind the embassy compound. Except for the noise of the blades, the city was quiet. A few Cambodians who had US connections were outside of the Embassy gates anxiously awaiting word whether there'd be room for them on a chopper. I captured the scene on film while Mariano hassled with Embassy officials to get permission for our Cambodian translator and his family to be evacuated. It seemed like Frank was taking hours. I shot what I could but thought I was missing a lot of the action at the helicopter landing zone. But once there, I'd be separate from Frank and we'd have no "goodbye Cambodia" stand-upper on camera.

So, I waited.

Finally, Frank got the permission and their names were hastily scribbled on baggage tags and pinned to their clothes. Baggage tags, that's what you needed to get out of Cambodia, to escape the nightmare to come. Frank did a quick on camera, we raced for the LZ, the Marines yelling at us, "You're late, You're late you're gonna miss the last boat out!"

And there, miracle upon miracle, was the US Ambassador, John Gunther Dean, with his chief military advisor, guarded by heavily armed soldiers. Up went the LW-16 (camera) on my shoulder. I was in gear now. At last, we had our story.

The ambassador was watching as the Stars & Stripes were folded and ceremoniously presented to him. He saluted and was escorted on to the last chopper. We followed and got on the same chopper.

Lift off. Phnom Penh shrank in the distance. The ambassador looked out in shock. His military advisor was weeping at his side.[3]

The whole sequence with the US Ambassador taking the flag and leaving was an exclusive for John Lower and Frank Mariano.

On the 25th anniversary of the end of the Vietnam War, former Saigon bureau secretary Loi Nghiem organized a gathering of all the old bureau staff. I asked Elmer Lower, my stringer president, what was his happiest moment during the Vietnam period? He motioned me close and said, "My most happiest moment was when my son John Lower returned safely from Phnom Penh having done his duty."

CHAPTER 26

FALL OF SAIGON

In the early days of the Vietnam War, everyone knew about the concept called the "Domino Theory." This was the American leaders' fear that if Vietnam fell to the Communists, that would lead to the Communists taking over in Laos, Cambodia, Thailand, and eventually Indonesia, and Malaysia. In the end, all of Asia could be a Communist bloc. The idea was that these nations were lined up like dominos and pushing one over would knock down the next and the next—this process continuing until the Communists ruled everywhere.

So far, this hasn't happened, but when I came back to Saigon from Cambodia, it certainly seemed to be happening in South Vietnam. The North Vietnamese had rearmed and retrained their army during the ceasefire, and now they were on the attack again: coming across the Demilitarized Zone and the Laotian border. The South Vietnamese lost their bases near the DMZ first and then it seemed that they just went from one defeat to another.

In the central highlands, 25,000 North Vietnamese soldiers attacked Ban Me Thuot and took it from its 1,200 South Vietnamese defenders in two days. All the major highways had been cut so the government couldn't resupply any of their bases and a badly planned and chaotic retreat began.

When North Vietnam had attempted to do the same thing in the Easter Offensive, they were held off in large part because of support from the US Air Force and Navy ships offshore. Now, there were no American warplanes in the skies nor battleships in the South China Sea and the defenses crumbled.

President Nguyen Van Thieu ordered the Army to make a tactical withdrawal and regroup. However, all the roads had been cut by the North Vietnamese days before so the South Vietnamese troops became just more refugees clogging the roads.

On March 16, the order came to evacuate Pleiku, a major city in the Central Highlands. Panic began to spread among civilians and the unsupplied and unorganized South Vietnamese troops now walking to Saigon.

By March 25, Hue City had fallen, and Troung Kha Tien and I accompanied Jim Bennett into Da Nang. The second camera was Joseph Lee with his partner Tran Khiem. We went out to the northern entrance of Da Nang to check the defenses but could only see thousands of refugees on foot walking down Highway One. There were no defenses.

That evening, Jim wrote a memo:

Tuesday, March 25, 1975

Tony & Lee

The evacuation charter will fly to Danang tomorrow (Wednesday) and you, Lee and Ca are to get aboard and fly back to Saigon. There will be absolutely no change in this plan. If Khiem wants to come that is okay also. Please stay in very close contact with Bruce Dunning of CBS at all times. He is staying at the Moderne Hotel. Under no circumstances are you or Lee or Ca to stay behind. We have definite word that Danang is in great danger of falling within the next 24 to 48 hours. I repeat, you are not to stay or think of any other means of getting out of Danang except by our evacuation charter. CBS, NBC, AP and UPI are under the same orders.

take care

Jim Bennett

(Courtesy Yasutsune Hirashiki)

My soundman had an elderly father living in Da Nang and he desperately wanted to get him on the last evacuation flight. Tien was hesitant to ask Jim directly so I asked Jim if there were any extra seats available for Tien's father. Jim explained that there was no guarantee of any extra seats since the planes were being shared by all of the press agencies. I told Jim that I could give up my seat for Tien's father and just stand or sit on the floor.

Everyone was tense but, to my surprise, Jim exploded with anger. He shouted at me, "You were always a troublemaker, never listening to me. You never obeyed my orders. You don't understand how serious the situation is in Da Nang. Why are you always against me? You did this in Phnom Penh too when I ordered you to re-base to Hong Kong. You didn't obey my orders and stayed there a few more days. Why?"

Then he asked a question that just made my heart go cold, "Do you still hate me because you think I let Terry and Sam be killed?"

I was stunned. I couldn't find any words. I didn't blame Jim for Terry and Sam's deaths, and I hadn't known that Jim had been blaming himself all of these years. He hadn't been responsible, and now I realized that he thought I hated him because he hadn't been able to stop Terry and Sam that day.

Now, I finally understood the wall of silence that had stood between Jim and me for the past two and a half years. I had thought that I was the only one suffering and had never guessed the depth of Jim's pain. The moment I heard his words, I immediately stopped arguing with him because I realized Jim was trying his hardest to protect his crew so events like those in Quang Tri would never happen again. He was determined to get us safely back to Saigon, and that was why he had written that severe memo to us. It was really aimed at me—Jim was trying to save my life.

We flew out of Da Nang the next day with Tien's father on board. Four days later, Da Nang fell. Jim Bennett's experience, his deep sense of responsibility and compassion had saved the lives of all his colleagues— even his troublemaking Japanese cameraman.

With war now spreading once again across South Vietnam, reinforcement correspondents Hilary Brown, Jerry King, and Ken Kashiwahara flew in along with fresh camera crews: the Fox brothers, Barry and Peter Fox from Europe; cameraman Syd Dobbish and his partner Jack

Grey from New York; and John Lower and Masaaki Ogushi from Tokyo.

Perhaps the most important person to arrive was former Saigon bureau chief, Kevin Delany, who returned and brought Hong Kong manager Pat Marz. Along with covering the story, their job was to gather ABC's Vietnamese employees and their families and make sure they were able to leave if they wanted.

★★★

After Da Nang, I was sent to the city of Quy Nhon with newly arrived correspondent Ken Kashiwahara. Ken is a third-generation Japanese-American, born in Hawaii, and one of the first Asian correspondents to get a job at the network level. Although he had the face and the demeanor of a Japanese gentleman, he actually didn't speak much more Japanese than I could speak English.

The North Vietnamese were continuing their advance down the coast, and Quy Nhon was the next big city south of Da Nang. Here, the South Vietnamese were determined to make a stand. We flew in in a light plane and landed around noon. We told the pilot to be sure and pick us up at the same time the next day.

Our first stop was the US Information Service building next to the tower. When we arrived, an American, a USIS employee I think, was busy packing and cleaning out the office. He was surprised when we came in because he thought everyone had left when the North Vietnamese troops struck the northern edge of the city. He was going to leave sometime that afternoon.

Ken asked if there were any hotels still open and he replied that everything was closed but we could stay at the USIS compound where there were beds, blankets, showers, and toilets—even a telephone service we could use for free. There wasn't anyone else planning to sleep there so we could consider it ours.

We happily accepted his gracious offer. The city used to be a small fishing port and, as refugees arrived over the years of the war, it had grown into a fair-sized city, one of the largest on the coast. It seemed now to be in "wait and see" mode as people were getting ready to leave but still waiting in case the South Vietnamese troops held, and they could stay in their homes.

We searched but once again couldn't find any defense line north of the city. No one seemed to know where either army was, but rumors were flying like crazy. We spent the entire afternoon walking, hitchhiking, and shooting film.

There were no restaurants open downtown so, since we were quite hungry, we walked down to the beach where there had been some excellent restaurants the last time I'd been here. Finally, we found one tiny restaurant and Tien asked the owner if there was any food left. The owner of the restaurant was quite an attractive lady in early middle age, and she set to cooking us a dinner. The place might have been only a bit bigger than a street stall but she brought out an amazing dinner, several kinds of very fresh fish and vegetables. The owner kept cooking dishes and bringing them out to us and when she finished she came out and sat with us.

While we were enjoying our dinner, Tien asked the owner, "Everybody has run away. Why are you still here?"

She answered, "Where should I escape to? I think anywhere is the same no matter where I go."

She told Tien that she had been a refugee since she was young, running from one place to another to escape the war. Now, she said she was simply tired of it, and the war was going to catch up with her anyway.

We thanked her for the food and the hospitality and headed back to the airfield. Tien wondered if the restaurant owner was actually calm because she'd been working for the North Vietnamese. There was no way to know.

When we returned to the USIS compound, the office manager had gone. We called the Saigon bureau on the old military "tiger line." Our call went through, and I heard the very worried voice of secretary Thuan Trinh. "Where are you now? We were very worried about you guys. The government just announced that Quy Nhon had fallen."

Ken explained that Quy Nhon certainly hadn't fallen, and it sounded as if the Saigon government was in such a state of panic they didn't know what was happening. Ken double-checked that the charter plane would be here early the next afternoon, and we went to sleep in the empty USIS compound.

Early the next morning, we walked to the center of Quy Nhon and found an entirely different city. There was no more "wait and see." The streets were crowded with traffic heading south, entire families piled up with their furniture and many with farm animals: pigs, chickens, ducks, even water buffaloes.

Now, it was certainly true that Quy Nhon was falling even though there were no guns firing, no sign of the enemy. We filmed a story of chaos and panic and returned to the airport a little earlier than the designated time. We waited for our charter plane until noon. Then we waited through the afternoon until about four o'clock. The weather was clear and calm, we'd had a good pilot, where was he?

The pilot told us later that he'd flown over the field but couldn't raise the tower on the radio and so couldn't get permission to land, and since Saigon was saying that the city had already fallen, the pilot was worried that the North Vietnamese had already taken the field. The fact was that all the engineers and soldiers who worked at the control tower had fled early that morning.

We were stuck—three new refugees sat on the empty airfield.

At 4:30 p.m., a large jet passenger plane landed and taxied to refuel right where we were standing. The name "Air Vietnam" was painted on the side. Tien and Ken negotiated with the pilot. The plane was chartered by a bank and already completely filled with their employees, but they said we could sit in the cargo section.

No problem! We had sat on the floor of just about every type of aircraft by that time. Before we took off, the stewardess even gave us candy. The metal floor was a little chilly and hard but at that moment, it was better than any seat in first class. Soon, the rhythm of the engines relaxed me, and I kept saying to myself the same phrase, "It's too good to be true" until I fell asleep.

After a nice nap, we arrived safely in Saigon and made it to the bureau in the evening. That plane really had been the last flight from Quy Nhon. From that time on, the battles were so close to Saigon that we didn't need to charter an airplane to cover them. They were at our front door.

The North Vietnamese continued their swift drive south until they hit Xuan Loc 60 miles north of Saigon. The South Vietnamese troops in Xuan Loc were surrounded and outnumbered, but they held out. President Thieu threw in his best units and called on them to stand fast.

It was a deadly battle with tremendous losses on both sides. The South Vietnamese soldiers had to be supplied and reinforced by air, and their warplanes were flying almost constantly to strafe and bomb the attackers. Xuan Loc held out from April 9 to April 25, and many analysts say it was the bravest battle that the South Vietnamese Army ever fought.

Like An Loc during the 1972 Easter Offensive, it was almost impossible for any press to get in or out of the besieged city. We would drive north from Saigon as far as we could and film what we could see.

★★★

One day, I drove up Highway One with a new correspondent, Jerry King, a tall, handsome Canadian. In fact, he was so tall that I took to calling him "Mr. Long Legs" and he retaliated by calling me, "Mr. Short Legs." He was a pleasant guy, liked to talk, joke around, and loved to drink Bacardi and Coke except, oddly, he insisted it be made with Pepsi and not Coca-Cola.

Jerry came from London where he'd been trained by George Watson. Before he departed New York, Jerry had met with his boss, Nick Archer, and my boss, Jack Bush, who gave him instructions on covering the Vietnam War.

They said, "Follow the camera crew, listen to their advice. You'll be fine. And Tony Hirashiki is quite dependable."

I was pleased to hear that my boss still trusted me lots.

On this first day with Jerry, my partner was Truong Kha Tien, who often worked with me during the final offensive. We knew that if we left Saigon early in the morning, we could arrive at the frontlines by 10 a.m., even if traffic was heavy.

When we arrived at the front, the elite Ranger battalion was setting up to break through the lines and reinforce Xuan Loc. One by one, these tough and experienced soldiers walked past along both sides of the road.

I shot them marching and got close-ups of faces and close-ups of boots, weapons, and wide shots of the long line of Rangers. Meanwhile, Jerry found a small hill where he could do a stand-up with the Rangers in the background. It was a good location for him but far too high for me. I needed him get lower, or he would have only blue sky in the background.

The other minor problem was that someone standing on a hill like that was a tempting target for an enemy sniper, and there was no place to hide if a rocket came in. Unfortunately, with my limited English, it was difficult to explain to Jerry all the problems with his choice of location.

Without his permission, I set the tripod up on a much lower hill, and we shot a series of good stand-ups with the line of troops in the background. I'm sure Jerry was confused by my refusal to use his location, but perhaps he remembered what he'd been told in New York and went along with me.

Right after Jerry finished, several shells landed nearby, and all of us took cover. As it happened, one of the shells had landed right on the hill where Jerry had wanted to film. Jerry looked at me with dirt and mud all over his face and asked, "Tony, how did you know the rockets were going to hit that spot? Somehow you knew it before the rocket landed there—that's why you changed the location. How?"

I couldn't explain, and he just shrugged and said, "Jack Bush was right! He said to just follow you, and you saved my life!"

When we got back to the ABC bureau, everyone in the office looked at us as if we were ghosts. Other press people had been nearby and said that Jerry King and his crew had been right under a shelling and were missing and probably killed. All the bureau was busy getting a rescue team together to look for our bodies up on Highway One.

I remember that it was nice to see the relief on Kevin Delany's face.

From the experience on that hill, I felt that my luck had returned. I went up near Xuan Loc to shoot almost every day and got good footage even though I never managed to get inside the town.

One day, I was covering heavy shelling, this time on Highway One. My camera position was just a bit higher than the highway on a tiny hill. There was no traffic, but once in a while, some refugees would run past trying to avoid the shells. At some points, I couldn't see the road at all, there was so much smoke from the explosions.

It was late afternoon, and we were about to head back when I saw two small children walking towards me. One of them was perhaps ten years old but no older. I thought that the other boy might be his brother; he was carrying a tiny suitcase.

Even though shells were constantly falling, they didn't run. They looked too tired to worry about it. I kept on filming in one continuous shot as they trudged past me and on down the road. Shells kept coming in, but the kids just kept walking, so tired that they didn't even look up at the explosions.

They threw a long shadow behind them from the late afternoon sun. Once again, shells came in very close, but the kids just kept plodding along under the rocket barrage on Highway One.

I knew that the daily news never used cuts that long—the maximum was 10 seconds, and the rest would be thrown away at the editing table but I kept rolling without stopping for more than three minutes until the kids disappeared from my lens.

Why did I film such a long shot that would probably never get used? Because, cinematically, I believed it was symbolic of the long sorrowful journey that everyone—Vietnamese, Americans, soldiers, journalists— had walked in the long Vietnam War.

On April 22, Xuan Loc's battered defenders finally crumbled. Saigon was completely surrounded. For months and even years, people had known that South Vietnam would fall and that they should prepare to evacuate. In the back of many Vietnamese minds was what had happened in Hue when the insurgents took the city during the Tet Offensive. The Viet Cong went from door to door with lists of those who supported the Saigon government or worked for American troops and took them away to be punished for "crimes against the people."

Kevin Delany, one of the last Saigon bureau chiefs, had the courage to protect his staff. It can be seen in this picture, taken in 1972, and in the way he orchestrated the evacuation of 101 ABC staffers and their families in 1975. (Courtesy Kevin Delany)

ABC had assigned Kevin Delany and Hong Kong manager Pat Marz the task of evacuating every employee, American or not, and their direct family members. It was a tremendous effort but, in the end, ABC moved all of the staff who wanted to leave and their families.

They gathered the evacuees in groups and began to bring them to the airport where a charter flight was waiting. The most difficult time was passing through the gates at the airport where the officials were being very strict.

Here's how Kevin Delany remembered it many years later:

> The evacuation of the Saigon bureau staff and their families was one of the things of which I was most proud. It was, of course, a team effort, and Pat Marz played a most important role. I can recall during that period almost nightly telephone calls from Stan Opotowsky in New York to my room in the Continental Palace.
>
> The first count of staffers and family members I recall giving Stan totaled about 60, but then every few days I would report to him that the number had grown larger, that "sons" or "daughters" had somehow been overlooked. He protested

that the ABC Board of Directors would not agree to any higher number, and I would have to point out that we were dealing in human lives. To Stan's credit, he always pushed the higher number through and we finally ended up with 101 staffers and their families.

Then the most difficult job still lay ahead—getting them out. The American Embassy was cooperating with us only because they knew that the American news organizations were contemplating all kinds of crazy schemes—from hiring planes and ships to smuggle people out from Vung Tau or the like. So the Embassy said that, if you will give up those crazy ideas, we will arrange to fly your Vietnamese staff and families out from Tan Son Nhut—provided we were able to get them on the base.

That was the choke point. As you no doubt recall, each day I had to go to the airport with a group of families in our van—and they would get to the gate and the ARVN MPs would look at our phony documents and shake their head, "No. You can't go through the gate." Then Minh or someone who had collected the money would push a wad of piasters into the MP's hand from underneath the papers and the MP would feel the piasters in his hand, and smile and say, "Oh yes, these papers are fine—drive right through."

And we would all breathe a great of relief, thinking "Thank God for corruption."[1]

★★★

After our Vietnamese colleagues and their families left, the Americans and the foreign nationals were the only people left. In the end, ABC decided that Hilary Brown, a Canadian, and Barry and Peter Fox, who were Americans with Irish passports would remain in Saigon after it fell and cover the aftermath for as long as they were allowed.

For years, I had taken my paycheck a few blocks from the Caravelle Hotel to the Bank of America, where I met a nice young Vietnamese woman named Anhue. As time went by, we got to know each other, fell in love, and got married. Now she was in Hong Kong with our little girl but her parents and six siblings still lived in Saigon.

I obtained passes for them and, in the days before the evacuation, went to persuade them to leave with the other ABC families. I even brought my soundman, Tien, to help interpret and reinforce my arguments.

My father-in-law, Nguyen Thanh Mac, was an evangelical Christian minister and had been assigned as a chaplain to the South Vietnamese

troops. He knew that this would make his life difficult under the Communists but he didn't want to leave and his children decided not to leave without their parents. I tried again on the night before the ABC evacuation but his mind was made up. He wrote a short letter to my wife, telling her that, as a minister, he simply couldn't leave his parishioners behind and care for his family only.

He paid a high price for that decision—more than eight years at hard labor in a re-education camp for his work with the Army. He never regretted his decision.

He was truly a great man.

Tony's father-in-law, Nguyen Thanh Mac was an evangelical Christian minister and refused to evacuate with Tony and the ABC staff in order to remain with his parishioners. Along with the rest of his family, he suffered privation and punishment during the post-war period. (Courtesy Yasutsune Hirashiki)

★★★

I was assigned to cover the official American evacuation, and Kevin Delany put my name on the list so that I would go out with the last flight of Americans. No plan is perfect, it was another week before the American evacuation occurred, a week during which we were desperately busy covering stories without enough people. ABC had to hire Vietnamese crews who used to do freelance—at least it was a last paycheck for many of them.

On April 27, rockets hit Tan Son Nhut airport and the city center. Several shells hit the densely populated area of Cholon, setting houses afire. You could see the light from the flames from anywhere in Saigon.

Now that Xuan Loc had fallen, the defenders were making a stand at a bridge in an area named Gia Dinh. Hilary Brown and the Fox brothers were covering this battle, and her report was done while she was crouching and even rolling flat on the bridge to escape small-arms fire only inches above her head. It was the last combat report ABC did from Vietnam.

On the 29th, the radio played "White Christmas" which was the signal for the official American evacuation. Kevin Delany said, "Ken and Tony, you have only 45 minutes to pack your personal things, take your gear, and meet us here. You guys are covering the evacuation. You can only bring personal luggage that you can put on your lap. That's it. Tony, don't separate from us. You have to cover every part of the evacuation. It's a very important duty."

I didn't mind remaining in the city—actually, I wanted to stay, but Kevin knew me well from all the years we had worked together, and I assumed that he wanted to make sure I got out safe. By assigning me to the evacuation, he knew I would do the job, and he could make sure I got on the plane.

I went back to my room at the Continental Palace Hotel and packed a small bag to carry, and put everything else in a suitcase. I left it with the bell captain to hold until I came back, along with a good tip. I paid my bill and was walking out when one of the room boys asked, "Are you leaving, too?"

I said, "I'll be back soon," but I felt guilty.

I was running away, abandoning people I had come to know, and a country that I really loved. I could escape and the others couldn't.

I told myself that I was just doing my job, but that didn't matter to the Vietnamese being left behind. To them, Tony was running away, and they were being left behind.

As I left the ABC office in the Caravelle Hotel, one of the cyclo drivers who waited outside said to me, "What are you are doing?" and I realized that these were old friends, guys that I would play chess with and usually lose money to. They liked me, and I liked them. They had always treated me as one of them.

"Hey Tony, are you leaving too?" someone shouted at me quite loudly. I sensed the frustration in his voice.

"See you soon," I said.

"Are you sure?" another driver said in a sarcastic voice.

The fact was that I couldn't look them in the eyes. Maybe they thought that since I was Asian, I wouldn't run away like the Americans.

"Uncle" Dang nodded at me with a faint smile and said goodbye. He could have come with ABC but he had a very big family and since they all couldn't go, he'd decided to stay.

I felt very small and sad.

It was only a few blocks from the Caravelle to the staging point where evacuees were gathering with their belongings. This time, there were American soldiers checking IDs and passes before we were allowed to board the bus. In the beginning, people stood in orderly lines and everything ran quickly and efficiently. I stood next to Ken Kashiwahara and filmed the scene.

Soon, however, more people began to arrive, and the scene became crowded and chaotic as people without IDs and passes tried to join the evacuation. There were not enough soldiers to control the crowd, and it turned into a mob scene.

Now it was our turn to leave but behind us, it was complete panic and confusion as people tried to jam onto the bus. I kept rolling film even as I was pushed back down the aisle. Ken was outside, helping other refugees get on board, and Kevin was at the top of the steps, helping mothers, children, and old people to find seats.

When the bus was filled, there was no room for Ken, and he remained outside, helping others. We all shouted at him to get in, but there was no more room.

Ken called, "I'll take the next bus. See you at the airport."

Ken told me later that he felt that he was doing the right thing and that Kevin and I should have not gotten on the bus but stayed with him. I'll admit that I didn't help anyone or think of others, I just kept filming the suffering and panic of the refugees from my safe place on the bus.

When the bus pulled out, crowds were chasing us, some on foot and some on motorbikes. Young men were yelling insults.

While all this was happening, Kevin Delany and I were waiting for Ken at the airport. The first wave of CH-3 helicopters, big machines that the troops used to call "Jolly Green Giants," swept in and landed. US Marines jumped off the choppers with grim faces and their weapons drawn and quickly proceeded to organize the evacuation, clearing landing zones and designating staging areas.

After the CH-3s, there were smaller "Sea Knight" helicopters that loaded from the back. As soon as they touched down, the evacuees—or perhaps they were just refugees now—would run to get on board. I could see other TV crews and journalists boarding and thought that Kevin's plan had succeeded. I was the only camera still filming at the evacuation point and so ABC would have the complete story.

We were still waiting for Ken so we watched and filmed as wave after wave of helicopters came in, filled with people racing from the shelling, and took off for the ships offshore.

Finally, a Marine commander shouted at us, "Are you guys going with us or not?"

Kevin said, "We're waiting for our correspondent. He was supposed to come on the next bus, so we'll wait and take the next helicopter with him."

"You can continue filming if you want, but this is the last flight. There are no more helicopters coming to land at the airport. The next rescue missions will be directly from the US Embassy. There is no way that your correspondent is going to make it in here anyway."

We had no choice and so we joined the last flight out.

While our helicopter was rising up, I could see that the airport was burning. We flew out over Saigon. I had flown over and filmed the city many times and thought it was beautiful from the sky. I had my last look, and we were out over the South China Sea. It was a bit like the day I went to Happy Valley all those years ago. But I had changed and the country had changed.

I finally took the camera off my shoulder. I had been shooting steadily from the time I left the Caravelle Hotel, only stopping to change film. I realized I was crying and that had been why it was so hard to focus my shots.

I cried quietly, not out loud as I did when Terry died. It was just lots of tears like a little kid who has been beaten. I turned my back to Kevin so that he couldn't see—he'd seen me cry far too often.

Now I was looking at a little Vietnamese child. I tried to smile, but I couldn't stop the tears.

Finally, this was my war.

As we flew, I cursed silently with every swear word I knew.

And cried.

EPILOG

Our Marine helicopter flew out over the South China Sea, and after an hour, landed first on the aircraft carrier USS *Midway* and then were transferred to the USS *Blue Ridge* —flagship of the Seventh Fleet. The *Blue Ridge* was jammed with thousands of evacuees and most of the Saigon press corps. It was good to see reporters and crews I'd known for years safe from harm.

I was filming a group of South Vietnamese soldiers and their families climbing from their small boat to the big American warship. As the people came up one by one, I got tight shots of their sad and exhausted faces.

A high-ranking officer put his hands in front of my lens. Before, it might have meant a haughty order but today, he just gently said, "Please..."

I knew immediately what he meant. I said, "Sorry," and pointed the lens at the floor. He thanked me in a very faint voice, like a man in a bad dream. I wanted to say something to comfort him but all I could think of was, "Good luck, sir" with a tone of respect.

In the early morning, American Ambassador Graham Martin and South Vietnamese General Nguyen Cao Ky were ordered flown to the *Blue Ridge*. Kevin Delany recalled that moment:

> Ambassador Graham Martin arrived about 5 a.m. on the last helicopter from the American Embassy rooftop helo platform. You and I were both on deck with a few other newsmen. I asked him only two questions.
>
> The first was, "Mr. Ambassador, did you get everybody out?"
>
> He replied, "Yes, they're all out." [A statement which I knew was likely not true ... many Vietnamese had been left back in Saigon.]

> He was munching on an apple and I asked him, "How do you feel now?"
> He said, "I'm hungry," and turned and went down the ladder.[1]

The USS *Blue Ridge* had prepared facilities for the press—a briefing room and telex machines. We were anxiously awaiting the first wire reports from Saigon. Even though hundreds of newsmen had left in the final evacuation, at least eighty remained to cover the story. Most were third-country nationals, English, French, and Japanese, but dozens of American reporters stayed as well. The first AP report was dispatched by Peter Arnett:

> North Vietnamese troops have officially taken over Saigon, had entered the city without bloodshed—a bloodless victory at Saigon. The Presidential Palace has been occupied by the NVA forces.

We had lost our correspondent, so Kevin Delany wrapped up the story, included a stand-up on the deck of the *Blue Ridge*. We shipped it off to Manila to be sent by satellite to New York. It was the first on-scene report of the fall of Saigon. His script concluded:

> AS SAIGON DISAPPEARED FROM VIEW, THE ENORMITY OF THE EVENT REGISTERED ON THE FACES OF THE 60 ABOARD—AMERICANS AND VIETNAMESE ALIKE. MOST WERE JUST STUNNED—BUT SOME BROKE DOWN AT THE REALIZATION THEY WERE PROBABLY LEAVING VIETNAM FOREVER.
>
> THE HELICOPTER PASSED OVER SMALL FLEETS OF BOATS LEAVING THE COASTAL CITY OF VUNG TAU—MORE FLEEING VIETNAMESE. THEN 30 MILES FROM THE COAST—A BEAUTIFUL SIGHT—THE FLIGHT DECK OF A CARRIER. CHOPPERS WERE DISGORGING AMERICANS AND VIETNAMESE—PEOPLE WHO CLEARLY SHOWED THE EMOTIONAL AND PHYSICAL STRAIN OF THE RECENT WEEKS.
>
> (scenes then followed on the USS *Blue Ridge*)
>
> AMBASSADOR GRAHAM MARTIN STEPPED ONTO THE DECK OF THIS SHIP EARLY TODAY AND IN EFFECT CLOSED THE FINAL AMERICAN CHAPTER ON VIETNAM. THIS CORRESPONDENT ASKED HIM WHAT HIS FEELINGS WERE, MARTIN WOULD ONLY SAY THAT HE WAS HUNGRY.
>
> KEVIN DELANY, ABC NEWS, ON THE COMMAND SHIP *BLUE RIDGE* IN THE SOUTH CHINA SEA[2]

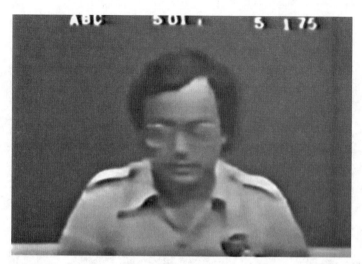

ABC News' Ken Kashiwahara didn't make it onto the same bus as Delany and Hirashiki and had to watch as a man tried to give his baby to a departing family only to trip and watch it die under the wheels of the bus he was traveling in. Here he reports live by satellite from Manila having finally scaled the walls of the US Embassy with hundreds of others. (ABC News off-air of Kashiwahara report)

Ken Kashiwahara's bus made it to Tan Son Nhut, but the Vietnamese guards wouldn't allow it on the field. Even though it was a US military bus and the driver was an employee of the Embassy, they were adamant that they were not going to open the gate and even went so far as to fire their rifles at the feet of the bus driver.

The bus drove randomly around Saigon, looking for another place where the passengers could be taken out to the ships waiting offshore. After many hours and innumerable obstacles, Ken, and the other passengers finally reached the US Embassy where Marines were keeping most people out but allowing those with papers and identification to climb over the wall. Ken laboriously climbed the wall, talked his way past the Marines, and was airlifted out by one of the Navy helicopters that were steadily shuttling people out to sea.

He landed on the USS *Hancock* and was sent to carry all the film to Manila. There, he was put on a live satellite feed to the United States and told of his ordeal—exhausted and shaken but calm and very critical of how the evacuation had been carried out. Hundreds of Vietnamese who had helped the Americans had been left behind, helpless against the Communists.

Hilary Brown left Saigon at the last minute at the request of her fiancé. This is one of the final stand-ups filmed on the evacuation fleet. (Filmed by Barry Fox; courtesy ABC News)

Hilary Brown did a great report on the following day from the deck of the *Hancock*, ending with, "This seems to be the last chapter in America's long involvement in Vietnam."

When I ran into Hilary Brown and the Fox brothers on the *Blue Ridge* later I was surprised. I thought the plan was that they would stay in Saigon. Much later, Kevin Delany told me a touching story about why this brave correspondent had decided to leave:

> For the record, Hilary and the Fox brothers said they would be willing to stay behind when Saigon fell and cover the events as the NVA/VC took over. But as I recall, it was a couple days before the evacuation when she heard from her English boyfriend, John Bierman—who I believe later became her husband— and he was very upset that she planned to remain in Saigon. She suddenly started crying in the ABC office.
>
> I had no idea why at first. But through tears, she told me that she felt that she was not being fair to him and would evacuate with the rest of us after all. Once

again, I felt it was unfair for me to influence her decision one way or another—and I told her that I accepted her decision and she should not worry about the issue further. So Hilary and the Fox brothers were added to the evacuation list.[3]

After I heard this, I respected Hilary even more for having chosen love over her profession and I was also touched by the compassionate nature of Kevin, who conducted the final evacuation so well.

Eventually, I was transferred to the USS *Iwo Jima* and later by helicopter to the Philippines. When I landed, I was so exhausted and emotionally beaten that I had no real idea where I was. I felt like just another refugee among the massive crowds of refugees.

I sat down and focused myself, because I knew this time was my turn to be their subject. Other journalists were going to focus in on me to see if I would cry, Soundmen would have their microphones ready for a good quote, Correspondents would ask me the question we had repeated so many many times during the war, "How do you feel?"

"Sorry comrade, don't waste your time and film, I won't cry anymore, my tears dried up long time ago. Besides my English is all dirty words and you won't be able to use anything I say on television."

When I got to the office, there were two telex messages waiting. One was from Ray Falk in Tokyo telling me that a Japanese TV station wanted to interview me. I was very polite but turned down their invitation. I was a loser. I remembered the South Vietnamese officer who had gently covered my lens with his hand. That was how I felt.

The other telex was from New York. When Saigon had fallen, ABC aired a special ninety-minute program:

TONY HIRASHIKI AMCOCAST HONG KONG HOLD FOR HIRASHIKI ARRIVAL

21302 HIRASHIKI WANT TO OFFER YOU MY PERSONAL CONGRATULATIONS FOR OUTSTANDING CINEMATOGRAPHIC EFFORT IN YOUR THOUGHTFUL FILMING OF SEQUENCE ON ROUTE ONE NEAR XUAN LOC APRIL 18. THREE MINUTE EDITED VERSION OF YOUR SENSITIVE PORTRAYAL OF SMALL CHILDREN MOVING DOWN ROAD WHILE ARTILLERY FIRE LANDING ON BOTH SIDES MADE POWERFUL VISUAL IMPACT PIECE WHICH

WE USED AS SHOW CLOSER IN NINETY MINUTE FALL OF SAIGON SPECIAL APRIL 29. IT IS WELL KNOWN THAT YOUR WORK IS CONSISTENTLY SUPERB BUT ROAD PIECE WAS EXTRAORDINARY ... BEST WISHES

ROBERT SIEGENTHALER EXECUTIVE PRODUCER SPECIAL EVENTS

ACKNOWLEDGMENTS AND THANKS

It took eight years to complete the English version of my memoirs—almost as long as I spent in Vietnam—so there is a long list of people to thank.

Terry Irving was the MVP of this book: editing, pulling a story out of the mess of the first translations, researching and back-checking the facts, and at every step proving his understanding of the war, the news business, and the people I wrote about. He has said many times that he is the editor and not a co-author because he never got shot at, and that his only interest was making the English edition as well written as the Japanese one. Oddly, Terry and I never spoke until the day we got the contract from Casemate. Everything was done in emails: happy emails, angry emails, emails with lots of red letters. We had quite a few arguments but we always ended up friends because Terry loved this book from the very beginning and all our fighting in the two years we worked together was only about making it better.

After we finished, it was about as big as an old phone book so Terry had to cut it in half but, as he said, that's what television producers do. I would be aching and wounded inside watching great stories and wonderful people disappear but Terry persevered without mercy or compassion (like Steve Bell, I think he has a bit of the "dictator" in him). However, he promised me that the book would be better in the end and he would always try to keep the stories I wanted the most. Well, now that it's finished, I believe it is a better book and I think more people will read it, like it, and learn about the brave people who brought you the "television war."

Without a doubt, this book would never have seen the light of day without the efforts of the legendary writer, lawyer, and literary agent Ronald Goldfarb. He said that he got Stanley Karnow's *Vietnam: a History* printed and made into a PBS series and he was determined to get this book published to "round out his career." He believed in the book and kept encouraging us even after one publisher after another turned us down. His delightful assistant, Gerrie Sturman, was as excited as we were when Casemate came through.

I understand how difficult it is these days for a company to choose which books to publish and so my grateful thanks go to Casemate for taking a chance on us. Choosing a book by an unknown writer about a long-ago war takes guts. Ruth Sheppard has been the Top Sergeant, aided by Hannah McAdams and Mette Bundgaard with the dramatic cover art done by Katie Allen. In addition, we know that Clare Litt, Michaela Goff, Tom Bonnington, and a host of others are preparing to sell the book—I just hope they don't want me to do too many interviews!

At ABC News, Vice President Kerry Smith and David Baker of Rights and Clearances opened the doors to the vault and Archivist Anthony Perrone and his team of film experts created the book's color photos from the original 16mm film I shot 50 years ago. I don't think it's ever been done before but it shows what was recorded in the camera instead of the foggy video you're used to seeing.

I spent 40 years at ABC News, from Saigon to the World Trade Towers, and there are so many friends and co-workers to thank that it would take a second book. Let me just say that every colleague at ABC, whether younger or older, taught me to be a better cameraman and a better journalist.

My personal thanks to my wife, Anhue, and all her family in Vietnam, my American children, my relatives in Japan, and friends and family here in America. Across three oceans, their support has been continuous, relentlessly encouraging, and deeply understanding.

I would especially like to thank my late father-in-law Nguyen Thanh Mac who taught me to become a Christian not just with words but with the brave example of his deep faith.

Finally, this book is dedicated to all those who, like me, went to "journalism school" on Vietnamese battlefields and especially those who sacrificed their lives, like Terry Khoo and Sam Kai Faye. Terry and Sam were special people and it was not only the way they died but the passion with which they lived every moment of their time on earth that was my first and greatest motivation to write this book.

Yasutsune Hirashiki

NOTES

Preface
1   ABC News press release (September 26, 1973). (Used with permission)

Chapter One
1   Ken Gale, e-mail (January 2, 2007).
2   Ken Gale, e-mail (January 2, 2007).
3   Ken Gale, e-mail (January 2, 2007).
4   Ken Gale, e-mail (January 2, 2007).
5   Yasutsune Hirashiki, diary (May 28, 1967).

Chapter Two
1   ABC telex (May 16, 1966).
2   ABC telex (May 17, 1966).
3   ABC New York telex to Roger Peterson (May 23, 1966).

Chapter Three
1   Roger Peterson, letter (August 6, 1987). (Used with permission)

Chapter Four
1   Richard Pyle, AP Wire Story "Amid Vietnam War, News Media and Military Fought their Own Battles." (Used with permission)
2   Don North, letter (August 5, 1988). (Used with permission)
3   Don North, letter (August 5, 1988). (Used with permission)
4   Don North, "V.C. Assault on the US Embassy," *Vietnam Magazine* (February 2001).
5   Bill Brannigan, letter (June 10, 1988). (Used with permission)
6   Bill Brannigan, letter (June 10, 1988). (Used with permission)

Chapter Five
1 ABC telex (June 1, 1967). (Don North Collection).
2 Dick Rosenbaum on Facebook (2016).
3 Dick Rosenbaum, quoted in "NEWSCASTING: Filling the Front Page," *Time* (NY, October 27, 1967).

Chapter Six
1 Sam Jaffe, quoted in "NEWSCASTING: The Men Without Helmets," *Time* (March 15, 1968); David Snell, letter (January 7, 1998). (Used with permission)

Chapter Seven
1 Phil Starck, e-mail (October 9, 2006). (Used with permission)
2 Jack Bush letter to Yasutsune Hirashiki (December 7, 1970) (Used with permission)
3 Steve Bell, e-mail (January 26, 2015). (Used with permission)
4 Steve Bell, e-mail (June 14, 2007). (Used with permission)
5 ABC News press release (September 26, 1973). (Used with permission)
6 Elmer Lower, letter (September 1974). (Used with permission)
7 Phil Starck, e-mail (September 10, 2006). (Used with permission)
8 Phil Starck, e-mail (September 10, 2006). (Used with permission)

Chapter Eight
1 Leonard Goldenson, *Beating the Odds* (New York: Scribners, 1991).
2 Ken Gale, e-mail (February 15, 2007). (Used with permission)
3 Ted Koppel, diary entry for Saturday, May 20, 1967—Dong Ha. (Used with permission)
4 Ted Koppel, diary entry for Sunday, May 21, 1967—Cam Lo. (Used with permission)

Chapter Nine
1 Liz Trotta, *Fighting for Air* (New York: Simon & Shuster, 1991).
2 Trotta, *Fighting for Air.*
3 Trotta, *Fighting for Air.*

Chapter Ten
1 David Snell, letter (January 7, 1998). (Used with permission)
2 David Snell, journal entry of June 9, 1966. (Used with permission)
3 David Snell, letter (January 7, 1998). (Used with permission)
4 David Snell, letter (January 7, 1998). (Used with permission)
5 David Snell, journal entry of June 14, 1966—Dak To. (Used with permission)
6 David Snell, journal entry of August 11, 1966—Pleiku. (Used with permission)
7 David Snell, journal entry of August 29, 1966—In Jet Heading to the States. (Used with permission)
8 David Snell, journal entry of October 28, 1967—New York. (Used with permission)

Chapter Thirteen

1 Kurt Volkert and T. Jeff Williams, *A Cambodian Odyssey and the Deaths of 25 Journalists* (New York: iUniverse, 2001).
2 Robert Sam Anson, *War News: A Young Reporter in Indochina* (New York: Simon & Schuster, 1989), p.198.
3 Drew Pearson, letter (April 2, 2007). (Used with permission)
4 Volkert and Williams, *A Cambodian Odyssey and the Deaths of 25 Journalists.*

Chapter Fourteen

1 Anson, *War News: A Young Reporter in Indochina*, pp.121–122.
2 Steve Bell, letter (July 28,1987). (Used with permission)
3 Steve Bell, e-mail (March 26, 2007). (Used with permission)
4 Steve Bell, letter (July 28, 1987). (Used with permission)

Chapter Fifteen

1 George Watson, letter (July 20, 1988). (Used with permission)
2 George Watson on ABC Evening News (March 29, 1970). (Used with permission)
3 George Watson on ABC Evening News (August, 1970). (Used with permission)
4 George Watson, letter (July 20, 1988). (Used with permission)
5 Sam Donaldson, *Hold On, Mr. President.* (New York, Random House, 1987), p.48. (Used with permission)
6 Donaldson, *Hold On, Mr. President*, p.48.
7 Donaldson, *Hold On, Mr. President*, p.48.
8 Irv Chapman, letter (September 2, 2006). (Used with permission)
9 Ann Bryan Mariano, Darby Fawcett, Kate Webb, Ann Morrisey Merick, Jurate Kazickas, Edith Lederer, Tad Bartimus, Laura Palmer, *War Torn* (New York, Random House, 2002).
10 Mariano et al, *War Torn*, p.44.
11 "NEWS COVERAGE DURING THE LAOTIAN INCURSION." ABC Evening News with Howard K Smith and Harry Reasoner (April 1, 1971). (Used with permission)
12 ABC Evening News with Howard K Smith and Harry Reasoner (April 1, 1971). (Used with permission)
13 ABC Evening News with Howard K Smith and Harry Reasoner (April 1, 1971). (Used with permission)

Chapter Seventeen

1 Ron Miller, letter (May 24, 1988). (Used with permission)

Chapter Eighteen

1 Drew Pearson, e-mail January 2, 2001). (Used with permission)
2 Drew Pearson, e-mail (February 2, 2007).
3 Drew Pearson, e-mail (February 1, 2007).

Chapter Nineteen
1   ABC NEWS Evening News (May 31, 1972). (Used with permission)

Chapter Twenty
1   Roger Peterson, letter (February 23, 1988). (Used with permission)

Chapter Twenty-One
1   My Dearest Sister,
    I hate to write this things for you now, but I have to do. First thing, please forgive me that we could not protect him during his last field assignment. No need to forgive me, just hate me, if can better to do so. I only know that my one hundred words seems to you nothing. When I hear first report from Lee "Sam was hit, then he asked Terry, Terry said, "I'm all right." It's lots of meaning for me. As far as I know, my Terry never escape without Sam. I had prepare worst situation that time. Then I came Hue first morning. Guam trip was cancel for this situation. Then I came to Hue the first morning. My Guam trip was canceled because of this situation. ARVN (Vietnamese soldier) witness said this morning that he was lying with his Auricon camera besides Sammy.
    He left you and me and all his admirers. He might say that it's life, it's destiny. But I just feel ... It's not fair ... very unfair. Actually, we had a nice time in Hue and filed as his last assignment. We had dined together with Morita, Thanong (Thailand boy) and Sammy. worked together, and he told us "I adore her. I'm loving her. She unlocked all my heart!" We all said congratulation him because we hear it first time officially, strongly. Shy Terry never talked like this before as you know. I was so happy that your love changed him. as told you since his affair, he was so moody and locked his heart and start hating people until having you. you made real Terry again that why I was so happy. We talked same night how you and Terry planning in future. He wanted to let you study business administration, then after that he wanted to study his way too. It was his last will. He was careful in this last assignment, but same time, he didn't want to give up his last responsibility too. I only can say if I was his position, I would do the same way what he did. And I'll do same way in future, too.
    The most important thing, the other night, he mentioned me during our conversation that he wrote a sort of will, which he gave to Phil or still keep in Villa. It said at the beginning, "If something happens to me, I don't blame any body ... don't blame any situation" Why he told me this, I don't know. This tragedy hit everybody ... nobody blame nobody, I agree. I just deeply regret I should kick him out from such dirty war that was my duty. Please forgive me.
    I'm planning to go to Singapore with them. Then I will go to Hong Kong seeing you. To tell the truth, I don't think I can see you. What can I say to you? Morita will give you more details of the incident. I do hope you will overcome this situation as Terry's so called Tiger.

Chapter Twenty-Two
1 Do Thi Thuy Hien Boase, e-mail (July 19, 2008). (Used with permission)
2 Larry Engelmann, *Vietnam: A Reader: A Newsman Goes To War*, p.281, and Larry Engelmann, "Another Top Newsman in Vietnam," Pushing On (September 6, 2009), http://lde421.blogspot.com/2009/09/another-top-correspondent-in-vietnam.html (Used With Permission)
3 Arnold Collins, letter (October 31, 2006). (Used with permission)
4 Arnold Collins, letter (October 31, 2006).
5 Arnold Collins, letter (October 31, 2006).
6 Kevin Delany, letter (October 12, 2006). (Used with permission)
7 Arnold Collins, letter (October 31, 2006). (Used with permission)
8 David Snell, letter (January 1993). (Used with permission)
9 David Snell, e-mail (June 17, 2006). (Used with permission)
10 Do Thi Thuy Hien Boase, letter (July 7, 2009). (Used with permission)

Chapter Twenty-Three
1 Kevin Delany, letter (October 12, 2006). (Used with permission)
2 Engelmann, *Vietnam: A Reader: A Newsman Goes To War*, and "Another Top Newsman in Vietnam." (Used with permission)
3 Kevin Delany, letter (October 12, 2008).

Chapter Twenty-Four
1 Arnold Collins, portion of ABC Evening News (July 28, 1973). (Used with permission)

Chapter Twenty-Five
1 Robert Capa, China 1937. Quote from a letter in Richard Whelan, *Robert Capa: A Biography* (Knopf 1985).
2 John Lower, letter (June 3, 1988). (Used with permission)
3 John Lower, letter (June 3, 1988). (Used with permission)

Chapter Twenty-Six
1 Kevin Delany, letter (April 26, 1988). (Used with permission)
2 Ken Kashiwahara, ABC News Live Broadcast From Manila (April 30, 1975). (Used with permission)

Epilog
1 Kevin Delany, letter (October 12, 2008). (Used with permission)
2 Kevin Delany, portions of report from ABC Evening News (April 30, 1975). (Used with permission)
3 Kevin Delany, email (November 2, 2006).

INDEX